THE TEACHING
OF LANGUAGE
IN OUR SCHOOLS

A Macmillan Guidebook
for Parents

Miriam B. Goldstein

SPONSORED BY THE
NATIONAL COUNCIL OF TEACHERS OF ENGLISH

THE TEACHING
OF LANGUAGE
IN OUR SCHOOLS

The Macmillan Company   NEW YORK
Collier-Macmillan Limited   LONDON

First Printing

Library of Congress catalog card number: 66–23928

THE MACMILLAN COMPANY, NEW YORK
COLLIER-MACMILLAN CANADA, LTD., TORONTO, ONTARIO

Printed in the United States of America

NATIONAL COUNCIL OF TEACHERS OF ENGLISH

Consultant Readers for This Manuscript

Mrs. Sheila Burt, Needham, Massachusetts
Martha Dell Sanders, Paducah Tilghman High School, Paducah, Kentucky
William Suggs, Jr., The Summit School, Winston-Salem, North Carolina
Marian Zollinger, Portland Public Schools, Portland, Oregon

Committee on Publications

James R. Squire, NCTE Executive Secretary, *Chairman*
Glenn Leggett, Grinnell College
Virginia M. Reid, Oakland Public Schools, Oakland, California
Frank E. Ross, Oakland County Schools, Pontiac, Michigan
Enid M. Olson, NCTE Director of Publications

To the memory of
my first teacher of English,
Lena Saltz Bludman

FOREWORD

Forces are at work to revolutionize the teaching of English: a swelling body of scholarly and pedagogical research, the new demands of a complex society, a heightened professional spirit among teachers. But if revolution is a fact in the teaching of English, so too is conservation. Changes are rarely as dramatic as enthusiastic proponents claim, or as sweeping as opponents insist. Even an overnight curriculum financed through a crash program and instituted by a task force has roots in decades of research, of insight, of vision.

The National Council of Teachers of English is grateful for the opportunity to bring to publication these three companion volumes: *The Teaching of Reading in Our Schools* by Ruth Reeves, *The Teaching of Language in Our Schools* by Miriam B. Goldstein, *The Teaching of Writing in Our Schools* by Richard Corbin. It is particularly grateful to the three authors, members of the Council and leaders of their profession, who show not only a grasp of the changing present, but an understanding commitment to the tradition and history that have led to it.

No other subject in the school curriculum commands more attention than English. In secondary schools most students give a minimum of five years to it. In elementary schools the content and the skills of English receive up to 60 per cent of the instructional time and effort. That this discussion of English required three books attests to the scope of English, but not to any natural separations in the subject. As the authors make clear, reading, composition, and language study are inextricably bound together; and the study of literature pervades all three. The National Council of Teachers of English is pleased to commend all three books to parents interested in English programs designed for their children, and to others who seek a clear and accurate picture of the present and the foreseeable future in the teaching of English.

Robert F. Hogan
ASSOCIATE EXECUTIVE SECRETARY
NATIONAL COUNCIL OF TEACHERS OF ENGLISH

PREFACE

Talk of the sixties:

Intelligent parents? I haven't met one yet.

—*My Friend Jim*

Why do so many youngsters murder the English language on paper and mangle it in speech?

Our theory is that most of the blame rests on the public schools, and that the remedy should not be too difficult to find and apply. That remedy would consist in the careful and persistent teaching of the grammar of the English language.

There are eight principal parts of speech in our language. They are the building blocks, the foundation stones and girders, the nails and cement, of the whole setup. Know how to use them, and you are equipped to use the language correctly and effectively.

—*New York Daily News* (November 27, 1960)

If English grammar is to be taught at all in the secondary schools, then there is little if any justification for teaching it in conjunction with rhetoric or literature; rather, such a study of language belongs in the area of science and general education along with psychology and anthropology.

—Robert B. Lees

In spite of the fact that "English" is supposedly the one subject required in every grade of the lower schools as well as in a majority of colleges, we can report no such satisfaction in the improvement of the teaching of English as we feel in that of foreign languages. . . . A majority of college students do not speak, write, or read their own language well.

—*Modern Language Association of America*

The present state of teaching in linguistics. In a word, chaotic. . . . The impact which the recent advances in linguistics have had upon the general public. Results to date: essentially zero.

—*Linguistic Society of America*

I have been much concerned that in this world we have so largely lost the ability to talk with one another. In the great succession of deep discoveries, we have become removed from one another in tradition, and in a certain measure even in language. We have had neither the time nor the skill nor the dedication to tell one another what we have learned, nor to listen, nor to welcome its enrichment of the common culture.

—J. ROBERT OPPENHEIMER

So do we build our Babels, with express elevators right to the observatory, with elaborate intercoms and walkie-talkies to shield us from silence. And as English has become a world language, our magic carpets jet us to the selfsame Babels in Brazilia, in Boston, in New Delhi.

The breakdown in communication between specialist and layman is one price we pay for unprecedented advances in knowledge. Another is the gulf between generations as the new learning begins to filter into the schools. What parent can hold his own in his youngster's world of CBA chemistry, SMSG math, PSSC physics, BSCS biology, and transformational grammar? Yet if we remain bewildered, we increase the silence; if we hanker for the old before examining the new, we increase the noise. Either way, we have contributed to the breakdown in communication.

Surely one place where the human dialogue must resume, if it is to resume at all, is the home, the beginning of all language. When parent and child can share common learning and understanding, good talk is under way. But the child-teacher is rarer than the parent-student. This book tries to bridge the gap between home and school. The time seems right, for we can no longer rely on recall or observation to appreciate our children's studies in English. By the time you read this page, almost 5,000 English teachers will be using in their classrooms and sharing with their colleagues the new insights and understandings gained from Commission on English and National Defense Education Act institutes in English. Training of new teachers, retraining of experienced teachers, an impressive restlessness and intellectual ferment.

New knowledge, new ideas, new experiences prevail. No matter how precocious a parent you are, things have changed since you went to school—not merely the changes you would expect: *Death of a Salesman* instead of *As You Like It* (not *Like You Like It*), Robert Lowell instead of James Russell Lowell, expository writing instead of "creative" writing, communication instead of belles-lettres. Nor are the new devices really significant: tape recorders, learning machines, electronic computers and translators. Nor the methods: team teaching, large-group instruction, ungraded classes, and seminars. What matters is what is being taught through these devices and techniques.

One fundamental change is language content, long the constant among many variables in English. Regardless of fads in reading and phases in writing and foibles in thinking, grammar, like the poor, we always had with us. Whether we lived in the North, where Sandburg's *Lincoln* had become a classic, or in the South, where it was still anathema, whether we cultivated the New England transcendentalists or blazed the trail with Wild Bill Hickok, we all learned some kind of grammar. Nor did we question it. Wasn't grammar the basis for all English?

The unexpected change, the one in language study, is the substance of this book. Since the undeniable contribution of linguistics thus far has been reasoned description in grammar and reasonable prescription in usage, I have concentrated on grammar and usage in today's classrooms. Similarly, I have stressed our new knowledge rather than its practical applications. To include or conclude more during this transitional period would be presumptuous.

When a subject is undergoing change (and which subject does not need to be reformulated from time to time?), we cannot talk unless we clarify our terms, both old and new. The *New York Daily News* means two things by *grammar;* Mr. Lees means something else. We also have to differentiate between popular and technical words. Our everyday use of *transistor* would make an engineer wince, and psychiatrists don't even look for a medical equivalent for the common garden variety of *nervous breakdown.* Therefore we shall have to note the linguists' use of words like *phoneme, dialect, colloquial,* and *grammatical* to achieve some common understanding. In order to present to the general reader new developments in English language study in our elementary and high schools, I have had to use some technical terms for new concepts and knowledge. Capsules and quickies may stimulate chatter but not good talk; often the technical term is the only tool for clear, precise communication. This book should help parent and child to speak the same language about language.

But in describing practices in the schools, I do not suggest an ideal course of study. There is no magic mold and there are no panaceas. We do know, now more than ever before, that good English teaching recognizes the strengths and needs of place and person, if the child is some day to feel part of his universe. Probably the greatest injustice to parent, to child, and to school would be to use part or all of this book as a basis for dissension or as a measure of excellence—especially in our culture, where excellence and diversity interact.

If this book does not try to popularize linguistics and if it offers no dowsing rods or yardsticks, what can it do? It can only tell some of the ways pupils are studying English today. It can encourage parental thought, reading, and responsibility. What better bases have we for communication between home and school? To revive some of the language of the tribe, I write this book for the intelligent parent.

The job has been awesome, but never grim. I owe thanks and apologies to the National Council of Teachers of English, who commissioned the book, left the planning and substance up to me, and waited with infinite patience for the manuscript. Without Robert Hogan, the waiting and the patience would have been in vain. But the mischief was already under way when, through a John Hay Fellowship, I left my own classes and invaded those of Werner Leopold and James Sledd. It assumed serious proportions when I turned the desk on two former students, Nancy Caroline and Barry Rosen. They read parts of the manuscript and offered useful suggestions. There was no retreat when my son Jonathan agreed to play parent and listen to sections. That gleeful tyrant has kept me this side of clarity. I have freely adopted and adapted classic examples from the lectures and writings of Noam Chomsky, Edward Klima, Robert B. Lees, and James Sledd. Many English departments generously shared their programs and materials; others whose work had not reached the mimeograph stage gave freely of their time. No one but Elsie McDermott could have made readable copy of my palimpsest. One name should lead all the rest: that of the scholar-teacher-parent whose criticism has been most helpful. But he'd hoot at hosannas and rail at rosters writ in books of gold.

Miriam B. Goldstein

CONTENTS

II
Grammar

III
Usage

IV
Implications

I

Literacy

WHEN I WAS A CHILD...

1

Education, like charity, begins at home. And "If . . . what educates deeply is the immediate experience of a child within each situation in which he is placed," says Harold Taylor, "then the family is what educates the most." Contrary to alarmists' fears, the most avant-garde linguists would agree. They not only praise the traditional virtues of noun, verb, and motherhood, but also suggest that the child's first and most important teacher is his mother when, in the child's intuitive grasp of the language system, they seek its universal laws. How a cell becomes a human being is no less mysterious and awesome than how a cry becomes a sentence, though one inquiry seems to start where the other one stops. As foetus becomes neonate, he exchanges protective amniotic fluid for disquieting air. A slap on the buttocks, and his new-filled lungs proclaim his birthright to language. Noises will hereafter surround him. Barring any physical defects or emotional blocks, he sorts out and repeats some of these noises; he begins to put them together according to a system. He grasps what he must imitate and what he can vary; he finally understands and utters sentences he has never heard. Without being told the rules, he is playing the language game. This learning feat has so far confounded both theoreticians and toilers in the classroom.

Though the father gets his genetic due, the mother gets most of the linguistic credit. Every language has its words for mother tongue. From her the child learns his language naturally by using it, not reasoning about it. Surrogate voices over TV and radio may compete with or drown out the mother tongue; the child's early communication with the world still echoes, with remarkably accurate nuances, at least the words if not the songs his mother taught him. Listen to, or if it's too late, recall your own child's first class. I can still hear the jabbering in one nursery school shortly after World War II, each child echoing *the* voice that had most eloquently spoken the universal language to some Boston G.I. That lovely Indian Summer every toddler played with, drank, and talked *water*. But David's *water* obviously came all the way from Cincinnati, Debbie's from Edinburgh, Roberta's from Blue Hill Avenue, Pamela's from Beacon Hill, Jonathan's from the Bronx, Scott's from Berlin, Alan's from Tokyo.

With varying success, each child approximated his parent's speech. How could he? And where did it all begin? These questions have teased man since earliest recorded time. Every culture has its oral and written myths explaining how language first came to man; William Golding's *Inheritors* is a recent version.[1] The farther back we go, the more do these theories attribute language to magic—to a thunderclap, to a god, or to God's first word. After Darwin, some of the old myths were revised; the language of Adam was no longer a little lower than the angels'—it was a little higher than the apes'. Finally, to end such fruitless debate, linguists banned from their meetings *all* papers on language origins. Since man probably spoke long before he wrote, his first words will be forever locked in silence and mystery. Cuneiform, the oldest script known, records comparatively recent events: the oral escapades of some Sumerian tradesmen or the physical exploits of a Mesopotamian warrior. Neither tape recorder nor time machine can take us back to the scene of man's most remarkable invention, language. Yet what starts in mystery has become man's greatest source of self-awareness.

[1] William Golding, *Inheritors* (New York: Harcourt, Brace & World, Inc., 1962).

Nor do the languages of "primitive"—nowadays called under-developed—societies tell us anything about how language began. Differences in perceptualizing and conceptualizing, in grammar, in vocabulary, in sounds, do not imply a shorter or longer history. These so-called primitive languages prove to be just as subtle, refined, and incisive as ours. Hopi verbs, combining the concepts of time and motion (for example, *ti'li,* it receives a slight jar, and *tili'lita,* it is vibrating), are remarkably Einsteinian. The Shona (a language of Rhodesia) scheme for naming colors in the spectrum is more useful in optics than are our own categories of violet-indigo-blue-green-orange-red; it divides the spectrum into three parts with specific gradations within each, including black and white.

If these languages bring us no closer to how language began, do they help explain how our children's language begins? TV westerns, Tarzan, and even James Fenimore Cooper's less noble savage try to equate the language of the "child of nature" with the language of the child. But it doesn't work. A baby calls *every* four-legged animal a dog or a kitty. A Laplander has many varied and precise words for different kinds of snow—just as Wintu has for cows and as English has for automobiles. As more and more of us take to skis to escape our automobile-choked cities, perhaps we, too, will need to refine our snow vocabulary. Will our language then be more or less developed or underdeveloped?

As linguistic detectives, specialists may be discouraged; the amateur never is. One ardent young mother, hearing her offspring repeat *aka,* could see the clouds of glory trailing from the grandeur that was Rome's. Every time baby said *aka,* Mama was ready to quench his thirst. The baby soon caught on. But *aka* was the first and last "Latin" word he uttered, until as a ripe teenager he tackled first year Latin. Mama's foibles are a little more forgivable than those of the seventeenth-century linguists whose international politics are revealed by the different languages they attribute to God, to Adam and Eve, and to the snake!

Suppose then we look at the child himself. If his language is not so sophisticated as the Bushman's, might it retrace the experience of all mankind? It might—except that the child learns the language in its *present* state from his parent. Instead of gaining some clues as to language origins, we find ourselves at the opposite end of the time line—not with first speaker but with the latest. And in the learning he in turn transmutes his native tongue. Instead of repeating, he is really modifying the history of his native tongue.

Looking at other languages and other times may be interesting, but we still don't know where and how man became a talking animal. In our own children's development, however, we can see what language is and what it is not. Shall we call the infant's first cry the beginning of speech? Like the rooster's crow, Junior's wail is instinctive, predictable, and eventually distinctive. Yet variations exist. The wet baby and the hungry baby *sound* different. Peristalsis has a contagious rhythm! The dog barks at his master one way and at the mailman quite another way. Even more variation appears as we try to reproduce what we hear. In America, the rooster greets the sun with cock-a-doodle-do; in France and in Israel, if we are to believe the songs, it's koo-koo-reee-koo. So far the little animal in the crib, though infinitely more beautiful, is no more or less eloquent than the little animal in the crate. Shortly, of course, he begins to imitate sounds; but so do some animals. Will the ape ever babble? Will he ever ape sound? Will the mockingbird attach meaning to his mimicry? The parrot can repeat whole sentences; but can he apply them to a specific situation? One parrot in a florist's shop punctures every swain's purchase with "You're a damned fool, you are!" Is the parrot a born misogynist? And currently it is the porpoise whose complex communication invites man's study. Is man to be driven from Eden again?

Yet another Eden awaits the child whose outstretched arms, smacking lips, and bear hug herald "I love you." And later, "I love*d* you once." Still later, "I *will love* you forever and a day." Then, "If I were tickled by the rub of love." And finally to "Love that moves the stars." How many expressions of love will the *animal* ever have to choose from? We can only say that human speech, with its infinite variety, its limitless potential, is a far cry from the animal cry.

The infant's physical maturation will be very much slower than his pet's. Yet how quickly the baby adds other kinds of expression to his repertoire of animal cries! Gestures, grimaces, grunts—all signs of how he feels in a particular situation. The animals can do more! The Cheshire cat grins, perhaps gastronomically. The bee, through an intricate dance language including dialects, guides his co-workers to the nectar. Mother Rabbit thumps her tail to warn the bunnies of approaching danger. All while the baby sends but does not seem to receive signals.

Both infant and animal will ultimately learn to respond to simple verbal commands (*No! Down!*) as well as to gesture, grimace, tone of voice. Some of these seem to communicate universally. That's why we enjoy foreign films, even without dubbing or subtitles. But gestures are quickly conventionalized: one man's handshake is another man's kiss on both cheeks is another man's smelling of both cheeks. And it is words that are most conventionalized. Is there any reason why *dog* means dog and *God* means God? why *chien* and *hund* mean dog? why *Gott* and *dieu* mean God? A social group's arbitrary acceptance provides the convention. And an innovator like Joyce in *Finnegans Wake* exploits such varied conventions to convey multiple levels of meaning.

From this point on, the infant leaves the animal far behind. Just how or why we don't know, but psycholinguists are trying to find out. Physiologically, the speech mechanism consists of secondary functions. Lungs, larynx, palate, nose, tongue, teeth, lips—all of these organs the child has used for survival long before he starts using them for expelling breath through certain organs to produce meaningful sounds. Sapir says these speech organs are no more primary than "the fingers (are) to be considered as essentials of piano playing or the knees as organs of prayer." Breathing, tasting, smelling, digesting are organic and instinctive; speaking is not; it is learned. Still, many of us never learn to play the piano or even feel the need to listen to a percussion instrument. And others of us learn to pray without genuflection, or are immune to all worship. Except through mental or physical disability or self-imposed silence, we cannot help speaking. According to Eric Lenneberg, who has written on children's language disorders, "Man may be equipped with highly specialized, biological propensities that favor and, indeed, shape the development of speech in the child ... roots of language may be as deeply grounded in our natural constitution as, for instance, our predisposition to use our hands." Speech, however, transforms those early instinctive acts, and even more, later acts such as walking and love-making. In turning instinct to intention, speech humanizes the beast in us. At least we enjoy, as Lenneberg says, a "progressive release from immediacy."

How this happens to our children is only a little less mysterious than how it happened to the first man. For one thing, speech is a much more complex act than breathing or digesting or walking. Its maturation is circular; it depends on a constant feedback of experience. How much of it is conditioned response? how much reinforcement? What happens to our theories of reinforcement when we note that sometimes the word or even the sentence comes without warning? Babbling, for example, thrives on auditory feedback. Yet we have reason to doubt that the babbling infant hears his own voice. During the first six months of life the babbling of the normal and the totally deaf child are the same. To complicate matters even more, we know that the child first learns language passively. Since we don't know when it occurs, how do we reinforce it? As specialists in psychology, neurology, and electronic communication theory tell us many new things, personal theorizing seems as futile as the classical aspirations of the ardent mother.

How can we adults, with our clearly defined reaction to our five senses and our ability to conceptualize those reactions, imagine a stage when we reacted synesthetically (our senses receiving one unified impression) and unself-consciously to signals conveyed to our senses? How can we recall a time when a word was not the name for a thing, but was the thing itself? when the word could be manipulated almost as another object in the environment? Preverbal experiences rooted in our unconscious undoubtedly affect our actions and feelings, but we cannot recall life prior to our own use of language; without words we had no means of holding on to these earliest experiences. This is perhaps what led the semanticist Alfred Korzybski to refer to the use of symbols as "time-binding." The wonder of it is that parent and child invariably succeed in this timeless game. We do not know how language comes to the child, how it gets from the outside world in and from the inside out; but we perceive sound, form, and pattern emerging. First, from the instinctive, symptomatic cry through gesture, tone of voice, grimace; then reaction to commands and requests; meanwhile gibberish, pointing, interrogatory sounds. And always the passive learning which surpasses mere listening and imitation. Imperceptibly, communication has been operating. The child is playing the linguistic game with us—though nobody ever told him (or us)— the rules. The baby may be a cryptanalyst, but soon parent and child are both encoder and decoder of a common system operating on a sound channel, and input and output of sound strengthen each other. Suddenly we realize that the human voice is operating in a highly complex system for the child. We understand each other.

At first, when he wanted out, he assaulted the front door pretty much as the dog did. Then, droopy diaper and all, he grabbed his sweater and waited mutely or bawled—depending on your type of discipline. A little later he said "Out" or "Bye bye" and no longer required the door or the sweater to tell us his wishes. Now you say to him, "Get the car key from Daddy" (But for convention, you might have said, "Teg the rac yek morf Yddad."), and he interrupts the last play of the World Series with "Car key. Mommie. Bye bye," or, if he's really caught on to the system, "Mommy want car key." He does not say "Want Mommy key car" or "Key car want Mommy." He has learned the English language, including the private patois invented by your particular family, or even a second language in a bilingual home, by hearing and speaking it. Almost intuitively, he has made the forms and patterns automatic. The language habit, a whole mode of behavior, consists not just of repeating but of creating new sentences and of understanding sentences never heard before. "We move, perceive, and think in a fashion that depends upon techniques, rather than upon wired-in arrangements in our nervous system," Jerome Bruner tells us. "The most important thing about memory is not storage of past experience, but rather retrieval of what is relevant in usable form."

A child may express himself suddenly in words or groups of words. More often he starts sometime before his first birthday with monosyllabic commands (*Up!*) or exclamations (*Hi!*) or names. From here on, according to the findings of psychologists Roger Brown and Ursula Bellugi, although imitation often helps the child to isolate individual words from the blur of sounds, he gains much more by "progressive differentiation" and by "induction of latent structure" as he hears words used in context. When context bewilders, he supplies his own. One little tyrant would not go to sleep until he had exacted his quota of lullabies from his long-suffering mother. One night, she mellifluously began

> I'll sing thee songs of Araby
> And tales of fair Cashmere . . .

only to be interrupted with "Puppy dog tails?"

As the child progresses from indiscriminate pleasure in expressive gibberish to a more coherent world in which word and object merge and then exist independently, he is learning *our* language. The rest of his life he will be sorting what *seems* from what *is*—on ever more complex levels of awareness. Do we thereafter *mold* his expression? Are the word play, the onomatopoeia, the nonsense rhymes and jingles confined to the nursery? Or can the sheer delight in sound, in experimentation with new forms and words, grow with the child? Do we listen to his sounds, his words, his ideas as we help him to

understand ours? What new worlds do we open to the child when he
begins to speak *our* language? What worlds do we shut forever—
except to the poet and the madman?

> "I bet people will think there's been hippos."
> "What would you do if you saw a hippo coming down our street?"
> "I'd go like this, bang! I'd throw him over the railings and roll him
> down the hill and then I'd tickle him under the ear and he'd wag
> his tail."
> "What would you do if you saw *two* hippos?"
> Iron-flanked and bellowing he-hippos clanked and battered
> through the scudding snow toward us as we passed Mr. Daniel's
> house.
> "Let's post Mr. Daniel a snowball through his letter box."
> "Let's write things in the snow."
> "Let's write 'Mr. Daniel looks like a spaniel' all over his lawn."
> —DYLAN THOMAS, "A Child's Christmas in Wales"[2]

Whether we are nurturing good solid citizens, madmen, or poets,
life becomes relatively simple when the baby learns our language! He
has reached a stage where he can control his instinctive responses
and cope with his environment by substituting word for object. Why
cry himself to sleep when talking himself to sleep is such fun? Gradually, he learns to dominate reality with language and, with every
conflict that he resolves, his world becomes ordered and meaningful
—*our* way because we have given him the language. But we need to
remember that *our* way is only one way of perceiving reality.

> We dissect nature along lines laid down by our native languages.
> The categories and types that we isolate from the world of phenomena
> we do not find there because they stare every observer in the face;
> on the contrary, the world is presented in a kaleidoscopic flux of
> impressions which has to be organized by our minds—and this means
> largely by the linguistic systems in our minds. We cut nature up,
> organize it into concepts, and ascribe significances as we do, largely
> because we are parties to an agreement to organize it in this way—an
> agreement that holds throughout our speech community and is
> codified in the patterns of our language.
> —BENJAMIN LEE WHORF, "Science and Linguistics"[3]

[2] Dylan Thomas, *Quite Early One Morning* (New York: New Directions
Paperbook, 1965), p. 29.

[3] Benjamin Lee Whorf, *Language, Thought, and Reality* (Cambridge, Mass.:
Massachusetts Institute of Technology Press, 1956). Reprinted in Harold B.
Allen (ed.), *Readings in Applied English Linguistics* (2nd ed.; New York:
Appleton-Century-Crofts, 1964), p. 62.

This view of language may be too extreme to satisfy scholars, but if we regard home and native tongue as the source of our way of life, Whorf's overstatement can do us parents more good than harm. Bruner says more cautiously, "Linguistic encoding places a selective lattice between us and the physical environment." Yet without a common code, mother and child could not communicate. As the baby's language falls into a clearly identifiable English pattern, we see the wonder of his innate capacity for language learning. At about eighteen months he can predicate statements: *boy-falling, kitty-meow.* Usually the present form satisfies his time sense. Tears flow copiously when Daddy leaves for work in the morning; words like *never, later,* or *tonight* have no meaning yet. Others that have limited use—what we identify as pronouns, conjunctions, prepositions—he does not really need. Plurals and possessives, on the other hand, come in handy. He usually limits adjectives to the tangible and generalizes them in rather bizarre ways. Word order (of noun, verb, adjective) and stressed syllables enable him to utter what we recognize as an English sentence.

The *I,* the identity, expresses itself early or late, depending on the love and assurance the child has known. When there is no one to love or be loved by, *I* may not even emerge. Eventually, the child's interior monologue gives way to dialogue, first with adults and older children, who can decode his telegraphic messages, finally with contemporaries. The frustrating *no* is a healthy sign of autonomy. So is the mother's *no!* Heaven help her if she tries to reason with Johnny as he's about to clobber Billy with a shovel! Even *no* is mastered in context of our categories of experience. A neighbor of mine had carefully taught his infant son that Daddy's books were off limits. Shortly afterward Mommie called me in to display her pedagogic prowess. "Where's the chin?" Eric pointed. "Where are the eyes? and the ears? Where's the nose?" Eric turns to Daddy's bookcase and stands in rigid forbearance.

But context is not enough. The child attaches meaning to objects in his environment as he recognizes their function—our simplest form of definition: a hole is to dig, a knife cuts. For some time Eric called both the electric clock hanging on the kitchen wall and the Wedgewood plates above the dining room dado "cock."

By the age of six, most children, with a speed, effort, and spontaneity never to be duplicated, have about ten thousand words in their recognition vocabularies (five thousand they can use); they have learned to repeat all the vowels and consonants of our language, to use the characteristic intonations, to build and recognize practically all kinds of sentences: commands, questions, statements, exclamations. Without conscious effort or formal terminology, some use and comprehend complex constructions: participles, infinitives, subordinate clauses, nominative absolutes, and objective complements. This is what we mean when we say the six-year-old has his grammar, for grammars exist only internally in human minds. He knows almost intuitively the rules of the language game; the rules for building an English utterance are implicit. He is becoming adept at playing our game. The grammar he will consciously learn has to be externalized, verbalized.

He still has a long way to go. Although he may pronounce some sounds perfectly, he confuses or barely approximates others. As he comes to know what English is supposed to sound like, words (as we hear him talk) take on greater clarity and stability. No longer do so many syllables (as we hear him talk) get lost or transposed, terminal consonants dropped, and sounds slurred. As his horizons enlarge, his vocabulary is only beginning to grow. He may talk a blue streak, yet he is not fluent; he hesitates, repeats himself, makes false starts, and throws in irrelevancies. He isn't on to the logical scheme of things. And it takes more than a kidnapper's patience to keep up with him:

> I like this fine. I never camped out before; but I had a pet 'possum once, and I was nine last birthday. I hate to go to school. Rats ate up sixteen of Jimmy Talbot's aunt's speckled hen's eggs. Are there any real Indians in these woods? I want some more gravy. Does the trees moving make the wind blow? We had five puppies. What makes your nose so red, Hank? My father has lots of money. Are the stars hot? I whipped Ed Walker twice, Saturday. I don't like girls. You dassent catch toads unless with a string. Do oxen make any noise? Why are oranges round? Have you got beds to sleep on in this cave? Amos Murray has got six toes. A parrot can talk, but a monkey or a fish can't. How many does it take to make twelve?
> —O. HENRY, "The Ransom of Red Chief"[4]

He is very much seen *and* heard; he interrupts his elders, even when he knows better. Egocentric creature that he still is, when he needs to speak, he doesn't seem to hear others. Nonetheless, his very linguistic failures show his competence. The child who says "We thank

4 William Sydney Porter (O. Henry), *The Best Short Stories of O. Henry* (New York: Random House, 1945), p. 190.

and thank" or "two ups" has drawn an analogy between *sink* and *think*, between *cup* and *up*. Or perhaps he has had his ups and downs. At any rate, he has abandoned more imitation and has begun to (over-)generalize rules that he knows implicitly.

And yet, though he has far to go, he has gone much farther than most of us at his age. Telephone, radio, movies, and especially television have supplemented the family and the story books that introduced us to language. In his own living room, he sees and hears the President and Captain Kangaroo; he travels the Great Wall of China and visits a rebuilt Hiroshima; he explores the pyramids and leaves Cape Kennedy with the astronauts. If his manners are primitive, his vocabulary and concepts are sophisticated. He has been bombarded with words, their sounds, their images. His two sharpest senses, sound and sight, have been whetted or jaded as never before in human history. "Get Cleft. Yes, Cleft. I mean Cleft; C-L-E-F-T. That amazing soap discovery, etc." has tied the spoken word (one symbol of reality) with the picture or letters (other symbols of reality). Mass communication, for better or for worse, is a kind of reading readiness that the school of the mother's knee could not provide, nor could kindergarten necessarily accomplish it. "Consider the child who knows the difference between a rocket trajectory and a satellite orbit, who can distinguish among hundreds of brands of cereals, soaps, and deodorants, who know families of mytho-poetic names, and don't offer him a cup of magic filled with tap water," warns Frank Jennings. But remember that exposure to the mass media is only a supplement to, not a substitute for, love and learning. Note the glibness, the stereotypes when TV becomes the marijuana of the nursery and the tranquilizer of the elementary years.

What has the child's experience told us about language? First, that it is acquired; it is not instinctive. Second, that it is vocal, though it may be reinforced by gesture or grimace. Third, that it is conventional, a form of social behavior. *Water* means water because a group of people have agreed to call it so; another group got along quite as well with *aqua*. Fourth, that the word is a symbol, that it arbitrarily stands for something; it is not the thing itself. Fifth, that sounds are put together in a system or code that operates through arbitrary, prearranged sets of signals and symbols called sounds, words, phrases, and sentences. The child latches on to this system. The language system, in turn, becomes the basis for the child's exposure to other kinds of reality—to the symbols underlying our

science and mathematics and logic, as well as to the symbols underlying our music and painting and poetry. Through all these symbols,
the child interprets his experience and imposes order upon a kaleido-
scopic universe. These are the symbols that civilize him.

But the preschool child is, in one sense, like prehistoric man; each
has only a spoken language. Where one was ready to *invent* the
secondary form of communication, writing, the other is ready to
learn it. The child's linguistic development will depend on many
variables: sex, intelligence, socioeconomic status, parental education,
experiences outside the home. But the greatest of these variables is
love, the source of the child's trust in others and confidence in himself. We parents may not be able to change what we are; but we
cannot ignore these facts. The six-year-old who feels loved is no
longer the nominalistic toddler or the schematizing four-year-old,
torn between fear and curiosity, dependence and impotence. He has
concrete awareness of himself as a person. His awareness of himself,
his identity, grows with him. It enables him to learn from others,
to become part of the traditions and thoughtways of his people.

He enters school with a natural, intuitive command of language
and an implicit feeling for its structure. School does not impose a
new way of speaking upon him; it builds upon and complements
the language skills he brings. It helps him to *use* language. To become
literate or educated, he may have to learn a new dialect, the one
that has prestige because it communicates most widely to educated
people. But unless he respects himself and his own dialect, learning
another will have little meaning and less joy. School also helps him
to *know* language. If he can become more conscious of the resources of his language—its potentials and its limitations—if his
experiences broaden and deepen, if he learns to think critically about
what he now knows only internally, then behavior which is at six
only a habit becomes science and art. But such learning takes a
lifetime and is never complete; school can only get him started.
How far and fast he will go depends most on the start he gets
at home.

2

The first day you let Johnny and Roberta share the same sandbox, your ascendancy is over. Heretofore, you have been chief model for all kinds of behavior, especially linguistic behavior. Now you are just one among many models. All too soon the *waters* mingle in the nursery school; and from trickle to gushing streams, they sound less like the parents'. These divergences are the earliest forerunners of "Mom, let's face it: you and I just don't speak the same language."

Still the child's language continues to grow naturally and unselfconsciously for the most part. He may become curious about new words:

"Scott wasn't in school. He has a G.I. infection."
"A what?"
"A gastro-intestinal infection. Miss Fidditch said so."

But reading and writing do not come naturally. They require conscious effort on the part of teacher and pupil. As speech becomes more and more natural and flexible, the child is ready for that next step: written language. No one writes the way he talks, but he learns to write from the way he talks. The correspondence between the spoken and written language will be the child's greatest ally as he learns to read and to write. This is why he needs firm footing on the spoken side of the plank before he can bridge the gap to the written word. And when family cannot provide this security, Operation Headstart tries to. If the spoken word is only the symbol for an object or idea, the written word is even more artificial—a symbol of a symbol. Lucky little Serbo-Croatian, for whom sound and written symbol correspond so neatly!

At best, writing can only approximate speech. Ordinary writing, for example, has no symbols to indicate stress, pitch, and subtleties of pause, accompanied by the raised eyebrow, the sardonic smile, the careless shrug. Thus the meaning of a sentence like *Lad is the clever dog* is clear when spoken, but it becomes ambiguous when written without capitals or explanatory parentheses or end punctuation:

> LAD (not Fido) is the clever dog.
> Lad IS (I insist he is) the clever dog.
> Lad is THE (the cleverest of the clever) clever dog.
> Lad is the CLEVER (as opposed to stupid) dog.
> Lad is the clever DOG (not cat).
> Lad is the clever dog. (I'm stating a straightforward fact.)
> Lad is the clever dog! (I'm quite amazed.)
> Lad is the clever dog? (I'm asking a question.)

For a while even the youngster who has mastered his phonics (grapheme-phoneme correspondences) and his phonemics (distinctive patterns of sound) gropes in vain in a myriad of squiggles and tinkertoys and worms sprawling all over the white page. Then his knowledge of the spoken system comes to his rescue. From his own experience and from the total context he supplies the pitch, pause, and stress that complete the meaning of the sentence.

Our symbols for vocal sound are also inadequate. Junior will find no one-to-one correspondence between the twenty-six letters of the alphabet (these smallest units or basic elements of writing the linguist calls *graphemes*) and the thirty or forty characteristic sounds of English. These smallest units of sound or basic signals of speech, the distinctive vowel and consonantal sounds, he calls *segmental phonemes* (as in *pat, bat, sat, cat, fat* or *pet, pit, put, pat, putt, pate, pot*). Pitch, stresses, and pauses that signal specific meaning in context (as in *mE! mE?; add'ress, address'; night'rate, ni'trate*) are called *suprasegmental phonemes*. The phoneme, then, is not itself a sound. It is only an abstraction or generalization based on the speech of many people, a minimal distinction between words. Like a musical chord, it is a bundle of various oppositions simultaneously involving various speech organs. The /p/ phoneme, for example, is nonvocalic as opposed to vocalic, consonantal as opposed to nonconsonantal, tense as opposed to lax, interrupted as opposed to continuant, and so on.

From their initial phonemes, for example, a native speaker hears that these are not English words: *YNGve, NGu, ZDrastvuiyte, XRBauizq*. To supplement the twenty-six letters of the alphabet the linguist can transcribe each of the thirty or forty English phonemes by drawing upon the symbols of an auxiliary writing system such as the International Phonetic Alphabet. The child can hear the different initial phonemes in *p*in, *b*in, *t*in, *d*in, *s*in, *w*in, *k*in, *f*in, and they sound like English words. *Yngin, ngin, zdrin, xrbin,* he as a native speaker rejects. *G*in we had better postpone—for many reasons. He learns the most common sounds corresponding to these alphabet letters, or graphemes, before we complicate life with words like de*b*t, *g*inger, o*h*, a*l*m, *k*now, *p*sychology, *vis à vis,* or *pince-nez.*

Soon the child learns the bitter truth: that the same letter represents several different phonemes and that sometimes it takes more than one letter to represent a single phoneme, as in *th*in, *th*ey, *sh*e, *ch*urch, ju*dge*. But the truth becomes less bitter when he sees the patterns underlying these combinations.

The vowels will be even less predictable than the consonants. The vowel phoneme in *eat* is not spelled as the same phoneme in sc*e*ne, bel*ie*ve, rec*ei*ve, mach*i*ne, w*e*, g*e*nius, or k*e*y. Nor does there seem to be any rhyme or reason why the following pairs don't rhyme: *lived* and *dived, cough* and *though, wave* and *have.*

English as She Is Written
"It's *rough,*" she said with a *cough,* as she sat on a *bough.*

> When the English tongue we speak,
> Why is *break* not rhymed with *freak*?
> Will you tell me why it's true
> We say *sew,* but likewise *few*?
> And the maker of a *verse*
> Cannot cap his *horse* with *worse,*
> *Beard* sounds not the same as *heard.*
> *Cord* is different from *word.*
> *Cow* is cow, but *low* is low.
> *Shoe* is never rhymed with *foe.*
> Think of *hose* and *dose* and *lose*
> And of *goose* and yet of *choose.*
> Think of *tomb* and *comb* and *bomb,*
> *Doll* and *roll* and *home* and *some.*
> And since *pay* is rhymed with *say*
> Why not *paid* with *said,* I pray?
> We have *blood* and *food* and *good,*
> *Mould* is not pronounced as *could.*
> Wherefore *done* and *gone* and *lone*?
> Is there any reason *known*?
> All in short, it seems to me
> Sounds and letters disagree.
> —THE YALE PANEL[1]

[1] Quoted in *Journal of Education,* **101** (1925).

Fortunately, the patterns of English words depend more on consonants than on vowels. *Brd, bttr, wtr, mlk,* if part of the spoken vocabulary, are easily read in context even without their vowels. But the complexity of our system of sounds, words, phrases, and sentences remains. And in our great desire to make life *easier* for our children, we might be tempted to improve the old alphabet or even to write a new one, with a one-to-one correspondence between grapheme and phoneme. Some teachers use an augmented alphabet to help the child with these anomalies and seeming inconsistencies until he is ready for our twenty-six letters plus a few printing conventions known as punctuation; for example, a represents the a in *cat; a,* the a in *barn;* and æ, the a in *same.* But in spite of George Bernard Shaw's bequest and in spite of President Theodore Roosevelt's reforms, our spelling system has not been revised.

How did our own alphabet become so "inefficient"? The blame isn't all ours. We got our writing system from the Romans, who got it from the Greeks, who got it from the Hebrews, who got it from the Phoenicians, who got it from the Egyptians, who got it from the Mesopotamians, who got it from where? Each heard the phonemes of his own language and adapted the writing system to it. Egyptian hieroglyphics were at first purely representational, with different pictures to represent different objects. Later, as picture writing began to symbolize words and finally sounds, there was bound to be some overlap among the symbols—with more than one symbol for the same sound. Suppose we had used a wavy line for *sea* and the human eye for *see.* When we decided to represent sounds, which picture would we choose for the first two phonemes in the word *seat?* To complicate matters, when the Greeks adapted the system they not only reversed the direction of their words, but they tried to add vowels; they did not, however, systematically treat the long and short vowels. Epsilon and eta, omicron and omega are the short and long *e* and the short and long *o* of the English alphabet. But the Romans in turn adapted and rejected some of these letters and handed us an alphabet that in turn had to accommodate five vowels to a great variety of vowel sounds.

As alphabet borrowing continued from one language to the next, sound and letter diverged ever more; for no two languages have a one-to-one correspondence among their characteristic sounds. But once adopted, the writing system sticks, even though pronunciation keeps changing. Long after we stopped pronouncing the guttural (or velar fricative[2]) in *thought* or in *daughter,* we retain the *g* in the spelling. Finally, and of great importance, English has so blithely borrowed—from Latin, the Scandinavian, the French, especially—that our spelling is a combination of all their systems.

To say that writing is more conservative than speaking, however, is *not* to say that spelling doesn't change. Speech and writing necessarily interact, as we can see in the development of American English. Initially it was the dialect of Renaissance London that became standard—when the speech of the economic and political capital signified affluence and success. It was a British spelling that became conventional—when the invention of printing demanded an end to whimsical and idiosyncratic spelling. Nonetheless we have modified these well-born conventions. We no longer follow the British spellings of *color, honor, labor;* we now sound the *l* in *soldier;* we have had little success in our attempts to force the *shall-will* distinction into our writing, since it never existed in speech.

The writing system, then, has been with us a long time. It is heavily in debt to its predecessors and neighbors. It is perhaps inefficient and inconsistent, confusing and deficient, and unable to keep pace with changes in the spoken language. But writing does change.

And somehow the child does manage to overcome the hurdles, to learn the system despite the apparent inconsistencies and confusions. He knows that words like *tloo* and *mer* are not English; he learns to accept the fact that spoken and written English are quite different. Yet he learns to reconcile the discrepancies.

No matter what the sequence may be, reading is a matter of sharpening the eyes as well as the ears, of responding to signals in space as well as signals in time. The letters of the alphabet have names; but the letters, not their names, suggest the sounds on the printed page. Matching these letters and sounds is phonics. Recognizing patterns among the letters is phonemics. Oral and silent reading reinforce the habitual response to signals. When the child can bring to the printed page an awareness of the signals which writing does not supply (intonation, stress, and some kinds of pause), his phonics and phonemics have served him well.

The child learns to attack and master the printed page, then, both by being able to recognize familiar words and by being able to spell them. The first five hundred follow the most common contrastive

[2] The sound made by friction of the breath as it passes over the back of the tongue touching the soft palate: most nearly the sound of *k* in English.

patterns of letters: single consonant + single vowel + single consonant, a single replacement at a time of initial letter (*at, cat, mat, hat,
fat*), final letter (*hat, had, has*), or medial letter (*bad, bed, bid, bud*);
then the digraphs (*than, thin, thing, shin, chin*); then a consonantal
cluster of phonemes replacing a single initial or final phoneme (*stop,
last, skin*); then consonantal clusters replacing two or more phonemes
(*clasp, strength, asks*); and finally doubling of letters (*full, pass,
fall*). He reads at sight in a familiar context and never looks at
letters and sounds without context. Thus reading and writing familiar
words become automatic habits.

What then do we mean by learning to read? If learning to read is
deriving meaning from the printed page, Charles C. Fries in *Linguistics and Reading* shows how the teacher achieves this goal through
different methods that reinforce each other.[3] One is helping the child
to recognize signals that differentiate lexical (dictionary) meanings.
He has to see how *tan, tin, ten* are alike and how they differ and what
that difference means phonemically before he can distinguish lexical
meanings of these words. Sometimes the context signals the particular
meaning of a word like *dressing,* which has several lexical meanings.
But to stop here is hardly to assure total meaning. Grammatical
structure signals other meanings to him. In *The men drove the cars*
the child has to recognize form classes (*man-men, car-cars, drive-
drove*), function words like *the* or *at,* and word order if he is to
make complete sense of what the printed page is telling him. Finally,
the child has to incorporate these signals into a pattern of social-
cultural meaning or significance. *A fairy made Cinderella beautiful:*
With a magic wand or with a hair rinse? Or *God drove Adam and
Eve out of the garden of Eden:* Was He an avenger or a chauffeur?

Every child has to learn to reconcile the discrepancies between
our speech and our writing system and to recognize all the signals
of meaning. The child who comes to school with a dialect other
than the prevailing one, obviously has to face two sets of discrepancies;
he has to hear his own speech and a somewhat different kind of
speech in his classroom and connect them both with the same printed
page. The first step, then, is to respect his dialect but also to acquaint
him with the prevailing dialect in the community. Then he will have
less difficulty hearing the correspondences between spoken and written
English. Finally he has to become so adept at handling symbols

[3] Charles C. Fries, *Linguistics and Reading* (New York: Holt, Rinehart and
Winston, Inc., 1963).

that he can tackle the vagaries of meaning not only through graphemes that signal sound but also through graphemes that signal a
total abstraction. $+$, $-$, 1, 2, 3—these have no aural correspondence;
they are ideographs, symbols that represent ideas rather than sounds
of words; i.e., they are *plus, minus, one, two, three,* in English; *de
plus, moins, un, deux, trois,* in French. Knitting, chess, or bridge
instructions similarly relate symbol to abstraction rather than to a
set of corresponding sounds.

At this point, the protective parent might say, "Why all this fuss
over written English? It's so abstract, so artificial, so ineffective! In
our world of mass communication, isn't speech enough? Aren't
radio, TV, tape recorder, and univac ample and more faithful records
than mere writing or printing?" To a large extent they are. And for
most parts of the world, as well as for many years of our own
history, the spoken word has been sufficient. Yet writing remains
more accessible than speech. When we need to communicate, the
pen is handier and less subject to breakdown than the transistor.
Although you may have missed the President's nationally televised
address, you can read it in tomorrow's *Times.* And if you want to
reconsider part of it, you can backtrack without disturbing anyone.
If you want to compare what he is saying now with what he said
last year, it is the written word that will damn him or save him.
Furthermore, everything antedating our era of mass communication
is available chiefly in written form. How many people could Shakespeare or Milton have reached if they had left no written records?
And if we had only their voices on tape or disc, how many of us
could understand their speech? Was it only awe and superstition that
gave the name *Scriptures* to the *Bible?*

Writing, as we have said, is much more conservative than speech.
And although it cannot stop change in language, it can slow down
change considerably. Differences in time, geography, social status
are less noticeable in written than in spoken English. Thus written
English is more general and more stable; it is understandable practically all over the world. And finally, because it cannot rely on the
signals of speech—stress, pitch, pause, and of facial expression and
gesture—written language must be carefully structured, more precise
and clear; it is a demanding science and art.

An awareness of these differences between speech and writing will
to a large extent be reflected in today's English classroom. The
reading teacher understands the relation between the two and can

help the child to use the signals of speech (sound patterns, word order, stress, pitch, pause) as he learns to read and to spell. Learning to sound words will not be enough. It is the *total system* that must emerge from the printed page. Hence the virtues of both oral and silent reading, of both phonics—learning to put together the sounds of a word, and look-say—to recognize the whole word or sentence rather than its parts. As he learns to associate punctuation with intonation and with other features of syntax which he now knows only intuitively, he will *hear* variations of pitch for different kinds of questions, statements, and requests. He will see punctuation suggesting these inflections—long before he worries about interrogatives, declaratives, and imperatives.

Reading and writing are mirror images of each other. The child assembles the parts to read meaning into the whole sentence. When he writes, he thinks the whole sentence and breaks it down into the smallest written parts. The better the teacher knows these minimal units of sentence structure, the more he can help the child every step of the way. The linguistically trained teacher also sees the larger relationships: that learning to listen and to speak were the first mirror images that grew with reinforcement. Now listening, speaking, reading, and writing reinforce each other.

From the simplest reading on, the child will see why writing the way we talk may be good, but not good enough. If he is to communicate with an ever expanding yet shrinking world, he has to learn how to "sacrifice the local for the general, the spontaneous for the permanent." He learns not by bowing to a series of fiats, of do's and don't's, but by being encouraged to create his own sentences, to make his own choices, and even to make his own mistakes. The first grade is not too early for individuality and responsibility in the use of language.

If style is the man, and style is linguistic choice, all we can do is expose the child to local and general, to spontaneous and permanent, in what he hears and reads. Education only enlarges his options. Let him choose the language that best says what he has to say where he has to say it; let him take the consequences; and teach him how to repair the damage if he fails. The first school year as it involves the child in literacy establishes important attitudes. With the simplest sentences, he can begin to see that good writing is the result of conscious choice, not decree. And since English is a living language, the range and choice must vary with time and place. As he matures, the *sound* of his writing will provide one of his best guides. If it sounds too much like his daily speech, it will be spontaneous but may not communicate generally. If it doesn't sound like him at all, it is probably too general to interest anyone. It will be anything but permanent. The spoken word links him to his contemporaries, his immediate world. The written word links him to the mainstream of history and the universe.

Such learning is not easy. But what is the alternative? If we impose a single standard on speech and writing, the pupil blunders into a no-man's refuge, where he guiltily tries to speak as he writes, and innocently tries to write as he speaks. He is learning not English, but classroom English. Better for him to know soon that when he speaks, success depends on his ability to adapt his language to that of the particular group; when he writes, he has to make himself clear to any reader anywhere. He need not sacrifice his individuality in order to observe the uniform writing standards of educated people. Only with this awareness does he enjoy language's two time frequencies, the spontaneous and the permanent.

SPELLING: THE BRIDGE BETWEEN
THE TWO R'S

3

"We are all over the shop with our vowels because we cannot spell them with our alphabet," said George Bernard Shaw. He was so annoyed that he left a sizable sum to anyone who would improve our antiquated, chaotic system. He even spelled out the way. "Design 24 new consonants and 18 new vowels, making in all a new alphabet of 42 letters, and use it side by side with the present lettering until the better ousts the worse." His bequest is still gathering dust and interest, and the twenty-six letters of our inefficient alphabet we still have with us.

Also the poor spellers. Despite the complaints of college presidents, editors, businessmen, parents, and teachers, the schools keep graduating poor spellers. (So do the colleges, for that matter.) Somewhere in the hierarchy of mortal and venial sins, errors in spelling abide and life goes on. A few see this problem as part of the general decline in standards in our time: in dress, in morality, in communication. Others see it as part of a temporary decline, another form of adolescent rebellion against conformity. They point to the gleeful assault upon spelling in the primary grades, to the spelling bees, to Junior's encyclopedic recall of spelling, geography, and history. Before he becomes disenchanted with school, he glories in indiscriminate, arcane memorizing. "Where is St. Ignatius Loyola buried?" he asks Mom just as she's lifting a soufflé out of the oven. Or "I'll bet you don't know the capital of Outer Mongolia," as he helps Dad lift the storm picture window. And when Grandpa rejoices in his youthful spelling of *antidisestablishmentarianism,* Junior asks, "But can you spell *floccinaucinihilipilification* backward in one breath?"

Then comes "the sturm und drang." Nothing matters; our adolescent's sloppiness in dress, in table manners, in writing appalls us. Give him time. When he wants to make a good impression, he can change the Beatle mop for a crew cut, the chain drive-in for the Four Seasons, and the spelling? No! Poor spellers abound in our world and the adolescent's. Poor spelling is unrelated to age or intelligence or education or occupation. The most obvious proof lies in the fact that most errors occur in simple, everyday words. Misspelling afflicts us all to some degree. The only one who is almost infallible is the trained professional proofreader.

Some people, especially those with good visual memories, find spelling easy. They're like those blessed with absolute pitch in music. Others, especially the ones with visual or hearing problems, are poor spellers, as naturally handicapped as the color-blind. And all of us can blame our spelling system if we want to. Who can deny the many foreign sources of our English words, the widening gap between our pronunciation and our spelling, and the seeming inconsistencies as we go from *pacify* to *pacific* and from *history* to *historical?* Since there are so many reasons for good and bad spelling, a single approach, pace, or method is useless. But because spelling usually improves with seeing, hearing, speaking, and writing, it is part of punctuation, pronunciation, and vocabulary study for all. Regardless of the cause, we cannot deny that incorrect spelling quickly damns the writer and sometimes slows down communication. The important goal is to help oneself. Only then can patterns and reasons facilitate learning.

First the poor speller has to stop rationalizing his disability. Although not the most serious error in communication, misspelling need not be dismissed as trivial or incurable. Since the invention of printing, idiosyncratic spelling has ceased to be a mark of individuality or distinction. Nor can the disability be dismissed by our saying modern English spelling is chaotic, that it is not phonemic. There never was a time when every single letter matched every single sound in our language—nor can there be one for long. Though Kemal Atatürk changed the Turkish method of writing and spelling to a phonetic Roman alphabet in 1928, students of the language note the changes in pronunciation that have even since then made the spelling system less perfect. So long as language is spoken, it will change. If spelling cannot prevent change, it at least standardizes and thus unifies and transcends the many dialects in a language.

The student is best prepared to face the phonemic-graphemic correspondences and differences if he first learns the regularities of our system and then the irregularities and their possible reasons. In a typical elementary school list of three thousand words, four fifths of the spelling is phonemic. Thus in the primary grades the pupil learns to recognize, to respond automatically to the major contrastive sets that represent the word patterns of our language. As we saw in the last chapter, he learns to associate sounds with patterns of letters rather than individual letters. Charles C. Fries in *Linguistics and Reading* lists these patterns in considerable detail.[1] Usually the pupil starts by noting the contrast when a single letter is changed in one-syllable words containing the same consonant and vowel sequences. Thus he identifies the various vowel phonemes in

at	it	——	——	——
bat	bit	bet	——	but
cat	——	——	cot	cut
fat	fit	——	——	——

From contrasts in the initial consonant (*bat, cat, fat*) he goes to contrasts in the final consonant of these one-syllable words (*bad, bag, ban*) and on to contrasting vowels (*bag, big, beg, bog, bug*), then to words containing final digraphs (*bath, ash, gush, bang*) to words with initial consonant clusters (*span, scan, skin, skid*) and final clusters (*ask, desk*) and multiple clusters (*branch, clamp, cranks*) and finally words with double consonants for single phonemes (*back, all, kiss*). Thus the pupil learns to respond automatically to the most significant spelling patterns of our language. He sees the connection between grapheme and phoneme. When he has mastered these one-syllable words, which provide the base for many polysyllable words, he is ready for more unusual sets of spelling patterns. But the reading habit does not assure the spelling habit. A good reader is not necessarily a good speller.

Wherever possible, teachers stress the positive approach. One way is to say what letters do appear in a word rather than what letters shouldn't appear but often do, as in *separate*. Mnemonic devices (like "when you sep*a*rate, you divide into p*a*rts"), dictation reviews, diagnostic and remedial tests may be of some use. Practice in dictionary skills, beginning in the early elementary grades, introduces pupils to suffixes, prefixes, homonyms, words in context, and common spelling rules. Drill in phonics—in digraphs, long and short vowels, dipthongs, double consonants, silent letters, and blends—often has to be reinforced into the high school years. Interesting word derivations make some words stick.

[1] Charles C. Fries, *Linguistics and Reading* (New York: Holt, Rinehart and Winston, Inc., 1963), pp. 171–182.

Another way to stress the positive is to offer a reasonable explanation for some of our spelling that seems to have no rhyme or reason. Thomas Pyles' chapters on the alphabet and spelling in *The Origins and Development of the English Language* (see Suggested Reading) offer many answers. There are historical explanations, for example, for our *c* before *e* and *i*, pronounced *s;* for *qu*, pronounced *kw*; for the insertion of *gh* in *right*. All of these changes can be traced back to Anglo-French scribes. Similarly many double vowels and consonants go back to a single text, the *Ormulum*.[2] The disappearance of silent *e*, the remnant of an old inflectional ending, goes back to the fifteenth century. The attempts to make spelling reflect word origins can be seen in some sixteenth-century "improvements" like the *b* in *debt* and the *s* in *island*. A knowledge of the systematic changes our vowels have undergone clarifies some of our questions about spelling. When we see how these sound changes characterize our language's growth, we begin to attach some meaning to arbitrary classifications like Old English, Middle English, Early Modern English, and Modern English.

Positive techniques and knowledge help; but what helps most is isolating the child's spelling problem. Often this diagnosis and individual treatment calls for a trained speech therapist rather than the regular classroom teacher; some schools have a full-time therapist on the faculty. Sometimes, however, the poor speller is a very logical person who is trying to impose order on our spelling. By the laws of analogy, he tries to regularize the language. His sins are certainly forgivable. But most often the poor speller has neither specific disability nor logical bent; he simply hasn't been motivated to do anything about his spelling. If he can be spared guilt feelings and can just see spelling as a custom commonly observed by literate people, he may want to improve. The following procedures may then help.

First the pupil has to listen, to know the meaning and pronunciation of the word he hears. If he doesn't know how to spell it, just guessing will only get him more confused. Trial and error is useful only when there is some underlying reason for the guess, when the pupil is learning to trust his intuitions. Looking, seeing, printing the word, with special emphasis on the unexpected or difficult part, should

[2] A fragmentary manuscript from the 13th century, in which the author, Orm, devised his own phonetic system of distinguishing short vowels by doubling the following consonant.

be followed by saying the word. Here any discrepancies between pronunciation and spelling should be noted and possibly accounted for. Underlining and saying the syllable may fix the word. The pupil may test himself by covering part of the word and writing that part or by covering all the word, writing it, and checking. When the pupil starts spelling this word correctly in his own compositions, he has really mastered it. Checking the pupil's weekly progress by dictating the words in sentences and encouraging the pupil to keep an individual spelling list have helped some. In Ralph M. Williams' class at Trinity College an average speller, by using these methods of practice, does not miss more than one word in a hundred in his compositions.

Much of this is old and just plain common sense. Yet technique and planned instruction have replaced random correction and arbitrary testing. The old spelling bee, picturesque as it is, has gone the way of the old oaken bucket. Today teaching spelling means more than testing spelling, and diagnosing spelling errors means more than separating the elect from the damned every Friday. And composition work is more than an excuse for teaching spelling. In other words, time is being set aside for spelling work in English classes nowadays. But such time justifies itself on the grounds of knowledge and results; there is no virtue in drill and hard work just for its own sake.

We know, for example, that some things do not help the pupil. Merely copying the word, trying to change the letters in a doubtful word, asking someone to spell the word aloud, or saying the word or uncovering it letter by letter has no effect because it contradicts whatever we know about content and method in spelling. All the well-meaning parent can do is to pretest words the child is learning to spell and then retest after he has studied them. If the child wants his homework checked, the parent can cross out the misspelled word and write it correctly for him to copy. The parent can discourage guessing and encourage reasonable hypothesizing about doubtful words. Most important of all, the parent's attitude toward spelling matters. He has to see it as a part, but only a part, of writing.

In addition to common-sense attitudes at home and at school, we have some real advances in knowledge about spelling. Some linguists, using the principle that speech is primary and writing only a representation of speech, have carefully analyzed our sound system, the basis of our writing system. Through refining the concept of phoneme and using signals of grammatical and lexical meaning, through isolating common sound patterns, these linguists have shown us the regularities underlying our whole spelling system. Now we have fewer anomalies to account for and fewer words to learn in complete isolation. Gradually we can abandon the old spelling texts that arbitrarily list words without context or with only thematic unity. Instead we are turning to spellers that recognize the relationship between speech and writing, that draw upon discreet items and lists that reveal underlying spelling regularities to the student. Robert A. Hall, Jr.'s *Sound and Spelling in English*[3] and Ralph M. Williams' *Phonetic Spelling*[4] are based on linguistic principles. Spelling lessons now have intellectual challenge and substance. Priscilla Tyler's work with teachers at Harvard University and at the University of Illinois has brought systematic, phonemically based spelling lessons to many classrooms throughout the country.

Finally Morris Halle and Noam Chomsky's forthcoming *Sound Pattern of English* may suggest the need for new advanced spelling texts for teachers who seek a rigorous analysis of our sound system and subsurface explanations for our spelling system. Thus far the work of Halle and Chomsky seems to show that English spelling is far less erratic than we had thought and that stress is predictable. Why do we go from long to short vowel in words like

cone	conic	esthete	esthetic
sane	sanity	kinesis	kinetic
serene	serenity	crisis	critic
divine	divinity		

and reverse the process in words like *study, studious* or *aqua, aqueous?* And is stress a matter of hit or miss in words like

telegraph	telegraphic	telegraphy
aristocrat	aristocratic	aristocracy

and in *copula, cinema, jalopy, tomato, Delaware,* and *tobacco?* What shall we call rules and what exceptions in spelling? The most insightful studies show that differences in spelling and pronunciation within a dialect and among dialects can be accounted for by the rules of the grammar of the language. Either the rules differ or they are being intuitively applied in a different order.

[3] Robert A. Hall, Jr., *Sound and Spelling in English* (Philadelphia: Chilton Books, 1961).

[4] Ralph M. Williams, *Phonetic Spelling for College Students* (New York: Oxford University Press, 1960).

Here again, we have another instance of how advances in theoretical knowledge enable the informed classroom teacher to reexamine his course content, texts, and methods. Only then can he be free to select what remains useful from our past spelling practices and to adapt what seems reasonable from current research. This is how the study of spelling has moved from virtuoso renditions of *antidisestablishmentarianism* to rote memorizing of random lists, even those pertaining to St. Ignatius or to Outer Mongolia, to phonemic analysis and on to powerful explanation of how and why we spell as we do.

When Mr. Shaw said we might just as well spell fish *ghoti,* he was admitting his unawareness of the simplest phonemic principles underlying our spelling system. Have you ever seen *gh* pronounced *f* anywhere but at the end of an English word? Can you think of a word other than *women* to justify Shaw's *o* with the short *i* sound? And where but within a word is *ti* pronounced *sh,* as in mo*ti*on or pa*ti*ent or conten*ti*ous? "We are all over the shop with our vowels" only when we choose to remain ignorant of phonemic spelling rules.

LEARNING A SECOND LANGUAGE:
THE TWO R'S IN A SHRINKING WORLD

4

For many children in our midtwentieth century, learning to read and write simply means learning to speak, understand, read, and write a *new* language. But if the first half dozen languages are the hardest, wherefore is English different from all other languages? And why worry about English as a second language? Precisely because a second language means not one among six or more but the one which is becoming the means of communication throughout the world.

Such a thing does not happen through any virtue of the language. English is in the ascendancy not because it is more precise than French, or more modern than Sanskrit, or more musical than Swahili, or more adaptable than German, or more teachable than Lithuanian. Just as the London dialect became standard English when this city became the political and economic capital of Great Britain, so has English become a world language as English-speaking peoples became the leaders in international politics and economics. If such leadership should pass to Kerala or the South Pole, the language of the new world leaders would become the new world language. Newly emerging nations, acutely aware of the need to communicate with the rest of the world, are naturally turning to English in their schools. Children all over the globe are today learning English. Often it becomes the language of instruction in all their subjects from the primary grades on.

English is also a second language for many a new citizen of the United States and even for many a native. A generation or two ago, when this country became the great European melting pot, the five-year-old from an Italian, Polish, Jewish, or German ghetto would leave the shelter of his small immigrant world to learn a new language in Public School 101 and to learn all other subjects—from gym to art—in this new language. In *Call It Sleep* Henry Roth has, with remarkable accuracy, recorded the variations within one such ghetto's dialects.[1] In our own time, Puerto Ricans in New York,

[1] Henry Roth, *Call It Sleep* (New York: Avon Books, NS2, 1964).

French Canadians in Maine, Mexicans in the Southwest, Cubans in Florida, Orientals in Hawaii and California, Indians in Alaska and the West present, as the Council for Public Schools well knows, "a growing challenge to the schools." They, too, are learning English as a second language.

At home and abroad the problem is the same. Every language we learn after the first, we learn against the backdrop of the first. To ignore this fundamental fact of linguistic life is to create obstacles for teacher and pupil. We cannot afford to think only of the language mastery we ultimately expect of the child and to ignore the language he brings to the second language. English presents one problem for the child who eats a bowl of "lice" or takes the "erebata" to the tenth floor. It may present even more problems to the one who asks for "baniira eisu Kurimu" and expects you to give him banana ice cream. The tense system in his language is no doubt much simpler than ours. Or it may have no definite article. Its idiomatic expressions are not ours. The teacher has to know the child's language, then, in order to clarify the important contrasts between the two. Even under the best circumstances English is not an easy second language. We isolate the peculiar problem of learning English in school only to see what teacher and pupil must do that does not ordinarily happen in a bilingual community. For wherever English is taught as a second language, it already exists, if only on the periphery or in garbled form. Language teaching and learning go on in the stores, on the radio, in the hospitals, and on the streets. The school has to do the same job more uniformly and efficiently. "Linguists are but midwives, without whom parturition would nevertheless take place; one function of linguistics, like that of the midwife, is to increase the convenience, comfort, certainty, and dispatch of a natural process." So says Peter Strevens, who has taught English in different parts of the English-speaking world.

But what do we mean by mastery? What shall we call the goals? What familiarity with the language shall we settle for? Being able to speak it well enough to find our way in a strange city or to listen to the radio or to read a daily newspaper or to study its classics or to make a livelihood in a trade or a profession? To the degree to which we know these goals, we can choose the appropriate means. For some, listening or conversing is enough; for others, reading and/or writing is a must. And always, listening to or conversing with whom? In each case, the particular model is important. Speaking

Burmese English in Toronto gets you no farther than speaking Kansas City high school French in Paris. Reading the *Rio Piedras Sheep and Goat Raiser's Daily* is not reading Cervantes or Lope de Vega.

So in teaching English today, the specific model or goal determines what will be included and excluded. English is so vast a subject that unless we limit the goals we can see only hit-or-miss results. This is where the art of second-language teaching lies. For the teacher must first master the description of the language in its oral and written forms in order to decide what parts he must filter for his pupils' mastery. The linguist can alert the teacher to varieties of English appropriate to a particular community. The teacher's job is to select and to teach from within that corpus or area. Then what grammar, vocabulary, and speech work will make sense for this particular class? And in what order to assure growth? Good texts try to answer these questions; the specifics are the teacher's.

The structural linguists, with their emphasis on the primacy of speech, on the direct approach to learning a language by speaking it, have opened the door. If the child has the chance to speak the language, he can become a fluent conversationalist. Unfortunately if he stops there, he is just as handicapped as the one who can read a printed page but cannot speak or follow a talk on radio or television. The saddest waste of all is that so many of us learned a foreign language moderately well enough to be able to speak and read. Then, through years of disuse, we find ourselves able to read aloud from the printed page without the slightest degree of comprehension. The languages we learn early and naturally, stick; the later ones we have to make stick. This is why a specialist like Strevens feels we need the linguist's knowledge or description of a language and the teacher's know-how in applying this knowledge to suit his students' needs. Learning a second language, he feels, depends on teaching methods and linguistic description, on what we know and how we teach it. Even this is not all.

Pauline Rojas has found that for the Dade County, Florida, public school teachers, brief inservice training is not enough. They have to be reoriented from problem-solving techniques in content subjects to the psychology of drill work in a skill. Many cannot or will not make this change—possibly for valid reasons.

So we are exploring and experimenting with new approaches and new materials, especially for English as a second language in the primary grades. The problem is to find the common core of learning any English teacher has to have and impart and then to find the specifics that will enable the little Peruvian schoolboy to learn his English as effectively as the little Afghanistan schoolgirl learns hers. In a land like India, with perhaps 200 languages and twice that number of dialects, English can bring this new generation national as well as worldwide communication.

New materials and texts are forthcoming: some from TESL co-sponsored by the Council for Public Schools and Columbia University with the help of a grant from the U.S. Office of Education; some from Project English in the research and materials at Hunter College; some from the *English for Today* series edited by William Slager for the National Council of Teachers of English and the U.S. Information Agency.[2] All of these build upon the pioneer work of Otto Jespersen's *How to Teach a Foreign Language*[3] and Charles C. Fries' *Teaching and Learning English as a Foreign Language*[4] and his *American English Series.*[5] Conferences, institutes, training programs abound. The American Council of Learned Societies, the Center for Applied Linguistics, the National Defense Education Act Foreign Language Institutes, UNESCO—all of these are helping to meet the challenge of teaching English as a second language.

Knowing the pupil's native language and being able to establish significant contrasts between it and English always helps. But a good second-language text can alert pupil and teacher to peculiarities of English that the native takes for granted and hardly thinks about. W. Stannard Allen's *Living English Structure: A Practice Book for Foreign Students* provides a good deal of exercise in forms that we use intuitively. These exercises are designed for the mature student. It then summarizes in tabular form what practice has made into habit for the pupil:[6]

[2] Published by the McGraw-Hill Book Company, New York, 1962–1966, for the NCTE and the USIA.

[3] Otto Jespersen, *How to Teach a Foreign Language* (New York: The Macmillan Company, 1904).

[4] Charles C. Fries, *Teaching and Learning English as a Foreign Language* (Ann Arbor, Mich.: University of Michigan Press, 1945).

[5] Pauline M. Rojas *et al., Fries American English Series,* Books 1–6 (Boston: D. C. Heath and Company, 1952).

[6] W. Stannard Allen, *Living English Structure: A Practice Book for Foreign Students* (4th ed.; New York: Longmans, Green & Co. Ltd., 1959), p. 44. Reprinted by permission of Longmans, Green & Co. Limited.

Obligation (must)	*Prohibition (mustn't)*	*No Obligation (needn't)*
Present		
he must go	he mustn't go	he needn't go
he has (got) to go	he isn't to go	he hasn't got to go
[he needs to go]		he doesn't need to go
		he doesn't have to go
Future		
as above, and	As above	As above, and
he'll have to go		he won't have to go
[he'll need to go]		he won't need to go
Past		
he had got to go	he wasn't to go	he hadn't got to go
[he needed to go]		he didn't have to go
		he didn't need to go
		he needn't have gone

NOTE: The forms in square brackets do not occur very frequently and need not be practised.

Still, good and bad texts, good and bad teaching will be with us for some time. Some people feel that a world language enables each culture to move directly into the twentieth century and so to help itself achieve real autonomy. They see no alternative. Others point to the breakdown of parental control and the weakening of family foundations when home and school speak two different languages. Or they point to the poor teaching that prevails when teachers are unprepared for—just assigned to—this necessary job. Ralph Long says, "In the public schools of Puerto Rico, English gets off to a bad start from which real recovery is exceptional." Some feel English, even when well taught, cannot really translate or express the thought-ways of some other cultures.

Compositions like these from an overseas high school make the difficulties—and the challenge—undeniable.[7]

Book Report

The most important person in this book is Akin. He is a young boy. He was a drummer. He is a tall boy. He wears long trouser, and a shot shirt. He lives at Lagos. He went to Akure before but he returns back to Lagos. He goes about to beat his drum to the people, and he was given a money in which he spends of. Even, a king asked him to come and play for him.

[7] These compositions were written by pupils in another country. Their teacher has given the author permission to reprint the compositions in this book, provided that they are not further identified.

"Ali"

The name of the most important in this story is called Ali. Ali was a clever man who was a Persia. Ali was a smat man and also brave, he live with his father and mother and his wife and son too. Ali was a tall man. He look like a pretty man, and then he was so beautiful. He known how there lanuage form by the accent people, he was too smart on asking question? Ali is a good man. On that day he was soon asleep and he saw Ja'afar who was is friend. Comes to Called him to Harun al Rashid. Harun al Rashid who lay awake, unable to sleep saw Ja'far comes he was so glad. So Ja'afar obey him and he was clever man. Ali beging to told them some story that he, has seen in his face and something that he had head.

The Election of St. Anselm's Football Team

There is one boy at St. Anselm's Grammar School. The name of this boy is John. He has one friend whose name is Peter. Peter, the friend of John is a very rascal boy. He wears dirty clothes and he doesn't care whether he is going to die today. He always play rough. When Peter's school is beaten in a match he will play roughly to score a goal. He is known as the best goal kicker in the school, because of this rough playing. John, who is very gently back in completion knows how to run very very very etc fast. He is the best runner on his school's football team. He plays a clean game and he always strugles to score for this team. According to Peter's rascality and his disobedien his father punishes him for not buying clothes for him. So he is always rough.

John is a very handsome boy and other boys jelous of him. He is always neat and his is intelligent. John knows book. O, you see, he knows science and he speaks good English O. you see.

John is selected as the captain of his school because of his good habit. He is not a cantekerous boy.

COMPLICATING THE TWO R'S

5

An even larger problem than English as a second language is the related problem of bilingualism. All we can definitely say is that we have no conclusive information—only conflicting theories—about its effects on children. Many children overseas grow up multilingual. In the Middle East many a normal six- and seven-year-old speaks four languages as different as Greek, Turkish, Arabic, and French. Here we have to get used to the idea of two. In our shrinking world wonderful careers in translation, television, journalism, teaching, and international relations await the bilingual. But at what price? We don't know.

Generalization is impossible because studies in bilingualism begin with many different definitions and proceed with many variables among measures of vocabulary, speech deviation, subjects, methods, and investigators. Larger variables in intelligence, emotional stability, parental background, and speech also complicate the matter. In different studies, bilingualism refers to simultaneous, alternate, or concurrent learning of two languages.

We know that the bilinguals we have with us range from the earliest Americans—the Indians—to the most recent immigrants, refugees from foreign lands, G.I. brides and Peace Corps grooms, United Nations personnel, world travelers, students, and salesmen. All of these have, with their lares and penates, brought bilingualism to their American homes. Nor is it confined to the large cities; increased travel and communication have given us bilinguals in rural homes in the Midwest and Southwest as well as in the cities of New York, California, and Hawaii. In many cases, there is no choice; the child is naturally bilingual because one language in his home differs from another in his home or community. Given a choice, among educated foreign families for example, should the child be confronted with more than one language?

Knowing in advance that bilingualism is never a sole cause of difficulty, we can only note some of the possible disadvantages. Speech environment is part of a much larger environment that affects the child. And to distinguish between nature and nurture is often as hard as deciding whether Johnnie can't read because his mother couldn't read when she was in the sixth grade or because she watches TV all day. At least that seems easier than deciding whether Papa's or Mamma's family is to blame. Nevertheless, some studies attribute poor speech development to a bilingual background. Poor articulation and pronunciation, for example, can result from the child's failure to distinguish the phonemes of each language. The Korean child does not hear the difference between "Amelican" *r*'s and *l*'s, but he laughs at our inability to pronounce his name, Chi. Many a native New Yorker approached the orals for a teaching position in his city, knowing only too well that his pronunciation of *New York City* might grant or deny him the license. Allophones (variants of the same sound, as the *p* in *pin* and *spin*) can be dangerous business. But pronunciation and enunciation are not the only hurdles of the bilingual child. Often the total melody of one language—the stresses and rhythms, the vowel lengths, and transitions—imposes itself on the second or simply confuses the second. Nor does age seem to solve some of these problems in speech development. The relationship between stuttering and bilingualism has often been noted, but the cause cannot be established.

In addition to speech, general fluency in language may be affected by bilingualism. Some studies cite the bilingual child's smaller active and passive vocabularies, his imprecise terminology, his unidiomatic expressions, his trouble with sentence lengths and patterns. These, in turn, can become handicaps—at least in certain intelligence measures. Some children, for whom learning two languages simultaneously is an impossible burden, do poorly on intelligence tests. Others feel secure in rote learning but avoid problem solving. From here on, bilingualism can become the cause of all of life's woes. It can retard educational progress, invite emotional problems, and produce anti-social behavior.

Other studies point to the advantages of bilingualism. They maintain that by the age of thirteen most bilinguals catch up with their "pure" American schoolmates. They can cite remarkable advantages in vocabulary and in greater resourcefulness. If there is trouble, a poor home environment or the attitudes of society toward the bilingual child may be the real cause. They also point out that family tension and alienation from home, church, and school are not confined to bilingual homes.

Within the past twenty years research seems to have moved from stress on the disadvantages to stress on the advantages of bilingualism. At least so J. Vernon Jensen found when he summarized them for *Elementary English* in 1962.[1] Where bilingualism does exist, then, the only sensible thing is to provide the child with an environment that will facilitate learning and avoid unlearning. This means a home where parents keep to a minimum differences that might produce tension, where they listen to the children and their problems, where they serve as good models of linguistic as well as other behavior. To avoid bewildering the child, parents are urged to be clear and consistent, to specify, for example, when and where each language will be used. One authority suggests, facetiously we hope, that the parents reserve one language for one floor of the house, the other language for another floor. Unfortunately bilingualism strikes indiscriminately. Princess Grace's children in the royal palace at Monaco have to live with it just as do the children of the migrant worker in the one-room shack in California. The most important thing is that the child mingle with people, lest his language difference become an excuse for isolation and withdrawal. In school, bilinguals need special attention, often classes where they can learn the second language through special instruction in phonetics, phonemics, ear training, sentence structure, and vocabulary. Such classes mean teachers qualified to handle the problems of the bilingual child.

Whether at home or in school, the child should learn his second language informally and incidentally—from the sound pattern to vocabulary. Games, stories, puzzles, riddles, pictures, puppets, pets, songs, rhymes, talk, and trips help him to use the language naturally. The adult's intellectual mastery of the language comes later. Wherever possible, the second language should not be introduced before the first language is firmly established.

Here, then, we have to stop to be sure that the child is not handicapped and heading for trouble with one language before we involve him in another. For language learning problems have a way of snow-

---

[1] J. Vernon Jensen, "Effects of Childhood Bilingualism, I and II," *Elementary English*, XXXIX (February 1962), 132–143, and XXXIX (April 1962), 358–366. Reprinted as *Effects of Childhood Bilingualism* (Champaign, Ill.: National Council of Teachers of English, 1962).

balling. To attribute them to learning a second language is often to miss the fundamental causes.

Yet if we cannot really generalize about bilingualism, we are on even shiftier ground when we try to discuss other problems children have in learning language. Dr. Eric Lenneberg, of the Children's Medical Center in Boston, in "Language Disorders in Early Childhood," points out the difficulties of defining the major disorders: "an unnecessary overlap of terminology" and "random criteria for classification." The disorders he isolates are deafness, mental retardation, childhood psychosis, congential inarticulation, and aphasia (loss of power to use words, usually from brain damage).

Because so few stimuli in the child's early environment are purely acoustic, early detection of deafness is virtually impossible. Even the congenitally deaf child babbles or vocalizes normally until his seventh month. The next few months the normal child develops only a greater variety of sound than the deaf child does. But such a difference is relative. Lenneberg turns to the child's play activity for the most telling signs. It just doesn't seem to occur to the deaf child to use his voice when he wants something. Instead, he resorts to poking, pushing, or gesticulating. Lenneberg says the Leiter International Performance Scale is the best test of congenital deafness in children. He also suggests the Los Angeles Tracy Clinic's correspondence course for mothers of young deaf children. Specialized preschool training can certainly help such a child. If, on the other hand, the child had normal hearing until the age of three, he has acquired language. Academic retardation cannot be attributed to "prolonged absence of language in early childhood." Often the interaction of social isolation and hearing problems is the real source of trouble. The parent's most important job, then, is to prevent the deaf child from becoming part of "a unique social minority."

Congenital deafness can easily be mistaken for mental retardation or psychiatric illness in the first few months. The mentally retarded child may have perfectly normal sensory development. He may sit, stand, walk, and say his first words at the expected time. Only when his cognitive skills (those acts requiring memory tied in with understanding) are carefully tested by a specialist does the difference in rate of development emerge. The mentally retarded child's early vocalization is perfectly normal and his speech and language develop —but they develop slowly and partially. By the time this child has entered his teens, his speech and language powers reach a plateau.

Lenneberg warns parents to leave this child alone, not to drag him "from one speech therapist to the next."

The psychotic child is usually apathetic—unconcerned with people or their affection—or he is hyperactive. His developmental history is not slower than the normal child's; it is simply less gradual. Although he may be mute, he understands language. Otherwise he could not respond to psychotherapy. If he talks, he may repeat words or sentences endlessly, or he may show "perplexing accuracy in mimicry." In other words, Lenneberg finds that the psychotic child has language skills but he is using them abnormally perhaps because of his motivational or emotional problems. Isolating the language problem is a necessary part of the child's psychiatric treatment.

The cry of the child afflicted with congenital inarticulation sounds abnormal from the start. The same is true of his babbling later. His repertoire consists of a few consonants and vowels that may be foreign to us. He sounds "as if his mouth is full of marbles." Yet he understands language: he can point to details in a picture or answer tricky questions requiring a *yes* or *no*. He is generally quick to react and eager to communicate. Speech therapy must not be rushed. It is best to wait until the child (at about the age of four) is motivated to improve his speech. Such therapy should be kept under twenty minutes per day. For even without it, this child's speech improves spontaneously during the first ten years. Lenneberg therefore suggests that the child be kept in a regular class and learn to read with a normal group.

Lenneberg calls aphasia "adventitious loss of language." He points out that any cortical lesions occurring early enough and confined to a single hemisphere of the brain do not prevent the child from learning language. In other words, there is no such thing as congenital motor aphasia and the acquisition of language and speech is not isolated; it involves the entire brain. Under any circumstances, Lenneberg urges that the child be allowed to recover naturally and spontaneously the first six months after the injury. But he admits the prognosis for recovery becomes worse with age. There is little improvement noted in teenage and adult aphasia after the second year of recovery. He warns that no one can work on all the deficits at once. Better to get the aphasic child started in his academic subjects and introduce articulatory drill later.

Language abilities and disabilities that present themselves in schools have many sources, including the child's interest, intelligence, emotional adjustment, and physical condition. On doctor's orders, removing the child's tonsils, balancing his thyroid, or correcting his vision or hearing often makes a difference. But when the child's difficulties in talking, reading, or writing persist, as they do for about 10 per cent of those who are failing in school, we have to get at the specific causes and the specific disabilities. We can't blame everything on environment or bilingualism and then wait for miracles.

Dr. J. Roswell Gallagher of the health department of Phillips Academy, Andover, Massachusetts, cites the need for early attention. Such disability exists among highly intelligent children from the most privileged homes, but often does not become noticeable until the high school years, when longer reading and writing assignments, frequent in-class compositions, or merely greater competition may reveal the pupil's handicaps.

Yet the signs, Dr. Gallagher finds, are clear enough. The child's handwriting is uneven, slow, and cramped. Or he may be a slow silent reader. Placement tests may show that he reads several grades below his actual grade. When he reads aloud, he stumbles. He confuses, transposes, or omits syllables; he reverses letters; he cannot tackle new words. Dictate a spelling test to him, and he comes up with numerous bizarre errors that may not yet be revealed in his own writing. He may be manually clumsy, he may do mirror writing, or he may have a speech defect. Often, Dr. Gallagher adds, the family history shows other poor readers, spellers, or speakers. And in school those subjects requiring verbalization are the ones he fails in first.

When these specific disabilities show up, the doctor tries to check all possible causes: family history, the relationship between the child's school age, chronological age, and physiological age, his general health including vision, hearing, and endocrine status, and—most important of all—his personality adjustment, which he finds the most common of all causes of failure. He also learns much from the way this child reads a short paragraph aloud, spells from dictation, and writes a brief description of a picture. Standardized test results are the last kind of evidence. Often the doctor finds the child's intelligence quotient and arithmetical ability to be far above his reading speed and spelling skill.

In some cases, then, recognizing the general and isolating the specific disability are the first steps toward speech therapy or reading clinic. In other cases, attacking the specific disability may not be enough; certainly not if the real need is psychiatric help. But in many instances, Dr. Gallagher points out, "The fact that the problem has been recognized and is to be given attention has considerable therapeutic effect. To have the cause of frustration explained and given attention may be all that is necessary." Then special practice in phonetics, spelling rules, or vocabulary building makes sense to the child.

Dr. Gallagher also mentions the debatable Orton hypothesis that reversals, mirror writing, and confusion of letters may be the result of failure to develop the dominance of one cerebral hemisphere. Here the remedy may be developing visual, auditory, and kinesthetic word associations in one area so that it will become the dominant one. Symbolizing means a close association between kinesthetic, auditory, and visual imagery. All of these are matters for specialists. But school and home can help by being alert to the child's language growth from the start. Obviously, we have to use common sense. Left-right confusion, mispronunciations, misreadings, hesitancies are a natural part of the child's growth. The hurdles he had to overcome in learning to speak may reassert themselves when he is learning to read and to write. We may need reassurance that the child's difficulties are "normal" for his age. On the other hand, early warnings may be very significant to the trained psychologist, neurologist, or reading teacher. All we can do is watch for these symptoms and report them to those who are trained to interpret them, to diagnose, and to recommend action. For the longer the handicap is allowed to develop, the harder it will be to repair.

A second language, then, is best taught orally at first in the classroom. But the child needs to feel secure in his first language. Such security comes usually when he is eight to ten years old. A later step, long after the second language has been introduced orally, is to use sound reading texts, especially those using contemporary literature. After ten, says neurologist Wilder Penfield of McGill, "speech areas of the brain begin to lose their sensitivity." If these recommendations seem reasonable, then the child's native tongue may be best as a medium of instruction in the early grades.

Ralph Long observes:

> . . . from both neurophysiological and psychological points of view, second-language learning can conveniently start when children begin their schooling. Obviously the teaching of a second language should not be allowed to undermine the teaching of the first language;

instead, it should be made to reinforce the latter. Obviously the approach in the beginning years should be unanalytic: what is needed is good models and genuinely interesting materials which put the language to use in ways appropriate to the ages and backgrounds of the children. Children learn spoken languages amazingly well when circumstances are favorable.[2]

These favorable circumstances are the combined responsibility of parents in the home, teachers at school, and specialists at the university. The better the communication between these groups, the more easily does every child—Wednesday's and Saturday's—learn to read and write in a shrinking and a bewildering world.

[2] Adapted from Ralph B. Long, "Second-Language Teaching in the Schools," *Elementary English,* XL (October 1963), 617–619, 622, 663.

WHAT PRICE LITERACY?

6

Intellectual revolutions do not occur in a vacuum; they are both cause and effect of social revolutions. So has it been in our time. The intellectual revolution has given new significance to the study of grammar, rebaptized with the status symbol, structure of language. But where shall we find the status symbol or the euphemism for that which the social revolution affects most deeply: literacy? In foundering for an adequate term to describe the target, our affluent society tends toward *d-* words, always linked with the word *culture*. For the most handicapped person in our society is the illiterate, the one who cannot assimilate our culture. The target created by the social revolution is thus called the culturally *d*eprived, *d*isadvantaged, *d*ifferent, or *d*ivergent child. As we become more aware of his needs and difficulties, the problem of nomenclature vanishes. The real problem is: How shall we make equal educational opportunity a fact?

To answer this large question we have to ask some smaller ones. Who are these *c-d*'s? How did they get that way? And what can the English teacher do to help? In other words, we have to see how the culturally deprived, disadvantaged, different, or divergent child becomes educationally disadvantaged. From the causes we may get some insight into the cures.

This child is easily identified in our schools; he just doesn't fit into our educational scheme of success. His parents usually come from the lower socioeconomic groups: the unemployed, the unskilled and semiskilled workers. By the age of two the child from a verbally poor home lags behind his age group. Maybe he does have someone to talk to at home. But if the talk is not English, he'll pay the same price as the nontalker from the first day of school. Both will have a hard time listening and talking, reading and writing; they will soon become handicapped in the basic skills underlying all verbal learning —and how much learning is not verbal? The language gap between the *c-d*'s and the others keeps widening from kindergarten right through high school. And then our identification of them is complete! Here is how one conference, held in a city committed to education for all, sums them up:

> They are not likely to go on to post-high-school education. They are likely to drop out of school before finishing grade twelve. They do not have known vocational or career goals and do not seem to know how to acquire them. They are unhappy in school because they do not find it a place where they experience success. In their after-life they are apt to (a) fall among the chronically unemployed, (b) require support assistance from the community, (c) become legal problems, (d) find themselves unable to take part wisely in making personal and civic decisions.[1]

Almost predictable language difficulties pinpoint our definition of these pupils. We have only the results. Marjorie Smiley of the Office of Instructional Research at Hunter College reports "There is little research on class differences in language and on class-differentiated language development." But the differences are there. These youngsters often have trouble with subject-verb agreement and with forms of the verb *to be*. They often substitute the nominative for the possessive case. What do such variants in usage tell us? Lou LaBrant, professor emeritus of New York University, points out that "It takes no more brains to learn 'we did' and 'we are' from a parent than to learn 'we done' and 'we is.' " Nor is this child's vocabulary as limited as it seems. Sometimes his words come from a dialect or even a language unfamiliar to most teachers, 95 per cent of whom are from the middle socioeconomic group, according to the investigations of W. Lloyd Warner, Robert J. Havighurst, and Martin B. Loeb. If the child's vocabulary deviates from the standard dialect, it remains untapped by our culture-bound achievement and intelligence tests.

One educator observes, "Their vocabularies are incredibly limited, except for obscenities and curse words which even kindergarten children use. A word like *steeple* they do not know, though seven are visible from their classroom window." They have not learned to lift up their eyes; they worship their God in a slum store. In spite of good intentions, the school, in its cultural blindness, often creates language problems for the child.

[1] Minutes of a conference of Newton, Massachusetts, school personnel working with terminal students, 1965. Used by permission of the Public Schools of Newton, Massachusetts.

Unable to use whatever resources his own vocabulary provides, he hesitantly follows directions, he gropes for descriptive or qualifying words, and he just gives up trying to understand figurative language. Although he uses more sentence fragments, fewer linking verbs, and fewer subordinating connectives than his more privileged classmates, it is not differences in structure but deficiencies in sentence flexibility which "make it almost impossible for him to formulate generalizations." The length and complexity of his sentences betray his socioeconomic background. But when his language deficiencies become so clear, all other distinctions go. He is now referred to as "the child with less power over language [who] appears to be less flexible in his thinking, is not often capable of seeing more than one alternative, and apparently summons up all his linguistic resources merely to make a flat dogmatic statement." So Walter Loban concluded from his study of the language of eleven kindergarten classes in Oakland, California, with 338 children from all socioeconomic groups in the city.[2] And since competence in spoken language appears to be a base for competence in reading and writing, the difficulties of these children can only increase—unless they get help.[3]

Too few of them do. Yet in spite of their disadvantages, in spite of the strengthening of defensive behavior patterns (speech, learning, recreation, and gang and sex habits are pretty well established by adolescence), these youngsters often become literate and successful, according to our measures. Some acquire basic skills essential for jobs. Some raise their intelligence, aptitude, and achievement scores and continue their education beyond high school. Some begin to recognize and realize their potential as human beings. Some, but not many.

Family, peers, neighborhoods, and schools share the credit or the blame. What can the school, and especially the English teacher, do to help these pupils succeed? The English teacher's obvious job is to make them literate, to develop those language skills which will make success possible, whatever the values and philosophy may be.

Almost invariably, in our commitment to life, liberty, and the pursuit of happiness, we expect children to adjust to a middle class

[2] Walter Loban, *The Language of Elementary School Children,* NCTE Research Report No. 1 (Champaign, Ill.: National Council of Teachers of English, 1963), p. 54.

[3] *Ibid.,* p. 85.

school. That is the surest road to success. So although we try to respect individual differences and meet the needs of each child, we find ourselves rewarding those who "speak as we do, read as we do, follow our customs, and adopt our moral values," according to the findings of Charles Calitri of Hofstra University. When they come to us, a confusion of family dislocations, isolation, on one hand and strength, endurance, and group solidarity on the other, the easiest way out of the dilemma is to "impose our language upon them, reject their mother-tongue or their peer group's meta-language," says Mr. Calitri. Thus we cut off "dealing with truths they will understand. We set before them models impossible of imitation." Teaching literacy in such a void only invites resistance.

Furthermore, we know that speech and writing skills are rarely if ever learned from rules or drill on independent words; that dictionary study, word lists, and prescriptive grammar (a grammar of rules) only give an aura of achievement; that even when such learning does occur, it is far away from sharing or expressing original ideas. This child will learn, then, only when he is motivated to say or write something that is important to him in his world. Language skills emerge from his need and his concern. Neither home nor school can bypass the fundamental steps: listening to the child, encouraging him, criticizing him in such a way as to strengthen his self-image. Then, when we have won his confidence, we can offer him an alternate model to imitate, what we call Standard, or correct, English. His speech tells the story; it tells us when he is beginning to substitute words for blows, when live-for-the-day goals are giving way to distant hope. This is the long and hard road to literacy.

But what alternatives have we? What happens when we decide to take the short cuts, to be "realistic" about these pupils' abilities, needs, and aspirations? The teacher who presumes to know what these are usually tries to impose literacy upon his pupils—for their own good. If he is realistic about his own goals in teaching, he will find himself frustrated from the start. The pupils may be going through the motions of obedience; they may seem quietly contented with their workbooks and drill sheets. But sooner or later the truth will out. Discipline problems keep growing as the school's expectations and the pupil's self-image decline. Sensing the teacher's authoritarian tolerance of differences, the pupils achieve less and behave worse. They regard the purveyors of Standard English with suspicion and rage. They feel the class bias in their texts and their tests. If they are in a large comprehensive school, they are the pariahs. The worst thing that can happen to such pupils is to be afflicted with a predominantly female faculty. Most of these deprived youngsters, especially the boys, hunger for a strong father image. Lacking Huck Finn's resources in Hannibal and in his own Pappy, they naturally rebel against the Widow Douglases and the Aunt Pollys. Only there's no territory to light out to! Geographical mobility is not the answer in our time.

The waste of energy on both sides of the desk is tragic. The implications of such waste are crucial. Allison Davis of the University of Chicago points out that our American way of life depends on social mobility within the lower income groups. He says that 70 per cent of the pupils in our large cities come from this group, that there is simply not enough potential in the rest of our school population to provide the engineers, scientists, teachers, and executives upon whom our society depends. We must develop the potential, encourage new values and goals in these "outsiders." It can be done and it is being done in more and more cities. He points to the improvement in I.Q. and aptitude of Negro children who had moved from the South to New York City or Philadelphia. He also mentions that "Negroes drafted in Illinois and New York City had a lower rate of failure in the education test used by Selective Services than did the whites in Virginia, West Virginia, North Carolina, South Carolina, Georgia, Mississippi, Alabama, Louisiana, Texas, Arkansas, Florida, Kentucky, Oklahoma, Tennessee, New Mexico, and Kansas." His source is the Government Printing Office Monograph No. 10, 1953. Much has been done in ambitious undertakings like Horizons Unlimited in New York City. What has been done in isolated experiments must become standard procedure. Our job is to provide the older pupil with every form of help and encouragement, to get the youngest ones off to the best possible start, and to keep reexamining our own values and goals in the light of our cultural diversity.

Schools that face up to the challenge usually find themselves involved in the following: a serious study of the school and the community (values, motives, feelings, needs); a reexamination of teaching resources (staff and curriculum); greater opportunity for pupil activity in the learning process; and integration of all groups in the school's extracurricular program. These involvements are simultaneous and interacting; there is no time to wait for the certainty that may never come.

The honest look at school and community is primarily a matter of communication between scholars, researchers, school, and home. Sociological studies and statistics are no more important than person-to-person talks and individual soul-searching. A united home and school front is the result of shared understandings, of the total involvement of school and community, of parent, teacher, and child in education. Regardless of local conditions, research means two things: new knowledge and more professional help. New courses of study avail themselves of the findings of modern linguistics; a logical, systematic approach to language can avert a return to isolated, mechanistic phonics programs and tedious drills. Additional staff means more teachers for smaller classes, specialists, psychologists, social workers, guidance counselors, and nurses. Another must is the inservice training programs where teachers can learn from each other and from outside scholars and consultants.

Aleda E. Druding summarizes Philadelphia's training program for teachers in eight schools:

> It starts with a group composed of the associate superintendent in charge, the district superintendent, the director of Philadelphia's Great Cities Improvement Program, the language arts consultant, and eight principals. The group meets monthly throughout the year to plan, evaluate, and replan. It moves on into each school through the school-community coordinating team. This team meets each summer and several times during the school term on Saturday in workshop sessions. In each school the training program, carefully structured, is put into effect by the language arts consultant, the language arts laboratory teacher, the reading adjustment teacher, and the consulting teachers—all working under the leadership of the principal who in turn keeps in close touch with the district superintendent, the director of the project, and the associate superintendent in charge.[4]

Most of these inservice courses stress the positive approach to literacy; they deemphasize conformity to middle class speech as an escape from illiteracy, delinquency, and unemployability. They urge teachers to read with and to children for the sheer pleasure of it. But they also differentiate between exposing a child to reading and

---

[4] Aleda E. Druding, "Selection and Preparation of Teachers to Serve in Schools in Culturally Different Areas," *Improving English Skills of Culturally Different Youth,* eds. Arno Jewett, Joseph Mersand, Doris Gunderson (Washington: U.S. Office of Education, 1964), pp. 192–193. Reprinted by permission of the U.S. Office of Education.

teaching him the reading skills necessary for word perception and between reading instruction and speech correction. Where necessary, they hire teachers trained to teach English as a second language. Reading clinics, language laboratories, libraries have to be kept up to date with new offerings. Most important of all, each teacher in the system has to see himself as a teacher of reading and writing. The job is not relegated to the English teacher alone. The teacher who is secure in his subject and in his human relations, who is good humored and flexible, succeeds with these children.

But the pupil is the real center of all this activity. In the pre-nursery schools in the slums, finger and muscle skills develop as the children handle crayons, pencils, scissors, books, and magazines. They look at pictures and become curious about words they hear. Often the child is read to alone by an adult and plays word games with an adult. He is getting the reading readiness his home cannot provide. Ungraded primary programs enable each pupil to learn at his own pace. Limiting classes to twenty pupils enables each one to express himself in small groups and in individual conferences as well as in reading, writing, and discussion among all. Such provision for pupil activity is often no more costly than the double English periods that some schools prescribe for remedial work. Double doses do not compensate for anything; quantity is no substitute for quality. What the pupil does is more important than what the teacher does.

The social revolution in the past decade involves linguistic performance; the intellectual revolution involves linguistic knowledge. Both are the concern of the good English course. Automation, integration, and urban growth demand literacy of everyone. But education does not aim to adapt the individual to the needs of the system. Through literacy and exposure to new ideas, the system itself becomes modified for the common good. When literacy becomes an end in itself, society becomes rigid. When it opens the doors to new experiences, society remains flexible. Only then does equality of education become a fact.

There is no one way, then, to achieve this goal. Here are two different ways, starting at opposite ends and hopefully taking the pupil as far as he will go. The first comes from Ruth I. Golden of the Detroit schools; the second, described in the following chapter, from two teachers at Newton High School, Newtonville, Massachusetts. Before we look at them, let's see what these programs do NOT want to do. Neither tries to "find a niche in the affluent society" for these pupils. Neither relegates these pupils to limited programs of remedial reading and practical arithmetic. Neither offers the following as "literature to enjoy": *A Tale of Two Cities, To Have and to Hold, Ivanhoe, The Gold Bug.* Neither gives students "instruction and experience in neatly and legibly completing bank deposit slips, checks, receipts, contest forms, subscription and mail order blanks, and applications for driver's license, employment, library cards, health certificates, and social security cards." At least neither boasts of these activities. Nor of "learning to give succinct directions, to request and offer explanations, to make introductions, to extend congratulations and apologies, to converse intelligently and correctly." Nor does either "suggest such places as parking garages, kitchens of large hotels and hospitals, maintenance departments of refineries and industrial plants, laundries, produce markets, and truck farms" as a "picture of the world which will one day be a part of their lives." Nor can either boast: "The affiliation of one project teacher with the American Legion enabled her to secure four $100 scholarships to a local beauty college."

Ruth Golden's report reads in part:

> The ideas I'd like to share . . . are partly those used in the experiment (a research project under Title VII of the National Defense Education Act) but mainly the result of almost 20 years of teaching in 4 Detroit high schools where there are culturally different students.
>
> Much of the success of an English language laboratory class depends upon the attitudes and the individual aims set at the beginning of the semester. In the orientation period, we discuss the purposes and the need for education. We discuss all aspects of language, stressing in realistic terms the need for effective language in all walks of life. To clinch the discussion, students write letters to the teacher in which they introduce themselves and state their aims for the semester. This setting of aims paves the way for breaking into speech drills later whenever the need arises. We plan introductory talks to be taped, and individual or group projects to be presented later to the class.
>
> These projects provide most of the composition work for the semester, although purposeful letter writing is engaged in as frequently as possible.
>
> A sheaf of letters, usually written to an individual or to an organization within the school, will actually be mailed so that good writing is made meaningful. Replies to the letters lead to some informal conversations later. The presenting of the booklets or other individual projects gives practice in strengthening needed forms such as "This picture" not "Dis pitcher" and in stressing agreement as in "This shows" and "It has."

To orient students to the use of the tape recorder for critical listening, we first give names or one-sentence introductions into a traveling mike from a relaxed sitting position. Even in so simple an exercise, we can learn the importance of emphasizing the surname so that it can be repeated in an introduction. Then we may try a sentence or two in "class on parade" order and hear a playback before giving introductory talks about our hobbies and interests.

"Class on parade" is a device I use frequently for many types of brief oral presentations. A whole row of students will rise at one time and take positions at the side of the class. Each student then waits for his turn, makes his brief presentation, moves to the other side of the room, and waits for his group to finish so that all can take their seats as the next group comes up. Barring illness, there are no exceptions. Anyone who is not prepared says so when his turn comes, but the moral support given when several rise at one time and the atmosphere of encouragement and informality seem to eliminate procrastinators.

This procedure works well and saves time during speech activities such as: the Inquiring Reporter, in which one student reporter asks each student two or three questions from a long list which they have all had time to consider; famous sayings, in which as a part of a unit on biography each student presents an adage or quotation and tells in his own words what it means to him; memory work, such as a few lines from "The Gettysburg Address" in a ninth-grade Lincoln unit; or the explanation of a rule of courtesy.

Other classroom speech activities include various extemporaneous talks, introductions, business interviews, and panel discussions. A taped business interview with questions designed purposely to bring out deviations, if used, comprised the second oral test of our experiment. For choral reading, with the ninth grade, I especially like Alfred Noyes' "The Highwayman" because my particular students need practice in improving the *ai* sound through the repetition of *highwayman* and *riding, riding*. The correction of this one sound may be a key to changing the entire speech pattern. As students change this frequently used sound, they are often reminded to change other less desirable usages.

We have made up a little nonsense story about "The Rat Named Kite" which introduces the idea of having the students write what we call "stupid stories" to bring in the repetition of sounds or usages they particularly need to practice. We emphasize final consonants and the past tense signal *ed* by listing substitutions for words like *walked* and *said* and by classifying these words according to whether they have a *d* or a *t* sound at the end.

Besides the taped group lessons for usage drill practice, we frequently spend a few minutes on general oral drill. If someone says, "favecent," we may take a minute to count in unison from "one cent, two cents," up to "ten cents," stressing the *s* sound. When trouble occurs in agreement of a third person singular noun and its matching verb, or if we hear "seen" instead of "saw," we may take time out to drill on the conjugation of the verbs, jazzing up the rhythm to make the activity fun as well as to reinforce it in the memory.

For extracurricular motivation, we participate in speech contests and put on plays and variety shows. In two schools we have organized a speech and personality improvement club called "The Teen Talkers and Tapers." One club sponsored a schoolwide Better Speech Campaign complete with Tag Day, daily homeroom lessons in speech improvement, and colorful hall posters and bulletin boards.

We now have some proof of success, but one never knows how truly successful such speech efforts are because so much of the learning may be a delayed action process. If we hold to high standards, yet make speech activities pleasant and memorable, there will be positive results. We cannot change the student's speech habits for him, but we can help him to become aware of the need for change by becoming a more critical and discerning listener; we can give him good examples to imitate; and we can encourage his efforts at self-improvement.[5]

[5] Ruth I. Golden, "Ways to Improve Oral Communication of Culturally Different Youth," *Improving English Skills of Culturally Different Youth*, eds. Arno Jewett, Joseph Mersand, Doris Gunderson (Washington: U.S. Office of Education, 1964), pp. 107–109. Reprinted by permission of the U.S. Office of Education.

IS LITERACY ENOUGH?

7

A REPORT ON HUMANISTIC EDUCATION FOR THE
GENERAL STUDENT[1]

A. The Student

Since *general student* may be a confusing label, we offer these
thumbnail sketches of eleven students who were enrolled in our program. These are in no way attempts at analysis or case history;
they are our consensus based on our classroom experience and other
available school sources. All of the eleven are atypical, but they do
in sum characterize the group of students we work with. Names only
are fictitious.

Fred is a tall, muscular boy with a violent temper. His father, a
construction worker, disciplines him by beatings. Fred is unpredict-
able. One day his good sense of humor and quick mind brighten the
class. Another day his eye begins to twitch; his controls are gone; he
is ready to erupt. His school history has been a series of low grades
and run-ins with authority. Fred likes the new course. He returns to
junior high to tell a teacher about it. Then the old problems reappear.
He fails to get work in and has occasional blow-ups in class. He hits
a teacher in the lunch room and puts a fist through a window. Still he
responds to his work sporadically, doing well enough to get an honors
grade one term in history. Throughout the year Fred receives special
counseling at the local psychiatric clinic. His guidance counselor and
housemaster in the school see him regularly to keep him out of trouble.
He makes it through the year and is to return in the fall.

[1] This chapter contains material adapted by the author from a paper she
prepared for the Commission on English, "The Potential in Potential Dropouts," which will appear in a collection of papers on English and English teaching to be published by the Commission on English of the College Entrance
Examination Board and is used with their permission.

This chapter also contains adaptations from position papers prepared by the
author and a colleague in 1962 and 1964, used by permission.

Ralph is a bright boy who could do college preparatory work. Like most of the others in the class, he is addicted to the mass media, but he has a rare affinity for the best programs on TV and film. He has not been lulled into unconscious ignorance by stereotype and cliché. He is the boy who always has the thoughtful questions and answers. Verbal and perceptive, he responds to ideas. Ralph's alertness, sense of humor, and easy-going disposition brighten the class. He is slow writing tests, but his answers are good, sometimes profound. Ralph doesn't do his written homework; he doesn't exert himself to a point where he realizes his potential. Intellectually he excels and he is aware of it, but not in a demeaning way. He sits next to Peter, Sicilian born, barely able to read and speak English, unable to write it, and having a history of failure in both Italian and American schools. Ralph helps Peter to understand assignments and class discussions. Toward the end of the year we try to encourage Ralph to go into a more difficult curriculum where he will encounter more challenging work and classmates. He refuses—he doesn't care—he doesn't even want to visit a class to see what it's like. He finally moves up a track but he is deeply suspicious of this type of aspiration. He knows only too well the social implications of the track system in a suburban community.

Sally is dishevelled, loud, and tough. Sally's parents are alcoholics, her younger brother has been classed as a juvenile delinquent, and she has been implicated with shoplifting. Sally does no work in school. She swears at her classmates and teachers and gets into fights. She is a constant troublemaker to the point of being regularly thrown out of class and suspended from school. A social worker assigned by the court works with the family, but the reports are not encouraging. A Big Sister has not been able to reach Sally. A schoolmate also with alcoholic parents is asked by the social worker to try to help. When Sally is again suspended, her parents withdraw her.

Mary is a sweet, well-groomed Italian immigrant. She has a gentle smile and a quiet manner. She works hard and diligently but has difficulty in reading, writing, and speaking English. She is easily confused, has trouble following simple directions, and shows little depth in perception. The Division of Instruction provides a tutor to help her learn English as a second language. Still, progress comes very slowly. Toward the middle of the year Mary discovers boys. She also discovers and befriends some of the wilder girls. She talks more and flirts in class. Her homework comes in late or not at all. In class and out of class she pays less attention to her studies. She has to be coaxed and prodded to finish the year's work with an average grade.

Jack likes cars and still seems unaware of girls. He is short and very sensitive. He wants to be one of the boys and act tough. He is extremely excitable and always seeks attention. He is the last in his seat when the bell rings, the first to ask a disruptive question, and the first to protest an assignment as too long, too hard, too easy, too stupid. When he is asked not to talk to his neighbor, he says he wasn't; then he continues the conversation. Jack receives psychiatric help at the local clinic; his problems are not new. More than anything he wants to go to the technical high school and learn about cars. But he can't pass the mechanical aptitude test. Anyway, his parents want him to take a regular, not a manual trades, course. In November Jack leaves our class; he has been admitted to the technical high school. In June we learn Jack has left trade school and will return to the regular high school in the fall.

Sarah seems quiet and docile. She is often absent, although her health is excellent. Throughout the school year she does very little work. Most often in class she sits blankly staring at the front of the room. When called on, she shrugs her shoulders or speaks inaudibly. Yet class tests show she is neither docile nor dumb. Her writing—when she does it—has unmistakable glimmers of comprehension, thought, and perception. There is a good mind behind that stare—how good, it is impossible to tell. Between classes, among friends, she is lively and vocal. Sarah is an enigma.

Gerry is an intelligent boy with a long history of trouble in school, but his parents refuse to allow him to receive special counseling. Gerry can be talked with individually. Once he asked quite seriously, "Do you think I'm nuts? My father says I'm nuts. You know what I want to do? Get arrested and thrown in jail so I can sleep all the time." Gerry is a tall, gangling boy who slouches as he walks and as he sits. He does no work. In class he sleeps, wisecracks, or surreptitiously incites others to disrupt the work. Finally, after an increasingly frequent series of outbursts, Gerry has to be removed from his English and history classes. He spends these periods in his housemaster's office and is tutored at night at the district's expense. Only then do his parents accept his referral to the clinic for counseling. In June we learn Gerry's parents have withdrawn him from the clinic.

Ray is an athlete: he has a powerful build, handsome features, is always well groomed. He plays football and baseball for the school teams. Ray is not a student. He has little use for the academic part of school and shows it by not doing his work and "horsing around" in class. He, Gerry, Fred, and Jack have "fun" in school. Ray is also a sensitive, perceptive boy, who, freed from Gerry's influence, finds some ideas interesting and worth considering. He likes to work with his hands—drawing maps and pictures—and finds that he can also discuss ideas. By the end of the year Ray is something of a leader in class discussions. He has read the material—at least some of it. But Ray still cannot get over the hurdle of really doing his school work. He does realize that he could do it if he wanted to. He takes his failing grade in English and history without bitterness, enrolls in summer school (at the sacrifice of a summer job) in order to get off to a good start in September.

Frances is a pretty, dark-eyed girl who likes boys and wants them to like her. She has not been a good student, sporadically handing in work and doing very poorly on tests. She can conceptualize and verbalize orally, but she cannot retrieve her ideas on a test. Exuberant, energetic, she is somewhat of a leader. Generally pleasant, she can be sassy and discourteous. During the year Frances becomes a good student. She is still a flirt and still fails some tests; but in class discussions and in homework she begins to show a type of intellectual leadership. She asks questions and volunteers information. She turns some of her energies to thinking about what is being studied.

Cindy is a pert, pretty blonde. She thrives on pulp fiction, TV, soap operas, and parties. She gets honors grades in the lower track and feels that academic activity, as she defines it, is worthwhile. She is somewhat taken aback when her traditional work is not enough; rote memory and neat papers cannot conceal her shallow reading and sloppy thinking. Both the content and the method of this new course become a threat to her security; her complaints are quite vocal: "When will we begin to study *English?* When will we begin to study *history?* Why do I have to write complete sentences for a history paper?" At the end of the school year, although she is still uneasy, she is asking thoughtful questions and achieving honors grades.

Jane is Fred's girl friend. She is pretty, fragile, a quieting and stabilizing force in Fred's life. She faithfully puts up with his flirting with Frances and with his explosive temper. Jane is a capable student. Her work is conscientious and shows understanding. She seems to know exactly where she is and where she is going. She sits quietly in class, taking notes and listening, rarely volunteering information or partaking in discussions. For Jane school is a place of only routine business. It is a job where you do your work carefully and well and you are rewarded. Jane wants good grades (*B*'s), and once when she didn't work very hard and received a *C,* she was quite concerned. She soon pulled the grade up. But Jane knows not to work any harder than she has to.

Some simple statements may unify the impression of the individual cases described above and set the background for our conclusions about curriculum for these youngsters.

1. Almost exclusively this student comes from the lowest socio-economic class in the community. He is not poverty stricken. Many, in fact, often seem to have extra money, good clothes and even cars. He is, however, constantly aware of his difference from the student of better means in a school system oriented toward college preparation, and he has apparent respect for his own class values. Although he shows hostility toward these wealthier students, he shares with them the hope of acquiring material prosperity. How does not seem to be a deep concern of his.

2. This student sees school as a place to be tolerated. Like his parents, he shows antipathy, a combination of awe and suspicion, toward school; yet he is committed to the necessity of "getting a diploma" as a pass to the outside world and economic opportunity. The general student who quits often "wants to" return. The resolution to the dilemma of school seems to be to work as little as possible— just enough to get by and to take a certain pride in his alienation.

3. This student is accustomed to failure. He has known almost constant failure in school and to some extent in the larger society, although he may feel some success in his small group of pals. He expects friction with society's institutions and their representatives: teachers, school administrators, police, etc. He makes up a large proportion of the disciplinary problems in school and has a high proportion of psychological difficulties unrelated to discipline. He finds it difficult to avail himself of the help offered to him by the institutions he feels so removed from. He feels that often people and institutions are out to get him. His resistance comes in the form of outward and overt hostility or a seemingly rigid placidity.

4. This student is not academic. He lacks basic skills of absorption and expression. Although he often tries to master them, he has a low

tolerance for sticking to a task and easily senses that he has failed again. Still, this student is intellectual in that he can and will handle ideas of increasing complexity if he tastes of success. He has good common sense and often uses it with candor and refreshing honesty, especially when he can force his classmates into critical reason. He can be creative in the sense of being able to sensitively perceive ideas and manipulate them as long as they are tied to the concrete and specific and relevant.

B. Conclusions about Education for These Students

From our perception of these students we have had to make some basic decisions about a sensible approach to teaching them. What do we mean by sensible? On the negative side, the course should help reduce the dropouts and discipline problems and chronic absenteeism. On the positive side, it should keep the pupil purposefully occupied in school until graduation.

The most obvious commitment is to an approach that will affect the self-image of the youngster in a positive way. He is pretty battered. He needs to have a sense of doing something well and worthwhile. He needs a curriculum with high standards and attainable goals. He is too sophisticated to be duped into thinking that any activity involves real achievement; he knows the difference between real output and busy work.

A second commitment is to a humanistic curriculum. This youngster needs to be exposed to and confronted with human existence as process and reflection. He needs to see the relevance of his life in terms of the problems and ideas of universal significance. He needs to see where he is and how he got there. Our aim is neither life adjustment nor preparation for the real world of job applications and tax forms. Our aim is a liberal perspective and sensitive perception of that real world in which the human animal exists.

Out of these two basic commitments has come a way of going about the job which will hopefully implement these beliefs:

1. The curriculum must have substance. In this sense we have been both traditional and revolutionary. There is a subject matter in the course which is to be mastered. This subject matter is selected from the best literature, history, art, and current linguistic studies.

2. The curriculum is centered on ideas of universal significance which are structured in a simple way. Starting with the pupil's reaction to simple ideas, we push him into ideas that are deeper and

complex but always the logical outcome of his earlier thinking. There must be a sense of clarity in order that the substance of the curriculum can be mastered.

3. The curriculum must be relevant to the life of this student. We do not use a "sex and cars" approach, but rather we try to show the student how the ideas he confronted in the course are relevant to him.

4. The classroom must be disciplined. We mean discipline in the broadest sense: knowing where one is going and how he can get there. The student must understand that there is a way to approach an intellectual problem and think it through. The major elements in this process are curiosity, questioning, evidence, and reasoning.

5. The curriculum demands a great deal of student participation. The student is involved in a constant oral and written dialogue with his classmates and his teacher. It is through this participation that he gets a sense of direction and achievement. His satisfaction comes not from having the "right answer" but from the reasoning involved in coming to his conclusion or the question he raises about another's conclusion.

We have found that by combining the English and history courses at the high school level we are in a better position to achieve our aims. By combining these two subjects we offer this student a consistent approach to learning in one third of his school day. But this is not a core program, where a teacher with a major in one subject or with general background teaches both English and history. Instead, we have insisted on the separateness of the two subjects and the preparation of each teacher. It is no accident that those who are in this program include four John Hay Fellows and five teachers of Honors or Advanced Placement subjects. The collaboration of the two teachers, does, however, give the pupil a double chance to master ideas and skills as the two classes run parallel courses. Moreover the student's problem can be more quickly identified and perhaps more effectively dealt with.

C. The Approach to Subject Matter

We have said success with these students depends on having substance in the curriculum. The basic outline for the substance we have committed ourselves to is as follows:

1. HUMANISTIC. Our approach to subject matter, whether historical or linguistic or literary, is humanistic. Our central theme for the three years is man as a creature with potential. By this we do not

deny the potential for either good or bad. We are not talking about progress; we are talking about man's potential as a creature to use his hands and brain to create. He may create, and he does create things both good and evil.

2: CULTURAL. Our approach is also cultural. By culture we mean that set of ideas and institutions which is generally accepted by a particular society at a particular time. We study individual men as part of a group who have created a total way of life at a particular time and in a particular place. This involves us with individuals and groups influencing and being influenced by their societies.

3. ARTISTIC. Our approach relies heavily on art to bring to life the basic ideas of the course. We try to find the finest examples of all art forms, traditional and contemporary. Much of the art we study comes from the historical period we are concerned with at the time, the reason being that the artist as a man of his time reflects the age in which he lives and also deals with the universal themes stressed in this course. Contemporary art places the theme in our own time.

4. HISTORICAL. The basic organization of the course is historical, but in a sense that must be defined. First the units fall into chronological sequence through all three years, but themes rather than chronology are the main emphases in each unit and in the total sequence. We hope that the students develop some sense of overall time, but our main goal is that they see how man, and particularly Western man, has developed over the course of centuries. We want to show major points in the experience of man: when he has used his potential to create or change. Within each unit the history teacher is concerned with a sense of time insofar as the students need it to understand change. The historical approach, then, is not a textbook approach. Above all we realize the need to be very selective. These students, and for that matter any student, can not be besieged with fact upon fact. He needs to have facts selected on the basis of the ideas he is to be concerned with. The danger here is obvious. We do not want to select facts to prove a point. We want rather to select facts on the basis of their relevance to the idea in question, whether the fact contradicts what seems to be the generalization or not. We want to show not only the consistent but the various.

5. LINGUISTIC. We feel that the study of language belongs in a humanistic curriculum. The approach to thinking about language can be intellectual without being academic if the pupil is encouraged to examine his own and his classmates' intuitive linguistic knowledge and

to externalize this knowledge. What must man *know* if he is a speaking animal? In other words, to study language is more challenging than to read *about* language. The three areas of emphasis are the nature of language, language change, and grammar. By nature of language we mean its universals and its particulars in English. What do we mean by the English language? By change we mean the history, varieties, and standards of English. What do we mean by good English? What do we mean by correct English? By grammar we mean structure. What finite rules do we know that enable us to utter and understand an infinite number of sentences? Transformational theory has reintroduced deep and reasonable insights into man's use of his mind. Such a study of language is both means and end in our survey of man as a creature with potential.

D. The Course in Action

The course is divided into five major units:

1. Man as a Creature with Potential
2. The Individual in Society
3. Man as Part of a Social Group
4. The Individual in the Renaissance World
5. The Emergence of the Scientific View

Here are excerpts from one teacher's report of how the program works in her English class:

As soon as we meet these youngsters, we make clear what the relationship will be. They know from the start that they are in a course which is being jointly taught by a history teacher and an English teacher. They know precisely what their obligations are: that if they try, they cannot fail; if they do not try, they will surely fail.

And rather than talk about what English will be like, rather than tell them what parts of their notebook will be devoted to spelling or composition, we get right into the act. We get into the act with the Maiziee game. Maiziee's kind of queer but she isn't crazy. She likes beets, but she can't stand carrots. She loves spoons, but she will not touch a fork. She loves Brookline; she keeps out of Newton. And we continue to play this game. Of course we have to recapitulate on the board. As soon as they see the two columns in writing, the hands go up. Then they give some more examples of Maiziee's likes and dislikes until everyone in the class is playing the game.

And this, we say, is what English will be like. From here on out, you're going to listen to your language as you never have before. You're going to observe it as sharply as you never have before, and the only thing you have to do is make a hypothesis or generalization that is based upon that sharpness of observation and concern. This will be English for the next year.

And it does become English. These youngsters are getting a course based on the best in literature, art, history, and current linguistic scholarship—so far as teachers who've come into the program can devise. But it's being offered to these students through avenues that assure success. Most of us, for example, smile at what the math people have been doing. It's so easy for us to sit on the sidelines and see third- and fourth-graders being teased into independent thinking or reasoning, only to emerge with very trivial generalizations which they might just as well have been told directly. And so we smile. And then we start rewriting our own courses, and we take that magic word "linguistics" and we say, "We will give these youngsters something in linguistics." But what shall we call independent thinking? And what shall we call significant ideas?

Here's how we've answered these questions. We've all heard that language has certain characteristics. And we've seen student films and texts which, in one way or another, say language is fundamentally an oral activity, that it is conventional, that it is symbolic, that it is acquired. But how to involve the students in these notions is another matter. In our classes, we start with selections like "The Far-sighted Cat," "The Wounded Cormorant," and Helen Keller's "Three Days to See." We observe the differences between animal and human behavior, particularly how each communicates. What do you call real in this story and what seems fake? These youngsters are very realistic. They tell you very quickly what is fake.

Then they start generalizing. A cat can't do this, a cat can't do that, but a human being can do this. All right. How useful is such a generalization? Let's test it against the facts, because that's only a story. So we bring a baby and a ball and a dog into the classroom. And we let the youngsters observe the actions of the baby and the dog, note those things which the infant can understand and say, those things which the dog can understand and say. And then the pupils realize that their generalizing on the basis of the stories they read was a little bit sloppy, because obviously this dog is doing everything that the baby can do. The dog *does* use his voice. The dog *can* use symbolic language. When you refer to something in the other room that he cannot see, the dog does get used to the conventions that you have taught him. And the dog can acquire more language. So far these youngsters have made observations that usually take a chapter in a text. But the most important observation is still to come. When they have come to the conclusion that there is no real difference between the dog's communication and the infant's communication, and they're perfectly right, we ask them to draw a big line on their paper.

"Now record the last sentence that you think this baby will be able to speak and understand five years from now, and record the last sentence that you think the dog will be able to understand five years from now." Obviously, they say, it's impossible. When that baby is five years old, there'll be no limit to what he can say and understand. They have then come to what is bedrock in current linguistic theorizing. What is this human capacity for creating an infinite number of sentences from finite sets of rules that we intuitively acquire? This is a pretty sophisticated concept, isn't it? And it sets some pretty ambitious goals for the year's work. Yet the approach is vivid and challenging. And it's anything but dull. This year we'll have a chimpanzee, a gibbon, and a spider monkey—all the same age as the human baby.

Then the next question comes. Do the concepts simply frustrate and bewilder these young people? After the excitement is over, does the trouble begin? Is it frightening to be told that the biggest questions are the ones that we are far from being able to answer? Then shall we spend a lot of time in the classroom on other things? Maybe we ought to go back to a little bit of spelling, a little bit of usage, which these youngsters call English. Maybe. We think not, and we are not.

We continue to look into the nature of language throughout the first unit, which is about six weeks, while the history teacher is doing the same kind of Socratic reasoning with these youngsters. The pupils noted, as they observed the baby and the dog, that man can *become,* for better or worse; that an animal *is.* Both classes are looking at man as a creature with potential. In history they study man as an inventor of tools. In English they are meanwhile studying man as an inventor of language.

They see a film, *The Hunters,* recording very vividly but simply the way of life of a primitive people in Africa. Again they are asked to observe very carefully just what this society has evolved, what a hunter has to know, what he has to do. This is the history teacher's concern: how does man control his environment, and as he controls it physically, what new problems are introduced with every advance? In *The Hunters,* we hear a strange language. It's the Bushman's. And yet, the youngsters realize as they look at this film, that although the Bushman may look a lot more primitive than we do, although his tools are certainly a lot more primitive, that his language is in every way as sophisticated as ours, that it uses every device that any other human being using language avails himself of. Careful observation of detail has led these pupils to another significant generalization.

This only leads to more questions. The youngsters say, "But this isn't really so. We write. We have books. These people can just talk." We ask the youngsters then to consider what these hunters could do better if they knew how to write. Is there anything in this hunting society that requires writing? And they see that the invention of writing is intimately connected with the community's geographical and social and even economic life. It's very easy, then, for these youngsters as they move along in history to discover why writing should have originated only with river valley cultures where record keeping and farming required some sort of improvement on the memory.

The youngsters, then, look into this whole business of the difference between speech and writing. As they observe the difference they are also observing some of the characteristic sounds of their own language. And as we observe these, we are still doing what we were doing the very first day. Most of these early written records have come down to us in hypotheses, which we call myths. The youngsters then read myths about the creation of the earth. They compare them. They hypothesize from them. What must these ancient people have been like? What were their values? What did the word *God* mean to them? What did excellence mean to them? Notice that these youngsters are constantly being involved in ideas that any card-carrying member of the human race has a right to be involved in. This is not baby talk. When these youngsters read myths, many of them will say, "Oh, we read these in junior high." Of course we did, but now as we reread them, we are finding out something about man as a thinking creature from their underlying assumptions or hypotheses. Why is the creation story of the Egyptians so different from the creation story of the Hebrews? Why does the epic of Gilgamesh tell the flood story so differently from Noah's version?

You can see the great books coming into this course. For in addition to the best in language study, these youngsters are given the best in literature. We never stop and say, "Can they read it?" If they can't read it, we will read it with them. And to them. And we will avail ourselves of all the visuals that we need. We will not assume that ideas can be communicated only by the printed page, surely not in our age of mass communication. Not when we think of previous ages, where profound ideas were being debated by people, many of whom were illiterate, too.

This is what goes on in the first unit when these youngsters become involved with the nature of language and the nature of hypothesizing. In the same unit the students' hypothesizing and the investigation fit into their writing.

The history teacher asks the pupils to create a tool. "Go out and find something from which you can make a tool. The only artificial device you may use is string or rope." And they bring in some pretty lethal instruments. But it doesn't stop there. They have to explain that tool. They have to describe it. Talking about composition with them doesn't work. But ask them to describe a tool, and before you know it, not the teacher but somebody else in the class will say, "Big? What do you mean big? How many inches? How many feet?" They, not the teacher, insist upon the accuracy of description. Similarly they hypothesize as to what the tool might have been used for and how it might have been used. They have to support their generalization with evidence, with reasons.

While they're making and hypothesizing about tools, we do exactly the same with language. We experiment with it. Can you invent a language? Many already have their own dialects and their own secret languages. How do they make it work? They manipulate various parts of the English sentence, without any reference to grammar whatsoever, varying one element at a time. They see, then, some of the surface structure of a sentence. They experiment with writing; they devise hieroglyphics. For example, it's easy enough to draw a picture of something like "The bird is in the tree," but what do you do when you want to say, "I think I see a bird in the tree"? This is where the youngsters see the need to move from pictogram to ideogram to some kind of syllabic or alphabetic system of writing. In other words, all of this is presented in a reasonable way that asks them to think through what they are observing.

The same thing is true in history; of course they are going to be exposed to archeology. They read about a Stone Age man, who seems to have been killed in some sort of landslide; he has buck teeth and one arm. The archeologist concludes that the man was probably attacked by a bear, had to have his arm amputated, and thereafter used his teeth and one arm to make tools for the tribe. The teacher asks for reactions to this hypothesis. They come with counter-theories. "Maybe his arm was severed when he was caught in the landslide." "Then where is that severed limb?" "Maybe he lost it in battle." "Does it look like a fresh cut?" In other words, the pupils are never encouraged to make or accept a quick, random guess. They weigh their hypotheses very carefully all the way through.

Similarly they create explanatory myths: why the leaves turn red, or why someone caught a cold last weekend. But they have to foot-note with a scientific explanation because a myth is only early man's attempt to order, understand, control his universe. This again, is quite an eye-opener to them. When they start checking with their biology teacher, they find that we do not have any very pat explanation for why the leaves turn red, that modern chemists differ, even among themselves. This is again giving them a much more sophisticated view of what hypothesizing really is.

In the unit on man as part of a social group, we try to get these youngsters to see what we mean by levels of usage. We do not say that expressions are right or wrong. We do, however, look at the nature of linguistic change and dialects. Again, this is never done didactically; this is never offered through textbook analysis, but rather through the direct experience. For example, in the unit on man as part of a social group, when we read and act out *Pygmalion,* they become involved with one particular dialect, one human being, and how she tried to become a lady by changing her speech. And they want to know: What is this dialect business? Why do people have them? How do they come? Why don't all Englishmen speak the same way? Why don't all Americans speak the same way?

So we look into the nature of dialects, hypothesize about how they arise, and see how they vary. The youngsters then have a much more positive attitude toward their own dialect. They realize that what we call "Standard English" or "correct English" happens to be the prestige dialect in any community. But they are no longer in terrible awe of it. They realize that perhaps acquiring another dialect is a useful thing, but there's no compulsion about it. We think this is very good for these youngsters. We think this liberates a good deal of their expression and a good deal of their communication with the outside world.

These youngsters go on several trips. They go to the museum. But again, we don't herd them into the museum to review a unit. We go in very small groups. We encourage them to linger and ask questions. And very often an observation may not be forthcoming until much later. For example, we had been to the museum after their unit on the individual in society. In reading parts of the *Iliad,* they had seen how a society shapes its heroes, molds its values, creates its rebels. In the museum the Greek vase paintings reinforced these ideas. Shortly after that, we were reading Stephen Crane's *Maggie.* We were at the part where Maggie, with her desire to make something of herself, goes one Sunday to the art museum; and Pete, who is trying to win her, accompanies her very reluctantly. "Look at all dese little jugs!" he cries. "Hundred jugs in a row! Ten rows in a case, an' 'bout a tousand cases! What d' blazes use is dem?" And one boy in the back of the room observed, "Do you know what's the matter with Pete? He can't connect with them jugs." It's these things that tell us that the course is taking effect. It's these things that show us that some of these youngsters are engaging in really thoughtful discourse with us. Our examinations are hard. They would challenge many a college-bound youngster. On the other hand, when we grade, we ignore errors in spelling, in punctuation, in usage: we look only for com-munication of ideas.

The youngsters, then, by direct exposure to the language and ideas of Chaucer and Shakespeare, develop a certain attitude toward the nature of language and a human being's relationship to language, to-ward linguistic change, and what we mean by good and bad usage. Later in the year, when these youngsters are studying the Renaissance and the seventeenth-century intellectual revolution, we see what has given impetus to our most recent studies in language. These young-sters then begin what could be labeled generative grammar. They do not need to become involved in frustrating abstraction in order to discover what the human sentence-making mechanism is. They don't just observe; they hypothesize from their firsthand knowledge as native speakers of English. They know a lot that they don't realize they know.

How do we form such a simple thing as a question, or how do we form negatives in English? Not where do you put the *not,* but what do we native speakers already know intuitively and automatically? How do we account for this extraordinary phenomenon that characterizes the human species? It's this sort of thing that these youngsters get involved in. They devise rules. They start testing sentences of their own creation to work out rules for converting a declarative sentence into a question. And they are pitted not against a prescriptive grammar but against each other. When their rules seem cumbersome, they devise abbreviations. They ask to create symbols. They are constantly testing, feeding these rules to their classmates, who play the role of computers. A machine cannot do anything except what you direct it to do; so those rules have to be more and more and more precise if they are to approximate not what the rules tell the pupils to do but what the pupils naturally do—in defiance of the rules—with an English sentence.

We don't push them far, but again we have the feeling that these youngsters could take a much more thoughtful grammar test than many a youngster who has been studying traditional classroom grammar. So we think these students are going far intellectually. How far remains to be seen.

On the other hand, not all their problems are intellectual. Some are very deep personal problems. The interesting thing is that as these youngsters taste of success, and as they become involved in really significant ideas, a few begin to see themselves in a new light.

And it erupts most unexpectedly. The history teacher had been making the transition from the age of craftsmanship into the age of automation, and to help them see what a human being goes through when he has to live through such a change, we were reading the short story by Galsworthy called "Quality." They were asked just one question: "What do you think is bothering Mr. Gessler anyway?" Well, this is where linguistics backfired. Their first response was, "He can't get used to change. He can't adapt himself." So far so good. "What evidence do you have of that?" "Well, there he is. He's been living in London all these years and he still speaks with a German accent." And then Kevin raised his hand and said, "Wait a minute. That's not such a problem really. We could line up all the phonemes of German for him and all the phonemes of English, and we could make him *hear* the differences." Then Sue, sitting down in front, asked, "Hey, isn't that the way kids learn how to read, anyway?" "I don't know. We're talking about two languages here. But would you like to see how people learn to read?" Not only was there a general "Yes." Sue picked it up immediately with, "If we could help Gessler, why can't we help those kids?"

As a result of this classroom activity, these youngsters did visit an elementary school. The guidance counselor alerted them in advance to some of the things they might look for in children's learning how to read. They visited classrooms in very small groups. Some of them worked individually with those youngsters. When they came back, they wanted to write thank-you notes to the principal who had arranged these visits. Some of them wrote those notes five times over. They wanted to impress that principal. They wanted to be sure that the letter was absolutely impeccable. When these kids need to write correctly, they will. But they've got to have a real audience. They've got to have a real motive for writing. They not only thanked him. They said, "May we help the teachers?"

Now notice what may happen to these youngsters in September. The principal accepts their offer. These are young men and women who have had remedial reading for years, and they are still handicapped readers. But when they have to sit down with a second- or third-grader and work on certain phonemic and graphemic correspondences with him, they are mastering for the first time that which has somehow eluded them. They are not *getting* remedial reading. They are getting it in order to *give* something of their own selves, their own spirit and their pride. That is far more important than learning the phonemic-graphemic correspondences.

E. Implications for the Total Education of the General Student

As can be seen from this general statement and examples from our course of study, such a blueprint means a great expense of money and effort. We are keeping our classes to a maximum of twenty. We are adding to our regular staff of teachers and guidance counselors a psychiatric social worker as liaison between home and school. For students who cannot adapt to a normal classroom situation we provide removal from class and individual work with a tutor who helps the pupil keep up with the course work until he is ready to return to the class. Providing materials for the curriculum has meant buying many sets of books, typing, mimeographing, and collating. Teachers responsible for creation of this course of study have had reduced teaching loads. Summer workshops and inservice courses of study have enabled teachers to engage in real dialogue, examining the materials, testing their efficacy, and finding additional ones. Scholars in residence and consultants should bring to the curriculum the theoretical knowledge and critical appraisal of informed opinion. The demands on the teacher are no less strenuous than the demands on the budget. Emotionally, these students drain him. Academically, they offer few returns. His only satisfaction can be exploring ideas and feelings that concern and affect both pupil and teacher as human beings.

We must face one fact: we are teaching an ever increasing number of potential dropouts. In this curriculum the word *potential* is far more important than the word *dropout*. We are committing ourselves to a curriculum that tries to reformulate the pupil's self-image. The ultimate proof that the pupil is gaining confidence in himself will come when he asks questions that enable him to discover for himself where and how he not only fits into society but can contribute to it. In order to ask these questions, the pupil needs perspective, an enlargement of his immediate horizons. We hope in the end the youngster needn't see himself as a cog fitting into a machine. He can see himself as a creature with enormous potential for better or for worse.

We don't know whether we are achieving these aims or not. But one thing we do know: for us there is no other choice. The inevitable job of educating these so-called "reluctant learners" is a long and painful process. The human effort is enormous; the expense is enormous. We think this investment is the best thing we can do for our young people. We call it a humanistic program because we do not believe a single humanities course or program can do all we have set out to do. And ours is only a beginning. We have no reason to feel, however, that such a program is for the general student only. The ways in which our materials have been borrowed and used in classes for the college-bound and the gifted at our school lead us to suspect that the needs of the reluctant learner differ from those of the successful student not in kind but only in degree.

RUMBLINGS OF REVOLUTION

8

The grammar test of yesteryear was a comfort to generations of American parents, pupils, and teachers. If composition grades seemed arbitrary and subjective, at least they were weighted with grammar grades that seemed completely reasonable and objective.

First the grammar test measured the pupil's mastery of a systematic description of English sentences. The description was supposedly based upon formal written English and the system consisted of sentence types, parts of speech, and phrases and clauses. Pupils who went on to study French or Latin in high school found this grammar, heretofore useful for identifying and classifying parts of an English sentence, even more useful for building sentences in the new language. If the declension of nouns in English seemed rather artificial (how many different cases are there for *girl?*), think of how real declension became when you had to learn at least seven different endings for *puella* in Latin? For the first time, words like *genitive, dative, ablative, vocative* came to life as the pupil built his Latin sentences. Then many a pupil would confess, "I never really understood English grammar until I studied French or Latin." What these pupils were admitting, perhaps unawares, is that their classroom grammar was closer to the facts of French or Latin than to their native English.

Why wasn't our grammar systematically describing our own language? Why did the pupil often have to ignore politely what he intuitively knew about his native language in order to analyze the sentences in an English grammar text or test? Any native speaker knew, for example, that *girl* remains subject and *moon* remains object in the following sentences:

> *The girl wanted the moon.*
> *The girl saw the moon.*
> *The girl hit the moon.*

According to the grammar, *girl* is the subject because it tells us what the sentence is about. The first sentence tells us the girl was spoiled; the second, that she was not blind; the third, that she was an astronaut. The grammar book also called *moon* the object, the receiver of the action of the verb. But nothing in the grammar verified what we intuitively knew about the differences in these three sentences: that the moon receives no action in the first sentence, that it does in the second sentence optically rather than grammatically (that the girl is really the receiver of the action), and that only in the third sentence is the moon the receiver of any action. The pupil who wanted an explanation for such discrepancies in the classroom definition of object soon learned to play the game: to seek reasonable explanations in subjects other than grammar. If he wondered why *girl* was in the nominative case in *The girl sees the boy* and in the objective case in *The boy sees the girl,* it all made sense when translated as *Puella puerum videt* and *Puer puellam videt.* And if he asked why we needed the article *the* when the Latin could do very nicely without, we simply said that was one of the differences between us and the Romans. Most important, this pupil knew better than to question the authority of the grammar; he just learned it and proved in his tests that he could memorize and regurgitate.

Another thing the grammar test measured was linguistic etiquette, conformity to the standards of classroom usage. It could clearly check a pupil's recall of the rules for *shall* and *will, who* and *whom, ain't* and *isn't, as* and *like.* The pupil could learn to assault double negatives, split infinitives, dangling participles, and whatever else was more honored in the breach than in the observance. Unfortunately, there was a curious side effect to such conditioning. No sooner had the pupil become sensitized to these violations of decency in the textbook exercises than they infected his own writing. Finally the metamorphosis was complete; he could write correct English, an idiom rarely seen or heard outside the school's jurisdiction. But the grammar rules, once learned, were like a benign infection. They could be ignored but never forgotten. Else how did we spawn a generation begging for a return to the rules of classroom usage? The people who worry more about the *like* than the taste in the cigarette ad may worry more about the plural of *sergeant-at-arms* than the pluralism of their delegations at a national political convention.

By the 1930's the English teachers themselves were worried. Grammar as a separate study of English sentence structure was NOT answering some fundamental questions about parts of speech, phrases, and clauses. And grammar as a guide to correct usage was producing only a classroom dialect.

The National Council of Teachers of English (NCTE) let *Facts about Current English Usage* in 1938 suggest the reasons for grammar's second failure. The most recent studies in the history of English, in grammar as a system, and in the usage of established writers and even English teachers themselves were simply contradicting the answer keys to our most objective, scientifically constructed tests. No wonder the pupils did not practice what the textbook and the teacher preached about usage anymore than they did about structure. They just learned the rules of test-taking.

As some English teachers began acidly testing our preconceived notions about language mastery, the defenders of classroom grammar became more strident. Only their grammar could improve reading and writing. A grammar that looked at the facts and questioned the fashions would merely encourage irresponsibility and sloppiness in language. Whatever is would be right! One might as well condemn marriage and motherhood as traditional classroom grammar. Yet how could test statistics and language statistics cancel each other out?

The intellectual ferment among English teachers is fairly recent; yet for a century and a half the verifiable facts of language had slowly been loosening the sacred foundations of eighteenth-century English prescriptive grammar, which had in turn reacted against the rampant individualism of the Renaissance. An age of rules—in dress and dance, in fencing and in foppery—had naturally evolved an etiquette in language. How else could the newly arrived bourgeois conceal his humble origins? As a rational human being, the late eighteenth-century English gentleman felt he had reached his neoclassical zenith. Nor had he any illusions as to further progress. His language only echoed this precarious perfection, and he was determined to keep it that way even if it meant chaining the winds and ignoring the actual usage of the best speakers and writers of his age. Many a handbook set the weary pupil to correcting the "errors" of well-known writers like Bunyan, Pope, Addison, or Dryden.

These prescriptive Latin-based eighteenth-century grammars did not appear suddenly. They went back to William Lyly's Latinate grammar of 1513, which became a model for other grammars until Ben Jonson's *English Grammar* of 1640. When universal literacy became a goal of eighteenth-century enlightenment, the English grammar book became a basic text. It followed two hundred years of Latin-based description but it added its own feature: rules of correctness that would keep English pure. Goold Brown's *Grammar of Grammars* in the midnineteenth century expresses the finality, the epitome of eighteenth-century tradition: rules and categories are the result of prescription imposed on description, Latin imposed on English, writing imposed on speech. A grammar school was a place where you learned classical grammar. This kind of grammar was the source for our classroom texts into the 1950's.

But the post-Galilean science that had produced the machine and the merchant also produced the linguist. Direct observation and experiment, empiricism, rationalism, and classification were yielding an objective description of language facts rather than fictions or fashions. In the Yankee the conflict between prescription and description was soon resolved: on the frontier actions spoke louder than words, but the mainland looked to the mother country for propriety in the mother tongue. If you wanted to pass as a gentleman, you had to talk and write like one. And you learned by following the prescribed rules. Although such rules produce a prestige dialect, they are only imposed on the rules that produce sound and meaning in a language. These deeper rules are the ones thinking man has long sought.

In the Western tradition, this deeper study of grammar really begins with Aristotle, who, in various writings, meticulously divided the Greek word into its component sounds and inflectional endings, and identified parts of speech by meaning and/or form and function.

The Romans followed his system of observing and classifying. But in concentrating on the glory that was Greek or the grandeur that was Latin, the ancients ignored the language of outsiders, or "Barbarians." So the classical world could discover few relationships that would characterize language itself. Furthermore, because they were unaware of the significant changes their language had undergone from earliest times, their analysis of words and word origins could only be sheer conjecture.

Barbarian looked like a compound of two Latin words: *barba* meaning "beard" and *rus* meaning "country." In fact, it has proved to be a direct borrowing from a single Greek word meaning "strange" or "foreign." To find the stem, the root, the inflectional ending, was a matter of hit or miss or wool-gathering, like that of the doomed Latin pupil who sees one common root in *duke* and *duck,* another in *leg* and *legislation,* and still another in *man* and *manufacture.*

The Alexandrian Dionysius Thrax is called the first Greek grammarian; he wrote the most complete treatise on classical grammar with its classification of the eight parts of speech. His deductive presentation became a model for Western grammars. Our first English grammars—like Lyly's designed for readers who knew or were getting ready to learn Latin, the international language of Renaissance scholarship—were naturally Latin based. The eighteenth century, in its classical revival, again appropriated Greek and Latin grammar as its English model but appended their own shibboleths as social discriminants.

During these very same periods, another study of grammar was emerging. Diverse languages had already come in contact, and comparisons were inevitable. The growth of Christianity was one force. Only through the native language of the heathen could the gospel be spread. Then the vernacular also came into its own as the language of literature. Chaucer wrote *The Canterbury Tales* in English rather than fashionable French, and Dante wrote *The Divine Comedy* in Italian rather than scholarly Latin. Before long, translations of the Bible and literature in the vernacular became the foundations for comparative study of language. The Renaissance, with its explorations into the Orient and the new world, with the invention of printing, brought even more languages into contact. At first scholars tried to trace them all back to a common ancestor, but the eighteenth century marks a complete about face from a search for characteristic differences. Empirical methods of direct observation were the start of our modern objective study of language, called linguistics. It begins with this systematic collection, examination, and classification of language.

The greatest impetus came when scholars like Sir William Jones grew familiar with Sanskrit and noted its similarity to Latin and Greek. Already the first Sanskrit grammars were suggesting the inadequacy of classical grammars. Sacred Sanskrit, handed down through strict oral tradition, was practically impervious to change. Whatever change had occurred had not disguised the forms of the Indo-European source. The stem of a word could still be clearly derived from its inflectional forms. The root could still be observed among several related words. Vowel changes could be traced in inflections and derivations. So Sanskrit grammar offered the first rational systematic analysis of its speech and forms. It provided the basis for a study of Indo-European languages, among them Romance and Germanic languages (including English) in various stages of their development. In this great age of archeological finds, inscriptions kept telling us more and more about both Indo-European and non-Indo-European languages. The Rosetta Stone is a famous example. With knowledge we saw that not all linguistic roads lead to or from Rome, that we must suspend judgment when we look at a language. Historical and comparative linguistics were beginning to undermine unreasoned Latin-based prescription. The dictionaries, grammars, and atlases that grew out of these studies, all proved that language is systematic and so is language change.

Languages that had no writing system and therefore no apparent history were another kind of challenge. In order to record such a language, the linguist had to know his phonology or sound system and he had to forget his Latin. He had to be objective, precise, and complete. Otherwise he could not describe the well-formed sentences of the language he was inductively studying. Surely he had to discover how people speak and write before he could say how they should speak and write. The questions he had to ask are the fundamental ones still facing linguists: How are sentences formed? How does the form lead to meaning? What, then, should a grammar be? What should it do? How should it be judged?

But it was the rare English teacher who heard of these questions until World War II was over. Workers like Henry Sweet, now immortalized as Shaw's Professor Higgins, were known only to specialists. Anthropologists like Sapir and Boas, linguists like Bloomfield and Jakobson, grammarians like Jespersen and Fries, although respected by scholars, rarely taught in departments of English. They were the first ones to note the shortcomings of schoolroom grammars, and they remained relatively unknown to prospective teachers of English and certainly to prospective administrators who had not majored in English. Derivative handbooks and prescriptive grammars, models of the eighteenth-century classical models, were the average English teacher's linguistic stock in trade. As early as 1924 Leonard Bloomfield had asserted: "Our schools are conducted by persons who, from professors of education down to teachers in the classroom, know nothing of the results of linguistic science, not even the relation of writing to speech, or of standard language to dialect. In short, they do not know what language is, and yet must teach it, and in consequence waste years of every child's life and reach a poor result."[1]

The shift to language as science was a threat to traditionalists. It was bound to raise naive alarm as well as serious questions. Yet if language is both physical phenomenon and social convention, then it can be studied as science as well as art. One deals with what language is; the other, with how it should be used. When long-established authoritarianism is confronted with new knowledge, when people begin to search for facts and reasons, to verify their hunches instead of accepting dogmas, conflict is inevitable. It is only natural to cling to traditional beliefs. The history of Western thought is a record of the initial collision, and of the ultimate reconciliation, between science and convention. And in our technological age the gulf between science and the humanities yawns from the Pentagon through the universities to the marketplace. According to men like C. P. Snow, the British scientist-novelist, our very survival depends on their reconciliation.

And yet when scientific knowledge impinges upon private behavior, there may be deeper personal reaction but less sound and fury than when it spotlights public behavior. For example, genetics, physiology, and biochemistry give us the facts or laws of human reproduction. These universal laws operate in the United States, in Russia, in Zambia, in spite of different conventions, laws, and taboos. Both natural and social law are man-observed and therefore subject to change. But we do not confuse natural laws of sexual behavior with social laws of sexual morality. We simply assume that the laws for

[1] Leonard Bloomfield, "Why a Linguistic Society?" *Language,* I (1925), 5.

conduct have some rational basis in the laws of science. Interpretation of both remains largely a private matter—somewhat more complex because of threats of the population explosion—than interpretation of the natural and social laws governing smoking.

Language, however, is both private and public social behavior. On the one hand speech and handwriting, like fingerprints, characterize the individual; on the other, communication would break down without conformity to conventions. We find it much harder, therefore, to accept the separateness of science and art in language. Witness the furor that greeted Webster's new unabridged dictionary in 1961. When Webster tried to report the facts of usage, many cried, "Who cares about the facts? Just tell me what is right." Such public outcry was the clearest indication of what many well-educated adults had learned in their English classrooms.

The laws underlying the production of language are studied and formulated by the linguist; the laws underlying the uses of language are studied by the rhetorician. We do not confuse laws of linguistic production with laws of linguistic etiquette. Yet we are uneasy. The English teacher's lot, then, is not a happy one. He must not only know language as science and art, but he must also know how to teach them separately; his prescriptions must be based on sound description. One pupil says, "She don't" and another, "She doesn't." A young Macaulay says, "Madam, the agony is abated" and his counterpart, "Mom, the pain's all gone." All of these utterances are linguistic events to be accounted for objectively by scientific rules. On the other hand, to know that such utterances are possible is not enough. The teacher must also alert his students to the problems of choice, to the consequences of using one version or another. Pragmatically, the second kind of knowledge is far more important than the first. The first test of English is literacy and conformity with a dialect accepted as standard. But education is more than pragmatics. If it were only that, then knowledge for its own sake—in all the sciences, and in all the humanities—would have to go. The rumblings of revolution had reached the English classroom. Linguistics, or the science of language, could not be ignored.

To some humanists, *revolution* is a harsh word. What may be a status symbol in modern math and science seems more a pragmatic acquiescence or scientism gone mad in English. But it was the methods, not the authority of science, that appealed to many an English teacher. Whenever science extends itself to an area which had thought itself immune, the first reaction is naive alarm. Yet thinking men know that all knowledge is relative. The euphemistically inclined prefer words like *reevaluation* or *progression* in the teaching of English. Call it what you will, the gaps and errors in earlier language study had become apparent. The conscientious English teacher wanted linguistic knowledge to help bridge the gaps and rectify the errors— often in spite of the cultural lag of school and community that asked only for a return to the good old days when everyone could read and write well because he knew classroom grammar. Within a decade the English teacher got more than he bargained for: not only revolution in the form of structural grammar but also counterrevolution in the form of generative or transformational grammar.

9

Both revolution and counterrevolution have had a healthy effect on language study. There is a good deal of questioning, bewilderment, and debate; a good deal of unlearning and learning going on these days. No one text or school of grammar provides all the answers; but the general direction has been away from the arbitrariness and prescriptiveness of schoolroom grammars to the reasonableness and descriptiveness of scholarly traditional grammar, structural grammar, and transformational grammar; from sentence analysis to sentence building, from rote memorizing to problem solving. As a science, grammar's unsolved problems and new frontiers challenge teacher, student, and theoretician.

The grammar underlying the wonderful feat of language is yet to be presented in its entirety. Meanwhile there are several grammars. A grammar is to *the* grammar as a map is to the landscape. The road map serves one purpose, the contour map another. So is it with the various kinds of grammar now being offered. Each attempts to describe the rules underlying an English sentence; each can be evaluated in various ways; for example, by seeing how well it corresponds to the given data. Traditional classroom grammars, in their prescriptions, described how English conformed to the logic and perfection of Latin and how we might perpetuate that perfection. If, for example, you could not split an infinitive like *amāre* into two words in the Latin language, then you should not hasten the deterioration of English which (alas!) has a two-word infinitive (to love). You should try not to further split the poor English infinitive. Scholarly traditional grammar, a natural outgrowth of traditional descriptive linguistics, is our richest source of detailed and varied examples of English sentence structure. It neatly organizes these examples, comments on them, and suggests how the student may construct similar sentences. All modern grammarians are still mining Otto Jespersen's seven-volume English grammar, one of the richest storehouses of examples of English sentences, one of the most provocative sources of modern theorizing. Jespersen's summary chapter in his *Essentials of English Grammar,*[1] for example, anticipates Charles C. Fries' analysis of grammatical devices. His chapters on junction and nexus have been picked up and expanded by transformationalists. The first stage of the revolution, then, is reflected in these early twentieth-century scholarly grammarians like Jespersen, Curme, Poutsma, and Palmer. Although some of these grammars originally taught English to foreigners, they still enlarge the understanding and appreciation of a language already known to many readers. Porter Perrin's texts (e.g., *Writer's Guide and Index to English*) incorporate much of this traditional grammar.[2] In many schools grammar is being quietly well taught through them. In others teachers are adapting to their students' level the rich fund of knowledge in Ralph B. Long's *The Sentence and Its Parts,* which incorporates contemporary scholarship in a traditional grammar.[3] What characterizes the best teaching of traditional grammar is the reformulation of knowledge. Scholarly traditional grammars always base their appreciation and prescription on an exhaustive description of spoken as well as written English.

The second stage of the development of linguistics—an outcome of the awareness of linguistic relativity, of differences in languages—sought to explain the uniqueness of each system. Structural linguists collected, classified, observed stretches of physical events called utterances as the botanist collects, observes, classifies plant life. The most subjective element in language making is obviously meaning; hence the structuralist not only refused to rely on meaning but he tried to exclude meaning from his analysis. The words "You drive me wild" may be a plea to a coy mistress or a blast at a termagant wife. The shift in meaning may interest all the neighbors, each of whom may have his theory as to how the transformation occurred. The grammarian also wants to find out how the change took place. In investigating the change, he cannot ignore the fact that speech is primary and has more signals of meaning than the written word has. Thus, though the written words remain the same, the spoken words have reversed their original meaning. But meaning is the outcome, not the method, of the structuralists.

[1] Otto Jespersen, *Essentials of English Grammar* (University, Ala.: University of Alabama Press, 1964). Originally London: George Allen & Unwin Ltd., 1933.

[2] Porter G. Perrin, *Writer's Guide and Index to English* (4th ed.; Chicago, Ill.: Scott, Foresman and Company, 1965).

[3] Ralph B. Long, *The Sentence and Its Parts* (Chicago, Ill.: University of Chicago Press, 1961).

Closely related to the problem of meaning is that of criteria for classifying elements of the sentence. Here the classroom grammars proved only circular, contradictory, and confusing. A sentence, we were told, is a group of words expressing a complete thought. But who tells the child what a complete thought is? How does he know? And if he already knows, of what further use is the definition? Or a sentence is a group of words beginning with a capital letter and ending with a period. The child can accept or recognize this in his reading. But how is he to use this definition to help him in his writing? Yet we speak and are understood without punctuation. The pupil who writes sentence fragments and run-on sentences has no trouble communicating orally. He knows more about a sentence than its traditional definition.

We can readily see *why* grammarians relied so heavily on meaning for classifying words as parts of speech. Since so many of our words had lost their characteristic inflections (case endings for nouns, personal and tense endings for verbs), we could no longer define them by form and meaning, as the Latinate grammars had. So we were left with meaning. *A noun is the name of a person, place, or thing.* Again, because the native speaker unconsciously knows more than this definition tells him, he rarely gets into trouble. Is a thing an action like *explosion,* an event like *revolution,* a quality like *mercy,* an animal like *dinosaur,* an object like *protoplasm*? Then why are *set* and *function* nouns? Note that my question does not include the possibility that *set* and *function* are nouns. It simply makes me seek a better definition of noun than the semantic one. And if a verb shows action or a state of being, where shall we draw the line between showing an action and naming it? In *They saw the fireworks,* where is the action? The interjection, according to prescriptive grammars, shows strong feeling. In *She adores him, adores* certainly expresses her strong feeling. Is it therefore an interjection?

If meaning was an unreliable criterion for some parts of speech, might overlapping the categories of function and meaning clarify our definitions? An adjective is a word that modifies a noun or a pronoun. But when *A bee stung Johnny and me,* both of us were modified by that bee. Is *bee* therefore an adjective? What does *modify* mean? An adverb is a word that modifies a verb, adjective, or another adverb. In *What did your brother's keeper use last year instead of his own money? brother* becomes an adjective, *your* an adverb, *year* an adverb, *last* an adverb. A pronoun takes the place of a noun. In *She and I are friends,* what noun does *I* replace? In *Nelson is my hide-away; I do my writing there,* is *there* a pronoun? If a conjunction is a word that connects words, phrases, or clauses, what shall I label conjunction in *He went from pillar to post?* And if a preposition is a word that shows the relationship between its object and some other word in the sentence, then in *John loves Mary, loves* must be a preposition. Since all of these definitions combine function and meaning, we do not know which takes precedence—according to the definition. Yet you know and I know in spite of the definition.

Because of these problems, structuralists decided that form and position were more reliable guides to function and meaning. Word order was paramount: *Man bites dog* makes headlines; *Dog bites man* is hardly news. But word order in turn demanded classification or identification of words. Structuralists recognized four large unlimited form classes (noun [and pronoun], verb, adjective, and adverb) and called the rest structure or function words (including determiners [such as *a, an, the*], auxiliaries, intensifiers, prepositions, conjunctions). We memorize function words naturally because they are limited in number and rarely change, yet through their position in the sentence they show structural relationships among the form classes that signal meaning. The ambiguity of headlines or telegrams disappears when we insert a function word like *the*: *Jam sticks in his throat* or *Police walk nightly.* So form and word order give a sentence its structure or grammatical meaning, which in turn is the basis for its lexical meaning.

In a sequence like *A raglump propagoodle hieraddles the aleurest ptolomaniacs ptaly,* the only two words that are unmistakably English are *a* and *the,* the only recognizable suffixes *est* and *ly.* Though there is an antique flavor about the roots of some of the other words, and *gl, mp,* and *dle* suggest the tone, we don't know what the sentence means. Yet the structural meaning is not so elusive. We can assume that what follows *a* and *the* are either nouns or noun phrases. Furthermore, the first noun phrase has to stop before *hieraddles,* because *a* signals a singular noun. So although *hieraddles* might have been a plural noun ending in *es,* and preceded by two adjectives (or what else?), it is more probably a singular verb ending in *es* with the preceding three-word noun phrase as subject. What follows *hieraddles* now looks like another noun phrase used as an object. *Aleurest* looks like an adjective in the superlative degree just as *ptaly* looks like an adverb; its position before the noun phrase used as object confirms our suspicion. We can assume all these things if the stress and pitch and pauses go along with this analysis. We can assume that the sentence consists of subject and predicate; that the subject consists of a noun phrase, the predicate consists of a verb, noun phrase used as object, and finally adverb, as in the sentence *A rabid demagogue addles the weakest voters usually.* Given punctuation, we might also see in these words a noun series consisting of *A raglump propagoodle,* (some) *hieraddles, THE aleurest,* (some) *ptolomaniacs,* and (a little bit of) *ptaly,* as in *a Santa Claus, gifts, the tree, cones, holly.*

To parse this sentence or noun phrase we have availed ourselves of the structuralists' criteria: inflectional endings, derivational prefixes and suffixes, word order, associated function words, and the suprasegmentals known as stress, pitch, and juncture or pause. In other words, by substituting the form classes and structure words in a test frame, we have arrived either at the sentence pattern or at the noun phrase pattern. These problems were clearly faced in such revolutionary texts as Smith and Trager's *Outline of English Structure* in 1951[4] and in Fries' *The Structure of English* a year later (see Suggested Reading).

Inflectional endings alone are no guide, but combined with other criteria, they confirm our intuitions about the way an English sentence goes. Nouns, for example, remain unchanged except for the possessive *'s* or *s'* and they usually form their plurals by adding *s* or *es* to the singular. In some words, replacement of an internal vowel by another (*man, men*) functions as a grammatical signal for the plural. Verbs are usually identified by their *ed, t,* or *d* endings for the past tense (or by the vowel replacement as in *sang* and *sing*) and by *s* or *es* for the third person singular in the present. When adjectives form their comparative and superlative by inflectional endings, those endings are *-er* and *-est*. Adverbs add the inflectional ending *-ly* to the adjective and *-er* or *-est* for comparative and superlative.

In addition to inflectional endings for case, number, person, tense, and degree, the four form classes have characteristic derivational endings: prefixes or suffixes. The most common noun endings are *-hood, -acy, -tion, -age, -al, -ant, -ism, -ness, -ess, -ist, -ster, -dom, -ment, -ence, -or,* and *-er* as in *motherhood, democracy, attention,*

---

[4] Henry Lee Smith, Jr., and George L. Trager, *Outline of English Structure* (New York: American Council of Learned Societies [Columbia University Press], 1951).

portage, survival, informant, totalitarianism, kindness, actress, jurist, youngster, kingdom, judgment, competence, actor, and *teacher.* Verb prefixes may be *un-, be-, de-, re-, pre-,* or *dis-* as in *UNdo, BEdevil, DEcontaminate, REsell, PREview,* or *DISapprove;* suffixes may be *-ize, -ate, -fy, -en* as in *agonIZE, activATE, rareFY, threatEN.* Adjectives have a long list of derivational suffixes, identifiable in words like *ghostLY, attractIVE, goldEN, cloudY, cloudED, hesitANT, competENT, beautiFUL, courageOUS, personAL, stationARY, argumentaTIVE, childISH, fashionABLE;* the commonest prefixes are *un-, a-, in-* as in *UNkind, Amoral, INeffectual.* The commonest derivational endings for adverbs are the suffixes *-ward, -time, -wise,* and *-ly* as in *homeWARD, someTIME, otherWISE,* and *heavenLY.* All of these derivational endings show us how a part of speech is derived from the root of the word: *agonY, agonIZE, agonizING, agonizingLY,* or *rariTY, rareFY, rare, rareLY.* In *rare* the adjective shows no derivational ending. These formal contrasts signal different meanings in *The dog's friendLY arrivAL* and *The dog's friend arrivED.*

But beyond inflectional and derivational ending, the four form classes can be identified by their position in the sentence and by associated function words. The usual patterns for nouns are shown in *The BABY* woke, *The BABY* woke his *MOTHER, The BABY woke his MOTHER* at *NIGHT, His MOTHER called the BABY a BRAT,* and *His MOTHER gave the BABY a BOTTLE. DICKY cried* and *MOTHERHOOD bored her* suggest some modifications to our tests for noun, since they do not ordinarily form plurals or take determiners like *a* or *the. A criminal lawyer* loses its ambiguity when we hear the stress.

The most common verb patterns are *The baby DRANK his milk, The baby CRIED loudly, The baby IS hungry.* If nouns are usually signaled by determiners, verbs are often preceded by auxiliaries like *be, have, do, can, will, may, shall, must,* and *ought.* Another way to distinguish noun from verb is stress. Listen to the difference between *con'duct* and *conduct', im'port* and *import'.* Noun compounds seem to follow the pattern of initial stress, as in *mad'house, egg'head, gun'powder, air'port, mas'termind.* Verb auxiliaries have weak stress except for *may, ought,* and *do.* Pause makes further syntactic distinctions. For example, it tells whether Herman is being spoken to or about in *Herman, the hermit is gone* and *Herman the hermit is gone.*

Similarly adjectives and adverbs are identified by position, associated words, and stress. Adjectives usually occupy positions as in *The dog is FIERCE. The FIERCE dog snarled. They thought him DANGEROUS.* Adjectives are often preceded by intensifiers; the same is true of adverbs. Stress frequently marks the difference between adverb and preposition: *He went up. He went up the stairs.* Or adverb and conjunction: *Speak to him; however, you'll offend him. However you speak to him, you'll offend him.*

Thus youngsters nowadays discover the word order or patterns which characterize the most common English sentences and which form the basis for more complicated sentences. Drill in such patterns is particularly helpful to those who are learning English as a second language. In these patterns, parts of speech appearing in parentheses may or may not appear in the sentence. Contrast, for example, *Experience* in pattern 1 with (*The*) *Experience* in patterns 6 and 7.

1. (Det) Noun   +   Intransitive Verb   +   (Adv.)
   Experience   *teaches*   *occasionally*

2. (Det) Noun   +   Verb   +   (Det) Noun
   Experience   *teaches*   *a lesson*

3. (Det) Noun   +   Linking Verb   +   (Det) Noun
   Experience   *is*   *a teacher*

4. (Det) Noun   +   Linking Verb   +   Adjective
   Experience   *is*   *costly*

5. (Det) Noun   +   Verb   +   (Det) Noun   +   (Det) Noun
   Experience   *taught*   *the boys*   *a lesson*

6. (Det) Noun   +   Verb   +   (Det) Noun   +   (Det) Noun
   (*The*) *Experience*   *made*   *the boys*   *men*

7. (Det) Noun   +   Verb   +   (Det) Noun   +   Adjective
   (*The*) *Experience*   *made*   *the boys*   *cautious*

The child learns to identify clusters of nouns consisting of a headword and various modifiers—such as determiners, adjectives, participles, adverbs, prepositional phrases, and clauses—each of which occupies a fairly predictable position in the sentence. Thus we say *A certain pretty little green-eyed girl with tawny skin that suggested her creole background,* and we know that the same details in another order alter the meaning: *A pretty certain green-eyed little tawny creole girl with skin that suggested her background.* The structuralists get at the complexity of analyzing and writing mature sentences by isolating layers of structural relationships from the largest cluster (or groups of words) to the smallest morpheme (units of meaning within the word), always correlating form with order.

Two great virtues of this grammar are the stress on inductive rather than deductive reasoning and the emphasis on synthesis rather than analysis. The pupil decides why he is calling a certain word a noun; he can account for his choice; he does not resort to rote memorizing or to unintelligent guessing. He also builds sentences from slots and patterns rather than takes given sentences apart. These sentences can grow in complexity as his need for expression develops. Sometimes, to wean him from earlier notions about parts of speech, he uses numbers rather than letters: 1—noun, 2—verb, 3—adjective, 4—adverb, A—auxiliary, D—determiner, P—preposition.

To make for sharper distinctions, nouns are indexed a, b, c, and so forth. The first noun in a sentence is indexed "a." All other nouns which refer back to this noun are also indexed "a." (*Mother is a teacher:* 1a   2   D   1a; but *Mother saw the teacher:* 1a   2   D   1b. When he has almost completed a standard text like Paul Roberts' *Patterns of English* (written for college freshmen but now used in junior high grades),[5] he can write sentences from formulas, for example:

$$\begin{array}{ccccccc} A & D & 1^a & 2 & D & 1^b & D & 1^c \\ \text{Does} & \text{the} & \text{doctor} & \text{give} & \text{every} & \text{patient} & \text{these} & \text{pills?} \end{array}$$

or

$$\begin{array}{cccccccc} \text{let's} & 2 & P & D & 1^a & S & D & 1^b & \leftrightarrow & 2 & 4 \\ \text{Let's} & \text{get} & \text{to} & \text{the} & \text{theater} & \text{before} & \text{the} & \text{feature} & \text{starts} & \text{tonight.} \end{array}$$

where S = subordinator and $\leftrightarrow$ ties units into agreement. We need only compare the definitions of *adjective, modify,* and *exclamatory sentence* in a book like James Sledd's *A Short Introduction to English Grammar*[6] with those in another text for teachers, Robert Pooley's *Teaching English Grammar*,[7] to see the structuralists' enormous advances in consistency and precision.

The pupil notices the effect of various kinds of sentences—statements, questions, and requests—on the hearer. He traces these responses back to their cause in the different structure words that have signaled the sentence pattern.

[5] Paul Roberts, *Patterns of English* (New York: Harcourt, Brace & World, Inc., 1956).
[6] James Sledd, *A Short Introduction to English Grammar* (Chicago: Scott, Foresman and Company, 1959).
[7] Robert C. Pooley, *Teaching English Grammar* (New York: Appleton-Century-Crofts, 1957).

These criteria of word order, inflectional and derivational endings, associated function words, suprasegmentals, and sentence patterns account for the different meanings of the same word. As native speakers, we know intuitively that *about* has several different meanings in the following sentences. We don't even need to refer to a dictionary:

1. He is *about* to jump.
2. She is *about* ten years old.
3. We talked *about* ten cave men.
4. We were given instructions *about* the work.
5. We wandered *about* the cave.
6. The railing *about* the tower is rusty.
7. I'm *about* ready to leave.
8. We moved the furniture *about* the room.
9. I spun *about*.

But in order to explain this intuitive knowledge, we need only examine the forms of words and their positions in these different contexts. Then we see how grammatical structure eliminates ambiguity. For example, *about* means *ready* only when it is followed by an infinitive. *About* means *approximately* when it is preceded by *is* and followed by countable nouns. When preceded by a verb of mental action like *talks* and followed by countable nouns, *about* means *concerning*. When preceded by a verb of physical action like *moved, about* means *around*. Grammatical structure, in other words, is an important part of what we loosely call *context*. We can talk about this fact, and use this fact in interpretation, not vaguely but precisely. Moreover, these principal devices for signaling structural meaning are one way to find several levels of lexical meaning in a poem like e.e. cummings' "anyone lived in a pretty how town," now a classic among pupils who have been taught structural grammar.

> anyone lived in a pretty how town
> (with up so floating many bells down)
> spring summer autumn winter
> he sang his didn't he danced his did.
>
> Women and men (both little and small)
> cared for anyone not at all
> they sowed their isn't they reaped their same
> sun moon stars rain
>
> children guessed (but only a few
> and down they forgot as up they grew

autumn winter spring summer)
that no one loved him more by more

when by now and tree by leaf
she laughed his joy she cried his grief
bird by snow and stir by still
anyone's any was all to her

someones married their everyones
laughed their cryings and did their dance
(sleep wake hope and then) they
said their nevers they slept their dream

stars rain sun moon
(and only the snow can begin to explain
how children are apt to forget to remember
with up so floating many bells down)

one day anyone died i guess
(and noone stooped to kiss his face)
busy folk buried them side by side
little by little and was by was

all by all and deep by deep
and more by more they dream their sleep
noone and anyone earth by april
wish by spirit and if by yes

Women and men (both dong and ding)
summer autumn winter spring
reaped their sowing and went their came
sun moon stars rain[8]

And as the pupil reads "You, Andrew Marvell," he sees how MacLeish's omission of the finite verb underscores the individual poet's awareness of time's passing within a timeless continuum:

You, Andrew Marvell

And here face down beneath the sun
And here upon earth's noonward height
To feel the always coming on
The always rising of the night

To feel creep up the curving east
The earthly chill of dusk and slow
Upon those under lands the vast
And ever-climbing shadow grow

---

[8] Copyright, 1940, by e. e. cummings. Reprinted from his volume *Poems 1923–1954* by permission of Harcourt, Brace & World, Inc. and Faber & Faber Limited.

And strange at Ecbatan the trees
Take leaf by leaf the evening strange
The flooding dark about their knees
The mountains over Persia change

And now at Kermanshah the gate
Dark empty and the withered grass
And through the twilight now the late
Few travelers in the westward pass

And Baghdad darken and the bridge
Across the silent river gone
And through Arabia the edge
Of evening widen and steal on

And deepen on Palmyra's street
The wheel rut in the ruined stone
And Lebanon fade out and Crete
High through the clouds and overblown

And over Sicily the air
Still flashing with the landward gulls
And loom and slowly disappear
The sails above the shadowy hulls

And Spain go under and the shore
Of Africa the gilded sand
And evening vanish and no more
The low pale light across that land

Nor now the long light on the sea—
And here face downward in the sun
To feel how swift how secretly
The shadow of the night comes on. . . .[9]

Structural grammar had not answered all the questions it set out to answer as to how we recognize and produce sentences, nor had it avoided all the pitfalls of semantically based grammar; but it liberated pupil and teachers from dull repetition and arbitrary routine. Structural grammar replaced the fictitious simplicity of a dead language with the complex reality of a living language. Careful observation, classification, and verification were beginning to make order out of chaos.

All of this may seem very complicated in its capsule form. Yet note how easily one parent, Professor Samuel B. Stone of Wayne State

[9] Archibald MacLeish, *Collected Poems 1917–1952* (Boston: Houghton Mifflin Company, 1952), pp. 58–59. Reprinted by permission of Houghton Mifflin Company. Copyright 1952 by Archibald MacLeish.

University, teaches grammar to his little girl. He starts with an awareness that "Beginning where the child is demands of a grammar that the language studied be the child's language, that the structures analyzed be his structures, that the categories established be categories having real existence in his native tongue." He also chooses "a logically clean grammar in which definitions are consequences of basic assumptions and in which identifications are really consequences of definitions, and not of intuition mixed with contradictory qualifications." But here is the story itself:

Last spring my oldest daughter, who was then only six years old, overheard my wife and me using the words *noun* and *verb* and some other grammatical terms. Later that evening, she backed me into a corner with the question, "Daddy, what's a verb?" I had never considered grammar an important subject for first grade children, but knowing Susie I sensed that it would be easier to answer than to evade her. Besides, like any dabbler in behavioral science, I find it impossible to pass up a good guinea pig when I see one. And so began an elementary study of parts of speech and sentence structure based on a mixture of structural and transformational grammar.

I started our little dialogue by saying, "In the sentence *The girls walk to school together,* the word *walk* is a verb. Now, notice that I can use *walk* in two other ways. I can say *Richie walks to school,* or I can say *Richie is walking to school.* All right, now, what have I done to the word *walk* in these sentences?"

She gave the obvious answer: "You've added *s* and *ing.*"

"That's what verbs are," I told her, "words that can add *s* or *ing.*"

To make sure that she really had grasped the idea and to ensure at least some retention, I gave her—still orally—six or eight more sentences and asked her to find the verbs and to tell why she picked them out. She was able to handle this little task without error, always reasoning, "Well, I can say *play, plays,* or *playing.*" At this stage, incidentally, the sentences were very simple, no past tense forms had been used, and *be* was not analyzed in any way.

Now came the introduction of the past tense. No explanation was offered—only a list of oral sentences containing verbs in the past, given one by one with instructions to find the verbs. The first sentence, *The boy dropped the ball,* proved to be a bit difficult; it took Susie almost thirty seconds and an encouraging, "You can do it if you use your brain," to come up with, "Is it *dropped?*" I asked her why and she replied, "Well, I can take off the *-ed* and say *drop, drops, dropping.*"

Having thus established the regular past tense endings as markers of verbs, we proceeded to the past forms of irregular verbs, again with a list of orally presented sentences and no advance explanation. The first sentence was *The sparrows ate all the seed.* After a few seconds' deliberation, the answer came: "I think it must be *ate* because *ate* is the same thing as *eated*, only you can't say *eated*, and you can say *eat, eats, eating*." The forms *sang, wrote, broke*, and *gave* were no trouble for her. "*Sang* is *singed*, and *sing, sings, singing*," crackled out with the brevity and precision of the "side, angle, side" of a high school geometry lesson. At this point I inserted the device *walk* + *D* → *walked* and *sing* + *D* → *sang*, which was grasped in a few seconds like most of the other concepts. We repeated these formulas orally as, "Walk plus D gives (or is) walked."

All of this had taken less than ten minutes, and Susie's curiosity was still not satisfied; she wanted to know about nouns. We started as before with some short simple sentences:

> Richie has a little sister.
> Eleanor has two sisters.
> His sister's name is Kathy.

I simply told her that the word *sister* was a noun and asked her what endings it could take. She immediately replied that it had an *s* ending but made no distinction between the plural and the possessive. When asked specifically whether *sisters* and *sister's* in the examples were alike or different, she said that the first meant more than one, but she could give no explanation—only examples—for the second; this, of course, was evidence that she knew what was involved. I then told her that nouns were words that could add "two kinds of *s*." Next, she was given a short list of sentences, orally as before, each containing at least one noun. The first three sentences had only regular nouns, but then a few irregular forms such as *child, tooth,* and *sheep* were introduced without either warning or special preparation beyond what she had learned in coping with verbs.

The regular nouns were no problem for her; she located each one and supported her identifications by showing that the word in question could be pluralized, could show possession, or could occur without an ending. For example, she justified *dog* as a noun because "I can say two *dogs* or the *dog's* bone." The word *child,* the first irregular noun in the exercise, failed to slow her down. "*Child* is a noun," she said, "because I can say *the child's shoe* and *children* is *child* plus the other kind of *s*." A few seconds later she was telling me that *sheep* plus *s* was *sheep,* that is if we were talking about two, three, or more sheep and not about the sheep's wool.

Later I constructed a set of exercises which I used to teach her complete subject and complete predicate. The first exercise consisted of twelve typewritten sentences with verbs in either the simple present or past tense and with some subjects in the singular and some in the plural. Susie was asked to put parentheses around such group of words that could be replaced by *he, she, it, we,* or *they*—that is, by nominative case pronouns—and to write the substitute word above the replaced group. Similarly, she was asked to put a second set of parentheses around the part of the sentence that could be replaced by *do, does,* or *did* and to indicate which one of the substitutes she had used in each case. At this point the terms subject and predicate were introduced and an exercise of five more sentences with the simple direction to put parentheses around the subjects and predicates was used to consolidate what had been learned.

The next exercise consisted of ten sentences, eight of which used some form of *be* as a linking verb. It began with the statement, "Some predicates can be replaced by *am, is, are, was,* and *were,*" and directions to parenthesize the subjects and predicates and to write in the appropriate substitute words. The predicate substitute in each instance, of course, was whatever finite form of *be* was present in the given sentence. One additional exercise introduced *have, be,* and the modals as auxiliaries and as predicate substitutes. For example, *The old man might come home tomorrow* reduces to *He might.*[10]

Professor Stone concludes with "Material that a six-year-old can handle should be a cinch for high school pupils." His observation is not a grammatical counterpart to those "Teach your baby how to read" ads that the *New York Times* nests between its "How to read the financial news" and "Why fear death?" ads. Had Susie in her infancy been confronted with cards reading "Mommie" or "toes" flashing from her Mommie's bosom, she would have known better at six; she would never have looked for trouble with "Daddy, what's a verb?" His observation does point out, however, the reasonableness and speed with which simple grammatical concepts can be learned when the pupil logically relates his automatic linguistic habits to a few simple cues that suggest a whole category to him. Grammar need not be taught repetitively and drudgingly year in year out. If language is a system, it can be learned systematically. Nor does Professor Stone suggest that this is the only way it can be taught. Had Susie begun with "Daddy, what's a question?" the story would have been entirely different.

[10] Samuel B. Stone, "Psycholinguistics and the Teaching of Grammar and Thinking," a paper presented at the 54th annual convention of the National Council of Teachers of English, Cleveland, Ohio, 1964. Used by permission of Samuel B. Stone.

10

Today's world depends more and more on the practical application of abstract knowledge. Few of us can any longer keep up with the fundamentals underlying the technology controlling our daily comfort and survival. Abstract theories, which are complex and deep and defy understanding through direct observation, can be expressed only in the most precise and concise language. The most famous equation of our time, $E = mc^2$, may affect the fate of all of us on this planet; yet, in spite of excellent popularizations, its meaning eludes most of us. If this is so in today's world, what can we say of tomorrow's?

The counterrevolution in grammar is part of this century's increasing concern with theory-building for its own sake. Instead of gathering data, discovering procedures, and classifying forms, the new grammarian constructs axiomatic theories and validates them. The transition from natural history to theoretical science is never easy. When a mathematician friend of mine came to a Nelson square dance, the indigenous folklore and tunes did not interest him at all. I thought he was indifferent to the rustics cavorting in the old town hall until I realized he was really bemused. Instead of trying to connect the caller's lingo with the intricate steps, this mathematician was studying their precise pattern and trying to derive axioms that would reduce the dance to a concise formula. And he succeeded! His knack of absorbing condensed information was matched only by his ability to express the underlying pattern or rules of the dance in a succinct equation. And while this mathematician found joy in the beauty of the dance's abstract structure, Nelson's citizens, young and old, found joy in the dance itself. Maybe we'll never tell the dancer from the dance. But we can tell linguistic knowledge from linguistic performance, and in our time linguistic knowledge concerns deep subsurface explanations.

At midcentury a single decade witnessed structuralist revolution and transformationalist counterrevolution. A new scientifically based grammar was to extend the frontiers and goals of structural grammar.

The twentieth century had seen an increasing interest not only in describing and predicting phenomena but also in explaining them. Many scientists in superbly equipped laboratories were still searching for rigorous answers from impressive data, while others were turning to a blackboard and a piece of chalk or a pad and a pencil to unlock some of the secrets of the universe. Both empirical-inductive method and theoretic-deductive methods of inquiry (described in James B. Conant's *Two Modes of Thought*[1]) were to make grammar a humanistic science.

The structuralists had made remarkable progress in collecting, classifying, and observing the physical facts of language. Their accomplishments were considerable in recording esoteric and unwritten languages and in teaching people how to speak a second language. Their grammars had made advances in analyzing linguistic sound systems and in classifying signals of meaning. But their syntactic or grammatical theories left many problems still unsolved, problems apparent in the discrepancy between acquiring a first and a second language. We simply do not learn our native language as we do later ones. We have to presume certain abilities in the first language in order to start learning the second. It is these assumptions and abilities that structuralists, in their rigorous empirical studies, could not take into account without bringing back into consideration a nasty four-letter word, *mind*.

In avoiding the vagueness of mentalism or intuition, in separating mind from matter (a separation with precedent going back to Descartes in the seventeenth century), they were following an established mode of scientific inquiry. Since we cannot observe what goes on in the mind, let us concentrate on the observable physical segments of utterances and note the causes linking articulation and sound waves. Since we cannot collect and manipulate the speech act itself, which exists in time, let us examine the record in phonetic script, tape, disc, X-ray photograph, or spectrogram. Knowledge obtained from such evidence can be especially useful to behaviorists and to neurophysiologists. But some grammarians, those concerned with the deep, subsurface discoveries which yield to theorizing, were not satisfied. To see sentences as elements put together in a sequence is to risk labeling without considering all the facts. Articulation and sound waves, phonemes and morphemes are interesting and revealing;

[1] James B. Conant, *Two Modes of Thought* (New York: Trident Press, Inc., 1964).

but they are only end products of those mental processes and internal capacities, the intuitive knowledge and judgments which enable speaker and listener to encode and decode a sentence.

The important thing, said counterrevolutionists like Noam Chomsky in 1957, is not discovering facts about the English sentence from a given body of data, a corpus of sentences representative of everyday speech. The important thing is explaining and predicting facts without ignoring other facts that stare us in the face: the total linguistic performance. We can't look into the head of a speaker for evidence of such performance any more than a physicist can directly examine a deuteron or an astronomer the solar wind. But we can hypothesize and see where the hypothesis leads us. We can arrive at an explanation intuitively and try to justify it logically.

We can, in other words, construct a model of the system. But we need the hypothesis. Without it, how can we match the behavior of the model against the actual performance of speaker and listener? We need to observe the logical consequences of our hypothesis.

Our proof, then, is not a matter of translating the theory into neurological terms like *synapses* and *nerve fibers* and *cortex*. Nor is it a matter of constructing a direct model which is an analogue to the human brain. The real test of our model's adequacy is whether or not it enables us to derive all the known facts and predict previously unknown ones. In other words, our model need only be a set of rules that will describe the structure of all and only well-formed or grammatical sentences which have been or may be uttered. Without ignoring what goes on in the speaker's and listener's mind, we can arrive at a more powerful theory of language than one which considers only the observable physical facts of an utterance. We can more adequately explain and predict linguistic performance.

To theorize is more than to predict. A farmer neighbor of mine is the best weather prophet I know. He can look toward Mount Monadnock through the morning mist and foretell the local temperature and humidity. Though his forecast is foolproof, it has nothing to do with an accurate knowledge or description of the events that a meteorologist must take into account. His predictions are useful but unrevealing. Neither he nor I can explain the weather through Monadnock's many guises; the farmer is combining years of observation with some intuitive hunches which could become a testable theory. A really powerful theory would describe and predict the weather in a manner that accounted for both meteorologist's and farmer's knowledge and judgment. Prediction becomes explanation only when it unifies a whole fabric of events, not just a few threads.

Theorizing in language is part of the philosophic temper of our age; it marks the counterrevolution in grammar. According to Emmon Bach, linguist from the University of Texas, its impetus came from logicians interested in abstract language systems, from telephone engineers concerned with codes and transmission systems, and from computer technologists involved in machine translation and data processing. The most precise, convenient symbols available happened to be those used in mathematics. Yet, as Bach points out, use of such symbols "doesn't make the [language] theory mathematical any more than stating a chemical theory in Spanish would make the theory 'Spanish.' " Some symbols are, of course, easier to work with than others. Try multiplying *XVII* by *LC*. The important thing, however, is not what symbols are used in setting forth the theory but "how well it fits into a broader theory of language that includes a theory of meaning and a theory of use." *Notion* is basic; notation is less so. A statement is no more valid when it uses algebraic signs instead of plain words; it is only more precise and concise, less subject to semantic confusion.

In order to understand, explain, and predict what language is like —at least what one's native language is like—we need, then, a general theory of language. The structural grammarians describe particular languages; the new grammarians look for the universals. They try to account for the variety of grammatical systems throughout the world, to explain the universal features of languages of the world, and to arrive at theories of specific languages. Simplicity, economy of statement, empirical consequences are the real tests. They suggest a task not yet completed by any theoretician or linguist. Yet language covers a relatively simple series of events. A linguistic theory should be easier to develop than a theory of biology or physics, which includes many more complex phenomena. And precisely on these grounds would it be even more unrealistic to teach traditional classroom grammar in the 1960's than to teach traditional pre-Darwinian biology or ancient four-element chemistry today. Nor do we wait for a single unified theory to engage the pupil in thought about biology, physics, or language.

Grammar as a humanistic science, a subject with its own intellectual integrity and autonomy, shares with other sciences the tentativeness and the partiality of theorizing, the readiness to admit change and variation. Traditional prescriptive grammar's first error was its claim to rightness. Its second error was its claim to eternal rightness. To justify its claim to eternal rightness or completeness, prescriptive Latin-based grammar had to ignore the facts of linguistic change or call change corruption. Nothing could be more unscientific, unhistoric, or anti-intellectual. Yet as a norm for correct classroom usage, punctuation, and spelling, this grammar served its purpose. A scientifically oriented grammar makes no such claims. But as an independent study it is bound to have more content, depth, and intellectual challenge for the student. The abstract symbols are no more difficult than those in elementary algebra. Yet they bring us closer to the way we understand and form sentences in that they formulate the rules we intuitively follow every time we utter or hear a sentence in our native tongue. These rules are abstractions only indirectly related to the physical output we recognize as a sentence. Grammar rules do not account for our choice of words or individual style; they only account for the structure underlying variations in word or style.

This set of rules revealing the underlying structure of our language system constitutes our grammar. If we follow the rules, whatever choices we make along the way, the result must be what we native speakers recognize as a well-formed sentence in English. Otherwise the rules are faulty. Furthermore, these rules reveal the relationships between our fairly simple and our most complex utterances, between one style and another of the same degree of complexity. Thus in the new grammar the student acquires a conscious knowledge of the major forms of sentences he invents and understands daily. He sees how the grammatical relations or structure of a simple sentence is the kernel or source which we rewrite or transform into alternate structures and combined sentences. What he has learned in traditional descriptive grammar proves extremely useful. What he has learned intuitively from you, his parents, is even more useful.

Let's see, then, what may have been beneath the surface of that language game you played with him in his infancy. We said, back in the first chapter, that somehow, in some mysterious way, parent and child, without any explicit knowledge, begin to play this game together and that the child latches on to the rules. Suppose Mother has just put out on the porch to cool a cheese cake which took an hour of her time and the last bit of her Grand Marnier for a special glaze. Suppose she's also put out on the porch to cool off a baby who's felt pretty neglected and despised during this culinary endeavor.

For a while silence reigns. Junior is playing with the cat, the cake is cooling on the table, and Mother is stretched out on the couch in the living room. All too soon, Junior begins to fuss again. Mother goes out to him and finds the cheese cake gone. "What happened to the cake?" she cries. And Junior answers "Kee kay." "The kitty ate the cake?" Mother asks. And Junior nods his agreement. If we were to break down the intuitive leaps into logical steps by which Mother created this sentence out of Junior's two syllables, they might look like this:

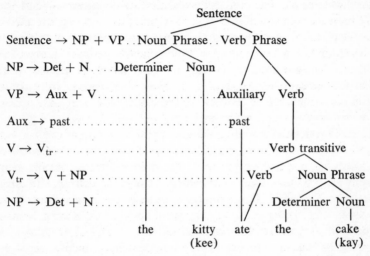

Step by step, but with a speed that defies analysis, Mother has figured out the baby's total sentence from the telegraphic parts that he has uttered. The more she repeats his fragmentary utterances by filling in the missing parts, which have less semantic content than his, the more do they play the game. The mother has figured out the latent structure of the child's sentence.

The latent structure of mature sentences is similarly apparent when we say *you* is understood in imperatives, and that some modal like *can* or *will* is, too, as in Mother's words to her guest that evening: "Help yourself to some Sara Lee cheese cake, won't you?"

In school the child's latent sentence building is consciously verbalized. He does not become self-conscious and suspect his own idiom as inadequate for the classroom standard of usage. He does not ignore his intuitive knowledge; he uses it to perceptualize, to discover and validate rules. He does not ignore meaning, but if he relies on meaning to justify syntax, then he is going around in circles, explaining the phenomenon by citing the phenomenon. Syntax helps us figure out how people decode a string of noises into a meaning. If the syntax makes assumptions about meanings, it cannot explain these same assumptions. *We won because we won* is only a joke. It explains nothing. Nor does *We won because they lost* explain why we won. Our ability to sense ambiguity also needs to be explained syntactically. It has nothing to do with our notions of reality. Whether or not there was a preface to the book *Doctor Zhivago,* whether or not there was a real doctor and a real Lara are irrelevant. "Lara read the preface to Doctor Zhivago" and "Lara read the preface to *Doctor Zhivago*" mean two different things when spoken and out of context. Therefore it is different from a sentence that doesn't mean two different things out of context. The ambiguity is explained by the fact that the same prepositional phrase comes from two different source sentences: Meaning derives from grammatical structure, which does not ignore intuition. "Intuition," says Chomsky, "is knowledge that comes to you without your knowing where it comes from."

If the grammar is to predict all and only the real sentences of English, it must meet the tests of any theory. It must be consistent; there can be no internal contradiction. It must cohere with other behavioral sciences. It must validly include all the known facts. It must be elegant, have a powerful generality. The rules must be short and simple, yet generate an infinite set of sentences. A grammar that required a separate rule' for every new sentence would be contrary to our experience with language, and totally useless. It must explain, not repeat, our linguistic intuitions. It must make explicitly clear whatever we vaguely and intuitively understand. And it must be able to stand the test of empirical consequences.

Robert B. Lees puts it this way:

> The linguistic units postulated by a grammar are constructed much like the concepts of proton, covalent bond, or gene: they are postulated because of the great predictive power which they lend to the theory, but they are not brought to light in the process of induction. And the theories by means of which we order our experiences, on the street or in the laboratory, are generated only by those flashes of insight, those perceptions of pattern, which mark off the brilliant scientist from the dull cataloger of data.[2]

[2] Robert B. Lees, "Review of *Syntactic Structures,*" *Language,* **33**, 3 (1957), 380.

An adequate grammar, then, would account for some of the abilities we take for granted in a native speaker. Why can we quickly memorize a nonsense sentence like *'Twas brillig and the slithy toves/Did gyre and gimble in the wabe,* or like *Sincerity eats pizza?* Why is it harder for us to recall a sentence like *Evil that the do lives men them after; oft their with good bones is the interred?* though we have heard every word in a familiar quotation? Such a grammar would account for the different degrees of grammaticality we feel in *an hour ago* and *a grief ago;* in *Portia seems sad, Portia seems sleeping,* and *Portia hits sad.* It would account for our ability to recognize the ambiguity in *Visiting in-laws can be a nuisance* or *Plumtree's Potted Meat.* It would account for all of these abilities through a method that is practical, objective, logical, coherent, explicit, economical, and verifiable, a method that commits us to follow our assumptions to their logical conclusion, wherever they may lead. The most convenient device may be algebraic; but the goal is consistency, cohesion, accuracy, and generality of our semantic statement about language. All the new grammar does is specify the patterns by which English sentences are formed. One way of specifying is to say that if X is an English sentence, then it must logically follow that Y derived from X through a series of transformational rules is also an English sentence. If not, why not? There is no limit to this "if—then" testing if we are to account for the richness and complexity of English sentences.

The grammar, then, consists of a series of phrase structure rules that formulate the abstractions underlying our simplest sentences and of transformational rules that formulate the abstractions underlying our more complicated utterances. They show us how to change one string of grammatical elements into another. The extent of their showing and the use of abstraction depend on the maturity and the ability of the pupil.

The elements of sentence structure are, for any pupil, no more words than the elements of mathematics are numbers. It is the equations, the functions or ratios, the interplay of elements that give them significance. The numbers zero to nine may be only counting devices, but think of what can be generated through their combination and interaction, from the simplest addition, subtraction, multiplication, and division to the most sophisticated operations performed better by computers than by man. If words were elements, how could we account for the total difference in meaning in *He weighed a tuna* and

He weighed a ton? Like any other game, the language game makes sense only when you know what each element is, what it can do, how it is related to other elements, how the action of one affects the pattern of the whole. Of course knowing the rules of the game of chess is no guarantee you'll win the chess tournament. But the rules explain the game. Phrase structure and transformational rules make sense of the linguistic game we've been playing since infancy. They do not make champions of us. Since they explain an infinite set of sentences that can be generated, they are often called generative grammar. Since transformational rules are used to explain our intuitions as to what is and is not an English sentence, they are often called transformational grammar. The important thing is that each sentence in an infinite set can now be assigned a proper grammatical description.

Transformational rules in themselves are not new. Old-fashioned grammar used them. Affirmative and negative statements, sentence transforms for questions and commands were clearly transformational in their basic nature. Most of us copied and memorized elaborate paradigms when we learned our first foreign language in high school. These systematized the language for us; they were extremely helpful, even though they might be arbitrary and subject to all kinds of exceptions and rationalizations. But more important than the classification itself is the transformational rule that justifies the classification, that differentiates the grammatical from the ungrammatical utterance. If transformational rules in the new grammar are part of the validation procedure, they must be systematic, coherent, and rationally ordered. They determine the structure of the sentence. Our present theories include the rule for passive transformation, for example, which must precede the rule for agreement of subject and verb, since passivization frequently changes the number of the subject. *He has bought a Jaguar on time payment* can be transformed to *A Jaguar has been bought by him on time payment.* But *He has bought three Jaguars on time payment* would be *Three Jaguars has been bought on time payment by him* unless the rule for agreement of subject and verb gave us *Three Jaguars have been bought on time payment by him.* We first have to see the object, turned subject, before we decide whether the new verb is to be singular or plural to agree with it. Thus the rules and their order, where tested against our intuitions, extend the grammar.

These rules move from the most abstract stage, the formulation of phrase structure rules for *any* conceivable sentence in the language to the most concrete stage, the formulation of morphophonemic rules that produce a particular utterance. The sentence may never have been heard before, but we recognize it as a sentence, regardless of its relationship to our notions of reality: *Last night the housemaster gave birth to four centaurs and three mermaids.* The grammar will not stop you from uttering such nonsense; it will provide you with the rules that assure their utterance. But change *last night* to *tomorrow,* and the grammar says NO! The grammar does not tell us about the world outside language; but once we have this information, the grammar tells us how to convey it by means of a sentence. The grammar, then, includes phrase structure rules ranging from the most general to the most specific, transformational rules, a lexicon, semantic rules, and morphophonemic rules. The lexicon provided for such a grammar would give much more than semantic information. It would also list rules for co-occurrence of particular words, restrictions as to environment and form of words. It would also have its sequence of categories. The grammar specifies possibilities of combination; the lexicon (like the dictionary we carry around in our heads) contains words fitting these possibilities. The utterance *boy,* for example, might be listed as noun, animate, human; *hit* as verb, transitive, takes human or animate subject, and so on.

The rules also account for the way we form numerous sentences from the basic or simplest sentences. *The man bought the peaches* can be transformed to *The man didn't buy the peaches, Did the man buy the peaches?, Who bought the peaches?,* or *The peaches were bought by the man.* More than one basic sentence can account for the derivation of a new sentence as in *The man who dared to eat a peach bought one.* Even more for *The man who wore his trousers rolled and dared to eat a peach he'd bought asked the overwhelming question.*

The grammar simply accounts for the fact that we as native speakers can do all these things to an English sentence; it provides rules for creating, altering, and combining sentences.

But it also explains why differences exist among sentences and how we interpret sentences. It tells us why we say either *He put through the call to Yoknapatawpha* or *He put the call through to Yoknapatawpha;* why we say *Holden called up his sister* or *Holden called her up,* but not *Holden called up her.* It explains why *The man that I spoke with left* or *The man with whom I spoke left* is an English sentence, but not *The man with that I spoke left.*

It verifies our ability to recognize ambiguity; it accounts for sentence homonymity. through derivation from two different source sentences for *They were assembled by the machine, The shooting of the hunters alarmed us, He cleverly opened the door, The routine scorn of the British telephone system is notorious, Hepzibah enjoys water-skiing, skin-diving, and exciting dates,* and *The lovers of the lake left the island.* It accounts for our sensing the difference that meets the eye and the ear in *They shot the man in the red fez* and *They shot the man in the right leg;* or *The pupil is easy to please* and *The pupil is eager to please;* or *The Macedonian lint gatherers are delightful to visit* and *The Macedonian lint gatherers are delighted to visit.* How do we know the first sentence tells which man was shot, the second tells where he was shot? How do we know when *to please* and *to visit* are active and when they are passive? How can the same word in the same form convey different meanings?

And if word order is a clue to meaning, if a declarative sentence consists of a subject followed by a predicate, how do we sort out questions from statements that follow identical patterns: *Dante had heartburn, Who had heartburn?* And how do we account for the differences in *Did Dante have heartburn?* and *What did Dante have?* when we note that both questions have the same pattern: predicate, subject, predicate?

Another thing we native speakers intuitively recognize is the different forms that convey the same meaning. We know that *bachelor* and *unmarried man* mean the same thing; that *Eustacia loved Clym* does not mean *Clym loved Eustacia,* but it can mean *Clym was loved by Eustacia.* The grammar accounts for our intuitive knowledge. It formulates rules we intuitively follow.

Many novices are first struck by the abstraction of transformational grammar, then by the far-fetched sentences cited by some grammarians. Neither abstraction nor weirdness is an intrinsic property of transformational grammar. The transformationalist does not dream these sentences up as a blessed relief from the boredom of his task. Nor is he suggesting that his examples are typical or standard or less ludicrous than some of the examples in classroom grammars. In citing the atypical or bizarre sentence, the transformational grammarian is testing. He is pushing regularity or grammaticality as far as it can go. He wants to see what rules produce a grammatical utterance, why certain sentences that follow the rules turn out ungrammatical according to the innate sentence sense of a native speaker. A sentence like

> Who said that I asked what John thinks the people whom you like who enjoy the game which you enjoy talk about?

would be shunned by the rhetorician but welcomed by the grammarian. Rhetorically—except under very special circumstance—the sentence is bad; grammatically it is not only correct; it is very revealing. Its extreme form shows that theoretically there is no limit to the cycle of rules which can be applied to a sentence but that there are restrictions on order.

A rhetorician might involve students in revising a sentence like

> The event prompted me to try to visualize myself forcing him to come.

The grammarian uses such a statement to clarify the rules for embedding one structure within another in an indefinite series. The aim nevertheless is to characterize well-formed English sentences. The grammar tells the student how to write and recognize a correct sentence; the rhetoric tells him how to write and recognize a good sentence. The two usually interact.

The aim is not to make a theoretician out of the high school student, but to engage him in basic and timeless questions about language and to teach him verifiable facts that accord with his actual experience with sentences. Many of these facts appear in scholarly traditional grammars, which described English syntax in rich detail but left much of the actual construction of a sentence to be supplied by the knowledge or ability or intuition of the person reading the grammar. The new grammar uses the facts of traditional grammar as well as the essential facts behind the innate abilities of the native speaker. A rigorous description of the syntactic structure of the sentence is basic to an explanation of the sounds we impose on the structure and the meaning we extract from the structure. A study of English syntax, then, is the basis for any study of sound or meaning.

The questions raised by the new grammar are not new: How can we describe explicitly the underlying competence of a speaker to generate an infinity of sentences from a few finite rules? In *Aspects of the Theory of Syntax,* Noam Chomsky points out that "a real understanding of how a language can 'make infinite use of finite means' has developed only within the last thirty years, in the course of studies in the foundations of mathematics." But he points out that if we are looking for the deep, insightful, explanatory hypotheses rather than the surface explanations, we have a long way to go. "It is quite apparent that current theories of syntax and semantics are highly fragmentary and tentative, and that they involve open questions of a fundamental nature. Furthermore, only very rudimentary grammatical descriptions are available, for any language, so that no satisfactory answers can be given for many factual questions."[3]

[3] Noam Chomsky, *Aspects of the Theory of Syntax* (Cambridge, Mass.: Massachusetts Institute of Technology Press, 1965), p. 148.

GRAMMAR IN THE NEW TEXTBOOKS

11

The result of all this revolution and counterrevolution is that different grammars are being taught in different schools today. The prepared teacher knows something of traditional, structural, and generative grammar; the new teacher, not knowing to which school he will be assigned, has to know them all. This need be no more bewildering to the teacher than knowing two or three schools of criticism in literature. Yet in both grammar and literature one interpretation or explanation will be more cogent than another, perhaps for different reasons or for different circumstances.

From the following excerpts from school texts—all designed for the same grade level—you can see what the pupil is asked to do and what he learns thereby about the English adverb. The adverb is a revealing example because it reveals much about a grammar's goals. Literally, *adverb* simply means one word added to another. It can, then, become a catchall for all the words that the grammar doesn't know how to account for. But it need not be.

Before we examine these excerpts, let's recall an assertion from the Introduction of this book: The new devices are not really significant. What matters is what is being taught through these devices. The selections from the three different texts enable us to test this statement as well. Although each deals with the same subject, the English adverb, and although each is designed for pupils of the same age, three different devices for teaching are being used. One text is completely programed. Questions, whether direct, multiple choice, or fill-in, are presented so carefully in such small, logical units or steps that the pupil who succeeds in answering one question cannot help answering the next one. The text or the teacher provides the answer after each frame so that the pupil knows immediately whether he is ready for the next step or whether he has to backtrack to master some information he needs in order to proceed with the frames. In this way the text becomes self-teaching. If the reader were not mastering the information being so slowly and logically presented, he could not proceed. If he is proceeding, he is using the knowledge provided by earlier frames.

The second excerpt is from a text that presents information in traditional form, that is, by discussion, explanation, lists. Although it is unfair to use just parts of chapters for our comparison, enough has been presented to enable us to see what information is being offered to the pupil. Usually such a traditionally designed text leaves questions for the end of the chapter.

The third excerpt is a compromise between straight programing and traditional expository presentation. Wherever the author feels discussion is necessary, he stops the frames and presents his information directly. Perhaps the best way to answer our first question, then, is to ignore the method and simply to list the things that you know about an adverb after reading the excerpt that you did not know before. Ultimately, this is what we're after. How we acquired the information is interesting but irrelevant.

JOSEPH C. BLUMENTHAL—*English 2600*[1]

We have seen how adjectives give us a clearer picture or idea of nouns by telling <u>what kind</u>, <u>which one(s)</u>, <u>how many</u>, or <u>how much</u>.

| <u>dark</u> cloud | <u>green</u> hat | <u>ripe</u> peach | <u>strong</u> coffee |

509 Do the underlined adjectives answer the question "How many?" or "What kind?"

| a. <u>clean</u> dish | <u>sharp</u> pencil | <u>fresh</u> eggs | <u>juicy</u> oranges |
| b. <u>this</u> dish | <u>that</u> pencil | <u>these</u> eggs | <u>those</u> oranges |

510 Do the adjectives answer the question "Which one?" or "Which ones?" in group <u>a</u> or <u>b</u>?

| a. <u>five</u> days | <u>most</u> cars | <u>some</u> schools | <u>no</u> trees |
| b. <u>warm</u> days | <u>fast</u> cars | <u>large</u> schools | <u>tall</u> trees |

511 Do the adjectives answer the question "How many?" in group <u>a</u> or <u>b</u>?

512 Words that modify nouns and pronouns are called _____.

513 Adjectives can modify _____ and pronouns, but they cannot modify verbs.

514 There is another class of words that answers questions about verbs in the same way that _____ answer questions about nouns and pronouns.

---

[1] From *English 2600*, Revised Edition, by Joseph C. Blumenthal, © 1960, 1962, by Harcourt, Brace & World, Inc. and reprinted with their permission.

515 John swam recently. Does the word recently give information about the noun John or the verb swam? _____

516 John swam recently. Since the word recently gives information about swam, we say that it mod_____ the verb swam.

517
a. John swam there.
b. John swam yesterday.
In which sentence does the underlined word tell where John swam? _____

518
a. John swam away.
b. John swam fast.
In which sentence does the underlined word tell how John swam? _____

519
a. John swam frequently.
b. John swam backward.
In which sentence does the underlined word tell how much or how often John swam?

520 Words that tell when, where, how, how much, or how often about verbs are called adverbs. Adjectives modify nouns and pronouns, but adverbs modify _____.

521 Notice that the word verb occurs in the word adverb. This should help you to remember that there is a close connection between adverbs and _____.

522 The dog ate greedily.
The adverb greedily tells (how, when) the dog ate.

523 The letter arrived today.
The adverb today tells (where, when) the letter arrived.

524 This pen leaks slightly.
The adverb slightly tells (how much, where) the pen leaks.

527 Floyd drove the car _____ (How?)
Underline the adverb that would fit in this sentence and answer the question printed in parentheses:

back   cautiously   regularly   sometimes

547 A serious accident occurred there.
_____ is an adverb because it tells where the accident occurred.

548 The children soon spent all their money.
_____ is an adverb because it tells when about the verb spent.

549 Tommy reads well for his age.
_____ is an adverb because it tells how Tommy reads.

559　Both adjectives and adverbs modify or change the pictures or ideas we get from words by making their meaning (<u>more</u>, <u>less</u>) exact.

562　a. The weather is cold.
b. The weather is very cold.
The added word which gives us the idea of greater coldness in sentence <u>b</u> is _____.

<u>very</u> cold	<u>so</u> cold	<u>rather</u> cold
<u>extremely</u> cold	<u>quite</u> cold	<u>slightly</u> cold
<u>terribly</u> cold	<u>too</u> cold	<u>somewhat</u> cold

563　All the underlined words increase or decrease the "power" of the adjective _____.

572　We have been working with special words that control the "power" of other modifiers. These words are adverbs. These special adverbs can modify both _____ and other adverbs.

PAUL ROBERTS—*Patterns of English*[2]

The reason that we say that adverbs are divided into these groups is not that they have three different meanings. Any adverb has a different meaning from another adverb. The reason is rather that adverbs behave differently in sentences according to which group they belong to. Notice that we can use an adverb from each group in the same pattern.

Headword 2	Modifier 4	Modifier 4	Modifier 4
went	away	quickly	later
looked	up	suspiciously	often
sat	down	unhappily	sometimes
stalked	out	angrily	usually
lived	there	thus	then

In other words, a quite common order is first the verb headword, then the adverb of place (there), then the adverb of manner (thus), then the adverb of time (then). To be sure, this isn't the only possibility. The order of adverbs is really rather flexible, and we'll see some other arrangements in a moment. But we can't scramble the three groups any way we want to. The following patterns wouldn't be used by native speakers:

went later away quickly
away went quickly later
looked often suspiciously up

[2] From *Patterns of English* by Paul Roberts, copyright © 1956, by Harcourt, Brace & World, Inc. and reprinted with their permission.

Neither do we ordinarily use two adverbs from the same group to modify the same headword (unless a word like AND comes between them). We wouldn't say "looked up out" or "stopped usually often" or "ate quickly greedily."

We do, however, have many other possibilities. Sometimes we put the THEN adverb before the headword:

Modifier 4	*Headword* 2	*Modifier* 4	*Modifier* 4
later	went	away	quickly
often	looked	up	suspiciously
sometimes	stalked	out	angrily
then	lived	there	thus

Sometimes, but not so often, the THUS adverb comes before the headword. When it does, we usually have just a THERE adverb after the headword, or no modifier at all after it:

Modifier 4	*Headword* 2	*Modifier* 4
quickly	went	away
angrily	stalked	out
reluctantly	refused	

The adverbs work into all the basic patterns, complicating the cluster. They all occur with the verb in Pattern One:

D 1 4 2 4 4
The men often went away quickly.

D 1 2 4 4 4
His uncle stalked out angrily sometimes.

D 1 4 2 4 4
His uncle sometimes stalked out angrily.

THEN and THERE adverbs occur in the cluster of Pattern Two:

1 4 2 3
She often looked beautiful.

1 2 3 4
She was happy sometimes.

1 2 3 4
She felt comfortable there.

All of the adverb types occur in the cluster of Pattern Three:

1 2 4 D 1
He was then my helper.

1 2 D 1 4
He was my helper unwillingly.

   1 2 D 1   4
He was my helper downstairs.

All occur in the cluster of Pattern Four:

   D 1   4 2 D 1 4   4
The quarterback always kicked the ball away vigorously.

   1 4 2 D 1 4   4
He generally took his dog outside reluctantly.

PAUL ROBERTS—*English Syntax*[3]

318	Adverbials of manner may, but need not, occur in verbals containing the following types of verbs: V_____, V_____, V_____, V_____.
319	We abbreviate adverbial of manner ADV-M. Then we can write: Verbal $\left\{\begin{array}{l} \text{VI} \\ \text{VT + NP} \\ \text{Vb + substantive} \\ \text{Vs + adjective} \end{array}\right\}$ + (Adv-m) The fact that an adverbial of manner may occur but need not is indicated by the _____.
320	Now take the sentence "Tom has a car." Like a VT, the verb HAVE is followed by a _____.
321	The sentence "Tom has a car" seems to have the same structure as "Tom drives a car." However, there are formal differences. One is that adverbials of manner do not occur in verbals when the verb is HAVE. Which of these is ungrammatical: (1) Tom drove the car recklessly. (2) Tom had the car recklessly? _____.
322	Which of these is ungrammatical: (1) Henry lifted the lid on purpose. (2) The lid weighed ten pounds on purpose? _____
323	Which of these is ungrammatical: (1) Sally slept peacefully. (2) The dress cost. (3) She bought a dress. _____
324	Verbs like have, cost, weigh are different from the others we have noted. Like transitive verbs and verbs of the become type, they are followed by NP's. But the NP is not an object for either the have type or the become type, and the have type will not take an adverbial of manner. In "Harry drank some milk," the noun phrase some milk functions as _____.

But some milk does not function as object in "Harry had some milk." We shall not give a name to its function but simply say

[3] From *English Syntax* by Paul Roberts, copyright © 1964 by Harcourt, Brace & World, Inc. and reprinted with their permission.

that it doesn't function as an object. We shall abbreviate verb
of the <u>have</u> type as Vh. In "The milk cost twenty cents," the
325 verb is a V‾＿＿＿＿.

We might say, loosely, that a VT shows some sort of thing
done to the following noun phrase by the subject, whereas a
Vh does not. This is a loose thing to say, because it is simply
an appeal to our feeling for the meaning of the construction
rather than to formal characteristics of the structure itself.
However, we have noted one formal distinction between the
VT and the Vh constructions: the VT construction can be
followed, after the noun phrase, by an adverbial of manner,
and the Vh cannot. We shall see other formal differences later
on. We shall find that the important differences in meaning
that we perceive in grammatical structures will usually be
supported in this way by formal differences.

326 In "The lid weighed ten pounds," the verb is a V＿＿＿＿.

Vh is the last main verb type we shall note. We now have:

$$\text{verbal} \longrightarrow \left\{ \left\{ \begin{array}{l} \text{VI} \\ \text{VT} + \text{NP} \\ \text{Vb} + \text{substantive} \\ \text{Vs} + \text{Adj} \\ \text{Vh} + \text{NP} \end{array} \right\} + (\text{Adv-m}) \right\}$$

This shows that an Adv-m may occur in verbals with VI, VT,
327 Vb, Vs. It does not occur when the verb is a V＿＿＿＿.

GRAMMAR IN THE NEW TEXTBOOKS

Another way to see what your youngster is learning in grammar
nowadays is to see how his text handles definitions and how those
definitions become useful. As a partial guide to a systematic analysis
of language texts, Jean Malmstrom suggests the following:

A. After examining the text's definitions of *noun, verb, adjective,
adverb, pronoun, preposition, conjunction,* and *interjection,* decide how useful these definitions would be to students for identifying the parts of speech represented by each italicized word in
the following sentences:

    1. Let's have a *go* at it.
    2. He uses too many *and's.*
    3. The *circus* lion was tame.
    4. Don't *nose* into my business.
    5. The play was fine, and the party *afterward* was fun.
    6. They came *in.*
    7. Miss Roget is my *French* teacher.
    8. Our friends *upstairs* like to play bridge.
    9. The *smoking* car is at the end of the train.

      10. Some men are wise and *some* are foolish.

      11. I always *oh* and *ah* at Mary's clothes.

B. After examining the text's definition of "subject of sentence," decide how useful this definition would be for convincing students that *fox* is not the subject of the sentence, "The cat was treed by the fox."

C. If "rules" are cited and then followed by "exceptions," how well can this procedure be explained to students to enhance their grammatical understanding of English?[4]

But perhaps the best way of all is to hear your youngster tell you a thing or two about the "new" grammar he's learning. From the preceding chapters, you should get some notion of where he's heading in his ability to describe the sentences of our language in a clear, concise, elegant fashion. And, perhaps even more important, you can sense whether he sees where grammar fits into his scheme of things. Is it a chore, a bore, or a quest in his young life?

[4] Jean Malmstrom, "A Progress Report on Textbook Analysis," *English Journal,* LI, 1 (January 1962), 42.

III

Usage

WE AND OUR DICTIONARIES

12

Perhaps the best clue to how we Americans feel about our language is how we treat our dictionaries, old and new. A Webster Unabridged, a uniquely American product, is only an extreme example of the ways of a man with a dictionary.

The Unabridged is a rare bird, found more often in libraries than in homes. Its gestation period equals its life span, roughly thirty years; yet it never shows signs of rigor mortis except to those who examine its insides. Libraries can afford to relegate old dictionaries to rummage sales, paper drives, or reference rooms. In private homes, dictionaries never die; Yankee thrift won't let them. When Aunt Hepzibah gives the Joneses the big Webster as a wedding present, she expects it and the marriage to last. In time, the table on which it rests may change from Tudor Oak to French Provincial to Danish Modern to Early American. But the dictionary the Joneses still have with them. A dictionary is not a table; styles don't change. And a dictionary is not a car; parts don't wear out—unless you turn the pages too often. Who, since Chaucer's threadbare Oxford Clerk, would beg or borrow to buy a big dictionary? There were none in English in his day. Our generation is less zealous. If and when we want to check the spelling, pronunciation, or meaning of a word any dictionary will do.

Why, then, the great fuss when the new Webster Unabridged came out in 1961? The first reviews in popular magazines and newspapers were written by journalists, teachers, generally educated laymen, and a few writers. They were largely unfavorable; the new dictionary was a blot on the Merriam-Webster colophon. Maybe only a Rohrschach blot. Some large city dailies wrote editorials warning their readers to beware of that dictionary. One civic-minded group gave away reprints of an eloquent blast at the new Webster. Later reviews in scholarly journals and second thoughts in the popular press were written by teachers and writers but also by scholars and linguists. They generally praised the new dictionary. The debate reached such proportions that ticker tapes fluttered and a casebook on the controversy became a popular text. Finally in 1963 *Consumer Reports* spoke out loud and clear between Stereo Headphones and Freezer Refrigerator Thermometers. To steer the customer to the best value in dictionaries, *Consumer Reports* chose experts in the history of English, its structure and usage, dialectology, and lexicography. This report had to be no less reliable than the ones on tables, cars, headphones, or thermometers.

Scholars and sciolists, friends and foes—all agreed on one thing: the big change in Webster was its new policy of labeling words. Purists felt Webster had abandoned all standards when it dropped status labels like *formal, informal, colloquial,* and *written.* Practical men felt Webster had let them down: abandoned its responsibility to the American public. For generations "Let's check it in Webster" ended all debate. Yet the new Webster, in listing many slang and new words without any warning labels, was really admitting them into the language as standard. Webster's judgment, heretofore unquestioned, had become suspect. To abandon the role of supreme authority was to court disaster. Those who expected the dictionary to tell them what words to use wondered how Webster could have abandoned all that it stood for. Those who expected the dictionary to tell them what words were being used wondered how the others could be so naive. Yet their debate was only the last in a long series between prescriptivists and descriptivists. The history of that debate is a very revealing chapter in American history.

And it all began with Noah—Noah Webster. Those who see the dictionary as lawmaker can cite precedent in the first Webster of 1806. So can those who see the dictionary as reporter of usage. For old Noah was the best salesman-lexicographer this country has ever known. The dualism began when he refused to accept the great Dr. Johnson's dictionary of 1755 as an authority for an America that had broken away from English domination. On February 17, 1785, this patriot warned, "I have too much pride to stand indebted to Great Britain for books to learn our children the letters of the alphabet." Interestingly enough, this staunch Connecticut Yankee had no sooner won his case on linguistic and patriotic grounds than he began to prescribe on patriotic grounds alone. The rest of his long and productive life he continued the fight, using prescription and description as the need arose. His legacy speaks for itself. For the past century and a half the Webster dictionaries have been thriving on authority and striving toward description.

Citing words like *appreciate, disorganizer, editorial,* and *sentimentalist*—not found in any British dictionary of the time—Noah protested on November 10, 1801: "It is difficult to see the crime of adding them to a dictionary with correct definitions." But after winning the first round with his *Compendious Dictionary* of 1806, he wrote Samuel Latham Mitchell the following year: "Perhaps this is the only country on the globe where men are determined not to have their errors disturbed, where men fix their opinions upon a particular standard without knowing whether it is right or wrong and grow angry at the man who proves it inaccurate." Those who persist in using British English as their standard must see the light. He also inveighed against the "obsolete, ungrammatical, and improper" terms in the seventeenth-century King James Bible—and proceeded to issue a "corrected" version. Webster blamed these corruptions not on "the vulgar, as is commonly supposed," but on "authors and writers, pretending to purify and refine the language."

Harvard's Professor John Quincy Adams, after examining this dictionary of 1806, admitted, ". . . if I deemed a new standard necessary, I know not where I could find one which I should prefer to yours. But I am not entirely convinced that one is necessary." For the Stonington bumpkin to have won even such faint praise from the Cambridge scholar was no mean victory. But a true lexicographer's work is never done—especially in a young, rapidly growing country where words are always being born, changing, and dying. On August 5, 1809, he wrote Thomas Dawes: "I have admitted one or two cant words, such as *caucus*." Other neologisms he defends are *accompaniment, acidulous, advisory, antithetical, statement, insubordination, expenditure,* and *subsidize*. By 1816 he had enough American citations to support his stand. He wrote in December to his stern critic, John Pickering (another Bay State patriot, and a lawyer, to boot):

> Nothing excites more rage among the nibbling gentry, than to find *test* and *advocate* as verbs. "Test," says one of them in the [*Monthly*] *Anthology*, "is a verb only in writers of an inferior rank who disregard all the landmarks of language." Then Washington, Marshall, Hamilton, Adams, Walsh, and almost every other writer of reputation in America is doomed to an "inferior rank."[1]

His words about *standard* have a familiar ring to those who followed the debate about *standard* in the most recent Webster:

> The reviewers are perpetually writing about a *standard* of *language*— a thing, in its own nature, impossible. In every nation there are certain authors whose writings stand higher in public estimation than those of others . . . the authors will not fix a standard. . . . How shall it be ascertained who are authors of reputation?[2]

He kept defending words in current use: *classification, simplify, diplomatic, payer, payee, substantiate, endorser, endorsee*. The people, not the great writers of antiquity, give authority to usage. His *New England Primer,* in spite of his Calvinist leanings, changed "In Adam's Fall/We sinned all" to "A was an Apple/made by the cook."

All this was prologue to the first great Webster, *An American Dictionary of the English Language,* 1828. The advertisement announced:

> I am convinced the dictionaries and grammars which have been used in our seminaries of learning for the past forty or fifty years, are so incorrect and imperfect, that they have introduced or sanctioned more errors than they have amended. In other words, had the people of England or these States been left to learn the pronunciation and construction of their vernacular language solely by tradition, and the reading of good authors, the language would have been spoken and written with greater purity than it has been and now is, by those

---

[1] Harry R. Warfel (ed.), *Letters of Noah Webster* (New York: Library Publishers, 1953), p. 346.
[2] *Ibid.*, pp. 388, 392.

who have learned to adjust their language by the rules which dictionaries and grammars prescribe.[3]

But the Preface sounded its own prescriptive note:

> It has been my aim in this work to ascertain the true principles of the language, in its orthography and structure; to purify it from palpable errors, and to reduce the number of its anomalies, thus giving it more regularity and consistency in its forms, both of words and sentences; and in this manner, to furnish a standard of our vernacular tongue, which we shall not be ashamed to bequeath to *three hundred millions of people*, who are destined to occupy, and I hope, adorn the vast territory within our jurisdiction.[4]

One way was to simplify the spelling system. To do away with the confusion of silent letters, he dropped the *k* in *physick* and *musick*. The *u* disappeared from *favour* and *honour,* the second *l* from *traveller,* the *a* from *bread* and *feather,* the *e* from *give. Ee* replaced the confusing pairs of vowels in *mean, grieve, speak,* and *key.* Similarly, *groop* made more sense than *group.* But the reforms which really outraged some of his readers were *bridegoom, canail, ribin, ieland, turky, tung, nusance,* and *nightmar.* Elsewhere he showed that "*notice* and *sanction* have become verbs in recent usage and are now well authorized."

Webster had done all he could to describe the American language accurately; he had succeeded in weaning his countrymen away from British dictionaries and he had justified the neologisms in his own dictionary. But when he tried to prescribe, he saw only too well the understatement of Dr. Johnson's prophetic words: "Englishmen are always moved by a spirit of personal liberty in their use of language. A policy of noninterference appeals to them much more than one of arbitrary regulation." In Noah's ark there is plenty of crow to eat!

The rest of Webster history records our country's fluctuating demands for prescriptive dictionaries. In a rich, democratic, rapidly growing land, where anyone can rise quickly, the correct word befitting a newly attained status becomes all important. As Webster satisfies this demand, it can afford to hire the best lexicographers. Because they know their business, their claims to authority become more and more cautious. And as their caution increases, the debate between

[3] *An American Dictionary of the English Language* (New York: S. Converse, 1828), unpaged.
[4] *Ibid.*

prescriptivists and descriptivists grows louder. Each new dictionary, as it refines its work, only extends the debate to another area.

In 1828, the fight was over new spellings and neologisms. Localisms in vocabulary and pronunciation pleased some patriots and alarmed all would-be gentlemen. In 1840, the new scientific and foreign terms met with mixed response. By 1847, the editor freely listed spelling variants, but neologisms and Americanisms were carefully labeled. In the 1850's, Webster's scholarly etymologies, thanks to German philologists, were so impressive that debate waned. Instead, Webster concentrated on its greatest threat, the competition of the Worcester dictionaries. It even had to introduce full-page color plates! The 1864 edition stressed conformity to usage of the best speakers; and new etymologies, citations, and science listings stressed the dictionary's role of historian rather than critic of the language. The 1890 edition was the turning point in Webster's labeling policy. "With the rapid increase in human knowledge," the editor explained what he was calling neologisms, slang, foreign words, sports jargon, and scientific jargon. He noted that his dictionary reflected the inevitable blur of standards for speech and writing. He explained his stylistic labels carefully. The 1909 *First New International Dictionary of the English Language* explained its own virtues; it did not try to compete with the volumes of the *Oxford English Dictionary:*

> The single-volume dictionary for the home and school and shop must have a larger element of the ephemeral or of the prevailing fashion of speech than the historical dictionary, and must omit many vocables that are becoming obsolete. . . . As a whole, the vocabulary of the New International is a more complete reflection of the multiform human ideas embodied in words than has ever before been included in a dictionary.[5]

The 1933 issue of this edition differentiated between cultural levels of cant, jargon, argot, and lingo; and functional varieties of slang, vulgarism, and colloquialism. By 1934, when the *Second International* appeared, the sales department and the editorial department were claiming two different kinds of authority. One used *authoritative* as *normative* or *official*. The other used it as *scientifically exact, recording the facts*. And the customer was not always right!

The *Second International* of 1934 offered no apologies for its word list. But it took status labels even more seriously than had the *First*.

[5] Preface, *First New International Dictionary* (Oxford: Oxford University Press, 1909).

As mass communication grew, *colloquial* became the most elusive label. With each issue the editor kept trying to clarify what it meant. The 1960 printing reminded us that "colloquial speech may be as correct as formal speech." It continued to quote Professor Kittredge: "Every educated person speaks his mother tongue in at least two ways, and the difference between the dignified and the colloquial style is considerable." "The so-called *standard* language," it quoted from E. S. Sheldon, "is not a fixed and infallible standard, but is itself constantly changing with the course of time, and is different in the different spaces where it is spoken."

If there were complaints about the lowering of barriers in status labels in 1934, they were drowned in the general applause that greeted the Webster Second. Nor were there cries of sabotage when the editors proclaimed their "eagerness to incorporate the findings of linguistic scientists" and asserted that "usage is still and must always be the standard." Yet some of the same statements as to form and usage, when repeated verbatim in the Third in 1961, dismayed the purists. Still priding itself on thoroughness and accuracy, and having gradually assumed the role of scientific recorder in spelling, etymology, definition, and phonology, Webster had only to take the final step with status labels to make the Third completely descriptive. And it did.

For people to turn to Webster as an authority on usage was perfectly natural. An Unabridged is exactly what it claims to be: not a complete list of all the words in the language (such a list would deny the primary fact of language: change), but a list that has not been cut down from any larger list. And a Webster Unabridged does represent an array of scholars and original research that no other dictionary maker in this country can boast of. Certainly, then, there's nothing wrong with the layman's "Let's look it up in Webster." Better that than "Let's not look it up in Webster."

For people to be unaware of Webster's long tradition of faithful description is also perfectly natural. Dictionaries do go out of print, and it is the rare library that has a complete set of the Unabridged Websters. For people to look to some group (whether in the mother country, the university in the old or new world, or among the gentry near or far) for its prestige dialect is perfectly natural. For them to resist change in spelling and vocabulary is natural, too. Language is a habit; we hate to have it disturbed unless we see some real reason. The way we assert our total need is to demand both freedom in our language and escape from freedom. At the same time, we want to choose our own words and we want to be told which are right. For the layman to turn to the Unabridged for compendious information is also natural. The many-volumed Oxford English Dictionary is for students interested in the history of the language, not for those interested in current usage.

But for the Second in 1934 to have satisfied the generally educated reader and critic and for the Third in 1961, proceeding on the same principles of accurate description, to have alarmed these people was not natural. It meant either that Webster had passed the bounds of reason in its reluctance to prescribe usage or that recent linguistic study had not penetrated the English classroom, even at the university level. How could it, when the experts called in by *Consumer Reports* —those who taught the history of our language, its structure and usage, dialectology, and lexicography—rarely worked with regular English classes? They taught from the hinterlands of anthropology, philology, psychology, linguistics, or schools of education.

The debate over the Webster Third, if it did nothing else, woke some English teachers up to these facts of linguistic life. Now they knew that we Americans—the Aunt Hepzibahs, the Joneses, journalists, writers, English teachers of the midtwentieth century, all of us— know what we want in the latest tables, cars, stereo headphones, and freezer refrigerator thermometers. But when it comes to dictionaries, most of us are antediluvian. We haven't even caught up with the facts that stared Noah in the face in the eighteenth century.

The debate over the Webster Third brought into the open what students of linguistics had been telling English teachers all along: that an educated American ought to know what a dictionary is, how it's put together, and how it can be used. It would be interesting to find out if in those communities where lexicography was already firmly established, usually in the tenth grade, reactions to the new dictionary were less frenetic than elsewhere.

The specific debate over status labels and standard usage also brought into the open something else that linguists had been telling English teachers since the time of Noah: the problem of standards cannot be simplified; it must be faced with linguistic facts, not fiats. Here was a double challenge to the English teacher. Was there room in the English curriculum for acquiring a knowledge of the facts in dictionaries and linguistic atlases? Was there room for a serious application of these facts to questions of usage? Could we teach—not preach—what correct English is and what good English is and how they overlap?

13

The gods of scientific tabulation had not decreed the change in Webster's labeling policy. For two generations, in two successive Websters, the lexicographer had been trying to describe distinctions in the language he was faithfully recording. Editors had explained *colloquial* and *standard* in their prefaces, defined and redefined in their entries, repeated Kittredge's statements about at least two standards. Status labels, made more explicit in each successive edition, could still not keep pace with usage. Distinctions between written and spoken English, when mass communication kept seeking the least common denominator, were becoming imperceptible without knowledge of context and situation. In a fluid society with unsettled style the only certainty is change. Pleas that we "slow up the inevitable process from substandard to standard" echo age-old demands: "Arrest the ceaseless tendency to change." The lowering of barriers, the overlapping and loosening of status labels, has been gaining momentum since 1806; it is part of the mainstream of Webster's and our country's development.

"Permissive principles" and "abandoning all standards of usage" cannot be blamed on new grammars or new dictionaries. Our mid-century commitment to accurate description is as old as the first Webster, though it seems revolutionary to some of us today. And some of the favorite whipping boys of the purists (the use of *finalize* and *awful,* of *each, everyone, everybody* with plural pronoun and/or verb) find sanction in scholarly nonstructural grammarians like Jespersen, Poutsma, and Curme, as well as in the *Oxford English Dictionary*'s quotations from "the established authors, the recognized masters of the language." The dictionary itself is not responsible for the fact that our current crop of quotations vindicates those who accept change in language and irritates those who abhor change. Webster does not prescribe usage; a listing does not order the reader to use a word. It simply alerts him to how the word is being used and by whom.

The purists' criticism that the new Webster too readily accepts dubious usage ignores the facts. In morphology, syntax, and idiomatic phrase, the editors have been most careful. No one who dislikes *finalize* needs to use it. He has a perfect right to reject it on matters of taste. But he cannot reject it on matters of usage. Not when the 1828 Webster sanctioned "verbs formed from nouns and adjectives by the termination -ize" and listed *methodize, systematize, moralize,* and *stigmatize.* If an "awful hat" and "an awful lot of talking" bother us today, we ought to remember that for one hundred thirty odd years "our common people [have] used this word in the sense of frightful, ugly, detestable"; and that in 1903 "an awful bonnet" was already in the *slang* category of Webster.

Each with plural pronoun and/or verb was acceptable in 1914 to Jespersen and Poutsma. In *Modern English Grammar* Jespersen cited Jane Austen's and Lord Byron's use of *each* with the plural.[1] "The substitution of the plural for the singular is not wholly illogical," observed this scholarly grammarian. Poutsma's *Grammar of Modern English*[2] quoted Charles Reade's use of *each* and added: "*They,* etc., in reference to *each, everybody, everyone* is often used because we have no third singular pronoun in common gender." Jespersen also justified *everyone* and *everybody* with plural pronoun and/or verb by quoting from Shakespeare, *The Spectator,* Swift, Shelley, Scott, Kingsley, Dickens, Ruskin, Wilde, Kipling, and others to show its widespread use.

Webster's acceptance of *different than,* as well as *from* or *with,* bothered some people. The new editors mention the widespread but unreasonable dislike for *than* and repeat the words of the Second in 1934: "The constructions with *to* and *than* have long literary usage to support them, but are considered incorrect by many." The fact remains that the *Oxford English Dictionary* cites the use of *different than* in the works of Addison, Steele, Defoe, Richardson, Goldsmith, Miss Burney, Coleridge, Southey, DeQuincey, Carlyle, Thackeray, Newman, Trench, and others up to I. A. Richards and Kenneth Burke.

Due to as a preposition is another favorite target of the old handbooks. Yet the First Unabridged of 1909 noted its currency and the

---

[1] Otto Jespersen, *Modern English Grammar on Historical Principles,* 7 vols. (reissued; New York: Barnes and Noble, Inc., 1954).

[2] H. Poutsma, *A Grammar of Late Modern English* (Groningen: P. Noordhoof, 1904–1917).

Second in 1934 said: "Prepositional *due to,* meaning 'because of' and introducing an adverbial modifier, though objected to by some, is in common and reputable use." Porter Perrin in the 1959 edition of his *Writer's Guide and Index to English* noted that *due to* has an imposing number of quotations from current writers cited in the Second.[3] Margaret Bryant of Brooklyn College, author of *Current American Usage,* was also cited: "In some thousands of pages of books, periodicals, and newspapers, *due to* as a preposition occurred in 56 per cent of the instances, *because of* in 25 per cent and *owing to* in 19 per cent." Reasonable man that he was, Perrin added, "A person may not care to use *due to* as a preposition, but in view of actual usage today he hardly has the right to deny it to others."

The *further-farther* distinction so long a-dying (distinctions stay with us so long as they are needed) is not even in the Third. It calls *irregardless* "probably a blend of irrespective and regardless." Then it adds the label, *nonstand. Like* as a preposition or conjunction is discussed in the Second: "*Like* with an incomplete clause is commonly used in colloquial style (he took to figures *like* a duck to water) but in the work of careful writers is usually replaced by *as.*" Again the usage is justified when we check quotations in Jespersen and the Oxford. Webster in 1961 notes Art Linkletter's "impromptu programs where they ask questions much like I do on the air" and Baton's "the violin now sounds like an old masterpiece should."

Some cling to the *shall-will* distinction. Yet way back in 1837 Macaulay asserted, with some chagrin perhaps, "Not one Londoner in ten thousand can lay down the rules for the proper use of *will* and *shall.*" And as late as 1958 one style book insisted: "I suspect the ignorant will win, and that their incorrectness in this matter will end by becoming correct English. . . . Meanwhile I shall, and will, continue to fight a rearguard action in defense of the older use of 'will' and 'shall.' " But who are the ignorant? Scholars have still to find justification—in other than the prescriptive schoolroom grammars—for the *shall-will* prescription.

The *who-whom* debate has more substance. Again Webster has been doing its homework. Jespersen listed examples of interrogative *who* in all cases except possessive in reputable writers of the latter half of the nineteenth century. Examples from the twentieth century abound. "I think many educated people never use *whom* at all," ob-

[3] Porter G. Perrin, *Writer's Guide and Index to English* (4th ed.; Chicago, Ill.: Scott, Foresman and Company, 1965).

served Sweet. The Oxford calls interrogative *whom* "no longer current in natural colloquial speech." Jespersen also called attention to
"the natural instinct, which has for centuries tended to use the form
who everywhere." How iconoclastic are we today when we accept the
Third's statement: "*Whom* is now often considered stilted, especially
in oral use"?

The evidence certainly suggests that the Third is a scholarly report.
What is in it can hardly be denied when we check our sources.

But something else bothers the purists. They object to the source
of citations in the Third. Are Linkletter and Merman and Eisenhower
equally reliable guides to proper usage? Webster explains its policy
in this way: the editors have in mind the "ordinary rather than the
literary reader" . . . in other words, citations have been chosen to
show words "in their common, general, typical and characteristic
senses and contexts, rather than in atypical uses often found in
imaginative literature, however interesting." Where the Second still
reflected a more aristocratic educational tradition by leaning heavily
on quotations going all the way back to the sixteenth century—it
clearly favored literary citations—the Third reflects the vast spread
of liberal education to subjects and students the Second never
dreamed of. After all, Webster was only doing what the Oxford had
been doing: getting a representative spread in its quotations.

Purists' objections as to dubious usage and citations, then, do not
really stand any tests. But the Webster labeling policy remains. It
admits the failure of a comparatively recent attempt to define usage
labels precisely. What will we call *standard?* In 1901, Greenough and
Kittredge, distinguishing between *popular* and *learned* usage, and
noting continuous gradation, called *standard* "the common property
of all but the absolutely illiterate; the regular medium of communication throughout the English-speaking world. Different persons speak
and write this standard English with different degrees of correctness
and elegance." In 1927, Leonard and Moffett began to air the whole
label problem in the *English Journal*. In the thirties, Arthur G.
Kennedy saw formal, dignified, and colloquial as only functional
varieties of the one cultural level of standard English. He out-Polo-
niused Polonius in his categories. But he did isolate two cultural levels,
substandard and standard. His functional varieties were all within
the standard group. H. L. Mencken included *colloquial* in his definition of standard. Perrin said general (unlimited use) is both spoken
and written; formal (limited use) is usually written. In 1948, John S.

Kenyon tried to summarize the problem in *College English*. He reminded us, in "Cultural Levels and Functional Varieties of English," of Murray's words in the NED (an abbreviation for the Oxford's original title, *A New English Dictionary on Historical Principles*):

> Level, when used to indicate different styles of language, is a metaphor, suggesting higher or lower, better or worse, more desirable or less desirable. What are frequently grouped together in one class as different levels of language are often in reality false combinations of two distinct and incommensurate categories, namely, cultural levels and functional varieties.[4]

Kenyon's functional varieties were *colloquial, familiar, formal, scientific,* and *literary.* "Yet cultural levels and functional varieties are not mutually exclusive categories." The important thing is that *colloquial* itself does not designate either the high or the low cultural level. Robert Pooley in *Teaching English Usage* had offered two other cultural levels, *illiterate* and *homely,* and three functional varieties, *standard informal, standard formal,* and *literary.*[5] In 1959, Perrin's third edition of his *Writer's Guide* admitted "There is no well-established system of naming these varieties of English, though they have often been discussed." He revised his earlier categories of General or Informal English to make four principal varieties: General English, Formal English, Informal English (the three together he calls Standard English) and Nonstandard or Vulgate English. Bergen Evans concluded in the May 1962 *Atlantic:*

> ... There is no standard for standard. Ideas of what is proper to use in serious, dignified speech and writing are changing—and with breathtaking rapidity. This is one of the major facts of contemporary American English.[6]

The Third's policy in status labeling is keen admission of sensitivity to this fact. The editors decided that rather than commit themselves to misleading labels, they would use only those that have not caused confusion. *Colloquial, formal, informal* obviously have; they must go. So the Third took the necessary step together with the inevitable risks. It brought thunder down upon its head. But it pointed to the

[4] John S. Kenyon, "Cultural Levels and Functional Varieties," *College English,* **10** (October 1948), 31.
[5] Robert C. Pooley, *Teaching English Usage* (New York: Appleton-Century-Crofts, 1946).
[6] Bergen Evans, "But What's a Dictionary For?" *The Atlantic,* May 1962, p. 62.

next and necessary stage in dictionary writing. The distinction between description and prescription, instead of collapsing in the name of pure science and objectivity, needs to be more subtly presented. Precise discrimination in standard usage need not be relegated to intuition by dictionary maker or user.

If the problem of standard and usage labels baffles the lexicographer, what does it do to the English teacher? Where does he go from here? How shall he teach correct usage? How shall he teach good usage? How can the Third be used for either purpose? The entire dictionary debate alerted many teachers to the need for re-examination and reformulation of their linguistic knowledge. Some realized the misconceptions they had innocently entertained and disseminated through indiscriminate use of handbooks. Others realized they and their classes could find some of the answers in a better knowledge of the history and structure of our language and through firsthand acquaintance with different kinds of dictionaries and linguistic atlases. The debate, in other words, indicated that there were still some big questions, but that we had a good number of answers, if we valued our language enough to find the answers for ourselves instead of turning to "God-given" authority. What had been relegated to the hinterlands now seemed to belong in the English classroom.

Another outcome was the teacher's more critical attitude toward the promise of any quick and easy answers to problems of usage. One large publishing company, after unsuccessful attempts to gain control of Merriam-Webster, announced that it was about "to recruit a panel of authorities" which will answer the editor's questions about usage and thereby enable him to issue a dictionary that does take a stand. Thus, within five years, this editor hopes to provide what Webster, the only permanent scholarly institution of its kind in the world, could not, after twenty-seven years. He warns that such a volume will be smaller than the Unabridged and cost the customer more. "It is silly for anyone to get excited about *ain't*," he adds. "It has been part of the language for centuries. The dictionary should say the word has never been accepted on formal levels, it is unused except in a joking or informal sense." Let the skeptical reader join the skeptical teacher. Let them turn to the Third's entry on *ain't* to see which is the more reliable guide. Maybe we've been cured of our childlike trust in Webster. Maybe we can start using it as it was designed to be used. Then maybe we'll have access to the choices that make us linguistically free.

LEXICOGRAPHY: ONE OF THE TRUTHS
THAT MAKE US LINGUISTICALLY FREE

14

For English teachers the Webster debate could not have come at a better time. Since World War II, linguistics had been gaining the respect and attention of English departments in schools and colleges. The Commission on English, created by the College Entrance Examination Board (CEEB), was preparing to offer new language study in its summer institutes for teachers all over the country. Throughout the 1950's and into the 60's curriculum revision had been in the air —not only in math and the sciences but also in English. The need for substance in language study, for more than incidental acquisition of the facts of linguistic life, was already felt. The dictionary debate only underscored the urgency.

Another stroke of luck was that classes did not have to wait for books to be written. The dictionaries, which had simply recorded usage and had often availed themselves of recent linguistic scholarship, were already there and ready to be used. This was not so in grammars or handbooks. The English teacher might have to wait to teach the new grammar or the new rhetoric, but the facts of language were there in the dictionary. And many publishers were more than ready with good study guides to accompany their particular dictionaries.

There was nothing new in all this except the need for systematic study. Dictionaries had been in classrooms for a long time. They were always handy for a quick check on the spelling, pronunciation, meaning, or even the history of a word. And this natural dictionary habit remains one of the best links between home and school. Curiosity about words can become infectious; but it can rarely survive carping criticism or harsh correction. The child who is marched off to the dictionary, whether at home or at school, to prove his ignorance or his parent's or teacher's omniscience, very soon finds out how to avoid these encounters. On the other hand, "Let's see what the dictionary says," opens doors for everybody. It's like teaching children water safety. You can prohibit children from learning to swim because they might drown. You can teach them to swim by shouting directions while you stand by fully clothed with a net in your hand. You can swap the street clothes and the net for a swim suit and still direct from the pool's edge. Or you can plunge right in alongside of them and teach them to swim. Children get into the linguistic swim pretty much the same way.

The natural dictionary habit is determined by the total linguistic climate in and out of school. It is certainly strengthened when the right dictionary and the right child are brought together. Here it won't do much good to check one publisher's output against the other's. It's like looking for significant differences in cars or soaps that have practically the same price tags. You can spend a lot of time and, in the end, save very little money because competition has forced every producer to gear his product to the same consumer. Lexicographers, despite their sales departments' jacket blurbs, are the first ones to admit that dictionaries can't be very different if they are to compete in price. If every customer wants the same thing of a dictionary—the spellings, meanings, pronunciations, and maybe histories and uses of a word—will a few pages more or less, a few entries more or less, new type, binding, or margin matter much? Either the lexicographer has to ignore all other dictionaries and start from scratch (he would have to live longer than Methuselah), or he has to build upon entries he finds in other dictionaries. He has all he can do to keep up with the present drift in language.

If jacket blurbs are no reliable guide to competing brands of dictionaries, the only way to bring child and book together is to see if he can understand and use it. The next time you are in a bookstore or library, spot check a word that interests you or your youngster. Look it up in one elementary, one junior high, one high school, and one college dictionary. See whether at each stage in his education the child can have a dictionary that will serve rather than frustrate him.

Many well-meaning friends and relatives give a Webster's *New Collegiate Dictionary* to celebrate a rite of passage in our culture: religious confirmation or graduation from grade school. Maybe they lack Aunt Hepzibah's fervor or affluence. At any rate, such a gift is only another example of how we respect the adult's rather than the child's needs on such joyous occasions. The proud parent may enjoy using the *Collegiate Dictionary,* but it is the rare thirteen- or fourteen-year-old who will. A single entry usually gets him going all around

Robin Hood's barn. For the definition of the word that bothered him in the first place is usually couched in terms that presuppose a college student's maturity. So the child has to scurry from one entry to the next in order to track down the meaning of the original word. He usually gives up after the third or fourth detour. Dictionaries for younger readers, on the other hand, usually have larger type, simpler citations, less detailed information, and more pictures, charts, and diagrams. One dictionary that tries to gear the definition to the maturity of the person apt to look up the word is the *World Book Encyclopedia Dictionary.* The title suggests how a dictionary has to modify its role if it is to be moderately useful to readers of all ages.

Being a knowledgeable shopper for dictionaries means examining the competing brands and trying dictionaries for size, as you would any other gift. Would you give the sweet girl graduate a heavenly blue sweater in size forty if she just tips the scales at ninety pounds? Why impose a dictionary on her unless you know her intellectual dimensions fairly well? The easiest way out is to send her a check. Everyone can use a page from that kind of book.

But what dictionaries shall we keep in the home if we want the dictionary habit to be naturally infectious? Surely the dictionaries that the youngsters enjoy using. But most families choose a good desk dictionary as a reasonable compromise, especially when an adult can come to the rescue in case of need. The most recent and popular desk dictionaries are the World Publishing Company's *New World Dictionary of the American Language,* Funk & Wagnalls' *Standard College Dictionary,* G. & C. Merriam's *Webster's Seventh New Collegiate Dictionary,* and Random House's *American College Dictionary,* all within the $5.75 to $20 range, depending on the binding, paper, edging, and indexing you're willing to pay for. The first is especially strong on etymologies and on midwestern pronunciations. The second is conservative, makes few pretensions to scientism, and appeals more to the nonscientifically inclined reader. Although it does not stress etymologies, it seems to do a better job than the others in synonymies and in collateral adjectives (like *daily* and *diurnal*). It includes Canadian English. It has discarded the label *colloquial,* but it carefully lists words that are *slang, illiterate,* or *informal,* with appropriate labels. Webster's Seventh, abridged from the Third of 1961, has simplified its capitalization and pronunciation system, is strong in new scientific terms, and remains compact chiefly because of its small type and cross references. The *American College Dictionary,* one of the earliest to avail itself of recent linguistic scholarship, is still deemed very reliable in pronunciation, etymology, usage, and definitions. All of these judgments come from the experts in lexicography who examined desk dictionaries for *Consumer Reports.*

But it takes more than an expert to make these desk dictionaries a vital part of the home; it takes curious, alive people. And the only way to know about dictionaries is to use them.

In English classes, however, pupils are getting more than this casual, spontaneous, positive exposure to dictionaries. Detailed, carefully planned units on lexicography have to supplement the natural dictionary habit. Had more of our citizens known this kind of training in the schools, there might have been less sound and fury over the Webster Third. Training in the use of dictionaries has to start early. It means learning to use many kinds of dictionaries, beginning with the simple picture dictionaries that accompany preprimer and reading readiness programs and working into the scholarly multivolume dictionaries in the twelfth and thirteenth grades.

The University of Nebraska's curriculum for English includes in *Language Explorations for Elementary Grades:*

> First graders do not read Webster's *Third International Dictionary* very often, but third graders can make up their own vocabulary lists, their own glossaries, their own records of pronunciation. They can use some quite good dictionaries. . . . Elementary students can accumulate and formulate information about words in the same way that the lexicographer does, and thus come to understand later just how it is that the dictionary maker goes about his job, what sort of product he makes, and what sort of service he offers. And fifth and sixth graders can do a competent job of using these services.[1]

One school system that did not need to be awakened by the Webster debate was Portland, Oregon's. For several years the Portland Curriculum Study, through the combined efforts of teachers and university scholars, had been planning an English curriculum rich in linguistic content. By 1961, the Portland Public Schools had already issued their own text, a pamphlet on lexicography. And by 1962, it was sharing with schools throughout the country its *Language Studies for English Classes.* This, in turn, was only excerpts from the guide used in grades nine through twelve. The tenth grade unit on lexicog-

---

[1] *Language Explorations for Elementary Grades,* from *A Curriculum for English* (Lincoln, Neb.: Nebraska Curriculum Development Center, 1965), p. 148. Copyright, University of Nebraska, 1965.

raphy and meaning includes pages of general information for teachers; suggested classroom tactics containing background and source materials; a bibliography of further reading for teachers; topics for discussion, writing, and further study; and exercises. This outline suggesting content and sequence, therefore, is not a mere directive. The teacher and class have the wherewithal for putting flesh on the skeleton:

  I. INTRODUCTION: MEANING
     A. What is a word?
     B. Minimum lexical units
     C. Meaning of utterance: expression and content
     D. Meaning and context
     E. Kinds of meaning
     F. Core versus peripheral meaning
     G. Process of lexical definition
  II. INSTRUCTIONAL TACTICS
     A. Dictionaries and etymology
       1. Semantic shift of common words
       2. Abbreviations and symbols of etymology
       3. Utility of etymology
     B. Variations among dictionaries
       1. Format
       2. Introductions and fine print
       3. Scope: single versus multiple-volume works
     C. Lexical processes
       1. Definition and denotation
       2. Citation
       3. Synonymy
     D. History of English language dictionaries
       1. Latin glosses
       2. Hard-word dictionaries
       3. Universal dictionaries
       4. Development of a plan
       5. Samuel Johnson
       6. Noah Webster and American dictionaries
       7. *Oxford English Dictionary*
     E. Dr. Johnson's "Preface to the English Dictionary"
       1. Johnson's intention
       2. Failure to purify and regulate English
       3. Problems of the lexicographer
     F. Shift of meaning
       1. Generalization and specialization
       2. Elevation and degradation
     G. Overtone and modification of meaning
       1. Connotation

      2. Euphemism
      3. Metaphor
   H. Dictionaries and usage
    I. Topics for writing and discussion; exercises[2]

An English class that devoted some of the tenth year to some of these topics could hardly be wasting its time. But there is nothing sacrosanct about the year and the sequence. Other schools cover the same topics at different times in other ways. The important things are substance and systematic presentation, pupil and teacher activity that lead to knowledge and concepts. Drill for its own sake may salve Puritan consciences; yet it remains tedious. Knowledge for its own sake is a different matter.

Whether the school has devised a well-thought-out program in lexicography, or whether it is still working out its plans, certain procedures seem more successful than others. Awareness of some of these may enable the parent to take the long view of dictionary work in the schools and may enable him to read school committee reports judiciously. The number of dictionaries a school or library owns may be very revealing to budget and inventory keepers, but it tells little about what the pupils are learning in lexicography. Because growth in the use of dictionaries often takes place within the school year, a single class set of dictionaries that sits on the shelves in one room is no assurance that God's in His heaven and all's right with the dictionaries. It merely looks as though God has provided generously for this particular class. The mobility of dictionaries, even with the attendant losses and damage, is a healthier sign. In September, for example, the *Thorndike-Barnhart High School Dictionary* may be just the thing for students who are learning how to use a pronunciation key and how to interpret the sequence of information in an entry.[3] But when this same class works on word history, the derivation and changes in meaning, the *New World Dictionary* is much more useful.[4] Thus, to ensure maximum use, sets of dictionaries are often stored in a central bookroom so that individual classes may borrow them for a unit or a marking period, or different kinds of dictionaries are assigned to different classrooms with frequent interchanges at the teachers' agreement.

    [2] *Language Studies for English Classes: Excerpts from Guide for High School English, Grades 9–12* (Portland, Ore.: School District No. 1, Multnomah County, 1962), pp. 131–132.
    [3] Published by Scott, Foresman and Company, Chicago, Illinois.
    [4] Published by World Publishing Company, Cleveland, Ohio.

No matter what the method of housing dictionaries, pupils soon learn by using them that the only way to exploit the strengths of each dictionary is to know the preface. In our machine age, we wouldn't think of ignoring the information booklet that comes with a new car or a new vacuum cleaner. But we usually plunge right into a dictionary when we're stumped. Yet the preface is the best guide to the dictionary's most effective use. Failure to avail themselves of this information (the dictionary's particular devices and short cuts for such matters as cross references, pronunciation keys, status labels, multiple meanings, etc.) embarrassed many hasty reviewers of the Webster Third. Yet if an editor does not offer these concise explanations in the preface, his dictionary could never condense all the information it does within its pages.

Training the student to use a dictionary intelligently does not mean forcing him at gunpoint through the preface. It does mean knowing what is in the preface and introducing him to sections strategically—when they serve a real need in the work of the class. Sometimes the pupil finds his way there because of a particular problem in vocabulary, dialects, stylistics, morphology, or etymology. Sometimes even this introduction is systematically handled for him. An ambitious array of problems and exercises can be found in the *Harbrace Guide to Dictionaries* by Kenneth G. Wilson and in *Dictionaries and THAT Dictionary* by James Sledd and Wilma R. Ebbitt.

The dictionary is a traditional tool for composition and spelling work. It is one way of connecting new words in student reading with new words in student speaking and writing. When dictionary study is tied in with literature, the students often need to turn from their smaller dictionaries to special ones like the *Dictionary of Americanisms* or the *Oxford English Dictionary*. All of these devices are helpful as supplements to careful instruction in lexicography. None is a substitute. Within the next few years, then, as lexicography becomes an essential part of many high school English courses, and as a pupil's work with dictionaries takes him into the larger scholarly ones, he may bring to his college classes a knowledge of the structure, history, and variety of our language that few graduates in his parent's generation could boast of.

LINGUISTIC GEOGRAPHY:
ANOTHER OF THE TRUTHS THAT
MAKE US LINGUISTICALLY FREE

15

Dictionaries are only one source—a very large source—of the truths or facts that make us linguistically free to choose our words. They tell us what we have to choose from when they report what words are in current use. A general reference like a popular dictionary cannot, however, give much space to variants in current use. Instead, it extracts as much information as it can from dialectologists' linguistic atlases.

Another way for the student to understand the choices available to him, then, is to get some of the facts directly from dialectology rather than indirectly from the dictionary. This comparatively recent branch of linguistics objectively describes variations among speakers of a language. The variations are distinguished by features in pronunciation, grammar, and vocabulary. Understanding these differences and the possible explanations for them can release the student from the tyranny, the false notion that there is a single Standard English which educated men speak. He can begin to see how language truly identifies the individual as he learns to respect individual differences in language.

Furthermore, dialectology is another way of making clear to the student some of the principles underlying the nature of language itself. ". . . the tendencies of language development are reflected far more distinctly in the popular dialects than is the case in the literary idiom, striving, in accord with its special functions, for a certain stability," notes Josef Vachek in his European-published dictionary of linguistic terms.

Dialectology can alert the student to wider choices than he had known, to deeper awareness of the nature of language, and also to the principle that underlies all his language learning from kindergarten on: the spoken language is the language. As we saw when the child learned to read and write, the printed page stabilized language for him while the spoken word assured dynamic change. A linguistic approach in the classroom stresses the importance of oral English throughout the school years to assure the pupil's knowledge as well as performance. And dialectology becomes a source of knowledge and performance. No matter how a school district divides the spoils between English teachers and speech teachers (the boundary is often established by local or state course requirements for certification), oral English comes into its own.

Dialectology has come into the classrooms very recently. There was little general knowledge of this subject, and there were practically no textbooks until a few years ago. Unlike lexicography with its long tradition in this country, even though that tradition remained arcane for a long time, dialectology is even now handicapped by publishing problems. But textbooks and classroom activities are beginning to show the strong contribution this subject can make to understanding and using English.

Although the language of the common man exists in the oral literature of every culture, serious investigation into the nature of popular idiom did not get under way until the eighteenth century. Two divergent forces contributed to the development of dialectology. On the one hand, the rationalists were pursuing empirical methods of direct observation. On the other, the romantics ignored scientific goals and glorified the individual's self-expression. The romantics drew attention to the enormous variety that exists in living languages; the rationalists did not ignore this evidence. They used it to classify languages and account for varieties within a language.

Rousseau's passionate concern for man as a child of nature had brought the language of poet and peasant together. In England, for example, Wordsworth strove for poetic diction through the speech of the rustics in his lake district. Burns's Muse stayed with him in his Scottish songs and stole away when he aspired to more literary language. And Coleridge turned to the medieval ballads for forms and subjects. Folk art, folk ways, mountain crags, and savannahs provided escape from factory chimneys and teeming cities. This return to a more idyllic past and to a more healing nature opened our ears to varieties of language long unheard or ignored. The dialects of English —regional, historical, social—spoke loud and clear, as did dialects all over the continent. Here were the raw facts of language that had heretofore been ignored.

Linguistic scientists were ready to use these facts. We have seen, in a previous chapter, how eighteenth-century scientific methods of careful observation and classification had led to nineteenth-century linguistic discoveries. Linguistics like Jacob Grimm (of fairy tale fame), Hermann Grassman, and Carl Verner had shown that sound changes regularly. These regular changes had revealed relationships among the known languages of the world. These linguists showed how the *k* pronunciation in Latin *cor, centum,* and *cantare* becomes divided into the *k* in *cordial, s* in *cent,* and the *ch* in *chant*; how *cent* and *hundred, pater* and *father, grain* and *corn, duo* and *two* are related. But they left unexplained the relationships within a language. If sound change was perfectly regular, how could they account for these exceptions? Why should babies pronounce *water* in so many different ways?

In the 1870's Georg Wenker took the first step to answering these questions. He decided to collect sufficient examples of these "exceptions" to standard speech. He sent forty sentences dealing with everyday subjects to school teachers in almost fifty thousand places in Germany and asked each teacher to transcribe as exactly as he could his students' pronunciation of these sentences. He was therefore gathering only variations in pronunciation, not in vocabulary or grammar. Plotting the replies on maps led to a first linguistic atlas. Although Wenker's work was never completely published, dialectology had begun in Germany. In France, the pioneer work of Jules Gilliéron produced the first linguistic atlas in 1910.

In our own country, with the founding of the American Dialect Society in 1889, serious study got under way. Since then, various groups have been gathering evidence that will eventually make up a Linguistic Atlas of the United States and Canada. Projects in New England, the North Central states, the Upper Midwest, the Rocky Mountain area, Texas and the Gulf states, the Pacific states, and the Maritime Provinces have divided the labors. The *Linguistic Atlas of New England* has already been edited and published.[1] So have Hans Kurath's *Handbook of the Linguistic Geography of New England*[2]

---

[1] Hans Kurath and Bernard Bloch (eds.), *Linguistic Atlas of New England,* 3 vols. (New York: American Council of Learned Societies [Columbia University Press], 1939–43).

[2] Hans Kurath (ed.), *Handbook of the Linguistic Geography of New England* (New York: American Council of Learned Societies [Columbia University Press], 1939).

and his *Word Geography of the Eastern United States*.[3] E. Bagby Atwood's *Survey of Verb Forms in the Eastern United States*[4] and Kurath and McDavid's *Pronunciation of English in the Atlantic States*[5] and Atwood's *Regional Vocabulary of Texas*[6] are only a beginning. But they should dispel any naive notions that a uniform pronunciation, grammar, or vocabulary can be hailed as Standard English in the United States.

If dictionaries are one thread of the fabric of our national history, linguistic atlases are another. Although we are too young a country to have the deeply ingrained regional and historical dialects that still separate speakers in European countries, and we are too democratic a country to have the social and educational distinctions that prevail abroad, the differences are there. Luckily, the likenesses among the various American English dialects outweigh the differences. But seeking a single standard is like hunting unicorns in our land. They're not native to the region, and they couldn't survive.

Teachers who understand these facts about our language can get their youngsters off to a much better start than those who assume a doctrine of correct usage that prevails among all educated citizens. It is never too soon to expose pupils to respect for individual differences in speech. Many respect themselves and their own dialects more when various dialects are enjoyed in the classroom. What might have become an embarrassment becomes something to be proud of. This is only another example of how prescription confines, while description liberates. Respect for self is the first step toward respect for others; to respect differences is a lot better than to tolerate them. Dialectology can contribute to this kind of learning readiness.

When children have learned to compare and share everyday household words—for family, pets, food, plants, furniture—the newcomer to the school is less likely to remain an outsider. People who talk like themselves are real people, whether they share the same reading table or are heroes in books. Paul Bunyan, Mike Fink, Pecos Bill, Feobold

[3] Hans Kurath, *A Word Geography of the Eastern United States* (Ann Arbor, Mich.: University of Michigan Press, 1949).

[4] E. Bagby Atwood, *Survey of Verb Forms in the Eastern United States* (Ann Arbor, Mich.: University of Michigan Press, 1953).

[5] Hans Kurath and Raven I. McDavid, Jr., *Pronunciation of English in the Atlantic States* (Ann Arbor, Mich.: University of Michigan Press, 1961).

[6] E. Bagby Atwood, *Regional Vocabulary of Texas* (Austin, Tex.: University of Texas Press, 1962).

Feoboldson—all these heroes talk their own way, and their talk can delight readers and listeners. Curriculum centers and teachers' texts now include such source material in readings, tapes, and recordings. Listening is better than reading if transcriptions of speech are a problem. Without a phonetic writing system, like that of the International Phonetic Alphabet, eye dialect can barely approximate living speech. Documentaries on film and TV provide authentic, dramatic material for class examination and discussion. One of the best lessons I have seen followed a documentary film on automation. On-the-spot interviews with people from different sections of the country and different walks of life gave the students an earful of what we call American English. The automobile worker in Detroit and the baker in Philadelphia shared the same worries about being displaced by machines. Both spoke the language of the common man, but the regional differences were there. Moreover the old worker, obviously an immigrant, and the young worker, obviously a native, sounded different both in Detroit and in Philadelphia. The speech of the union leader in each plant was equally revealing: articulate, intelligent, yet bearing regional and social distinctions. Even the executives of the two large corporations spoke different dialects. Urbane, obviously well-educated, each spoke English that was Standard for his part of the country. But the regional differences were unmistakable. The history teacher then tried to help the pupils figure out why these people felt the way they did about automation; the English teacher, why they spoke the way they did. To explain the obvious is often impossible; sometimes the struggle is enough.

Dialectology, then, can provide both substance and tone for classes on all levels. But there is a sequence which makes sense and determines when the obvious is merely to be noted and when it has to be probed. In the early grades, the child enjoys dialects. His ear can be sharpened, his humor aroused, his respect for differences strengthened, his horizons enlarged. But he is not ready to analyze what he hears or to investigate underlying causes. The real distinctions that characterize dialect cannot be discussed in a vacuum. They can be understood only in terms of vocabulary, pronunciation, and grammar. In other words, he needs precise terms for more than surface observations.

Formal study of dialect, then, is fruitful when the pupil is equipped with the precise tools provided by his knowledge of dictionaries and grammar. Then the student is ready for serious and sustained inquiry into what a dialect is, what we mean by variations in dialect, what the principal dialect areas in the United States are, how we justify these classifications, how information is gathered from these areas, what this information can tell us about settlement history, migrations, population and social changes, and geography. Political, cultural, intellectual, religious, and economic history converge and often emerge in dialectology. Students may, on the other hand, narrow down their interests to their own bailiwick.

The mature student is also ready to cross boundaries within his own subject. The handbook that answers his questions as to usage and form when he writes his compositions did not come from Mount Sinai or even Mount Olympus. It was written by someone. On what did he base his rules?

Although the handbook takes no stand on *spider* versus *skillet* or *frying pans* and doesn't care whether you cook *pancakes, flapjacks, fritters, slapjacks,* or *latkes* in them ("whatever goes into a man cannot defile him"), it usually does care about such matters as *shall* and *will, lie* and *lay, who* and *whom, like* and *as, further* and *farther, can* and *may, less* and *fewer, try to* and *try and, the reason is that* and *the reason is because, in back of* and *behind,* and *ain't.*

When Jean Malmstrom checked fifty-seven usage items against 312 language arts textbooks containing statements about at least one of these items and all published between 1940 and 1955, she discovered the following:

> First, no textbook discusses all the fifty-seven items. Second, the lower the grade-level of the text, the greater the number of items omitted. Third, no textbooks discuss identical sets of items. Fourth, the distinction between speech and writing is not strictly and consistently maintained in the textbooks. Fifth, textbook writers do not agree with each other on the meanings of the terms "colloquial," "standard," "nonstandard," "formal," "informal," and "vulgate."[7]

In view of the fact that so much of our communication nowadays is oral, these are sobering discoveries. The student has a right to know these facts so that he will not expect answers to questions about usage from some oracle. He also has a right to know where to look for answers to some of these questions. Atlas findings confront him with objective evidence for accepting or rejecting the prescriptions that he finds printed in his handbook. Such classroom discussions inevitably

[7] Jean Malmstrom, "Linguistic Atlas Findings versus Textbook Pronouncements on Current American Usage," *English Journal,* **48** (April, 1959), 193.

take students from the question of correctness to the question of effectiveness, which is the heart of the matter in speaking and in writing.

Final answers, then, are not yet forthcoming. But the student who can examine the facts of language dispassionately has overcome his provincial attitudes toward usage and is ready for the next step: a sense of personal responsibility and commitment in language. When, for example, we discover that many of the features of upper-crust Atlanta speech in the midfifties were also found among Oakland's migrant workers, we realize that what is prestigious speech in one section of the country is hardly that in another. Dialectology, then, alerts the students to differences and forces him to confront the essential differences between speech and writing. It also teases him into trying to account for some of these differences. Is it mere accident that laborers in one section of the country speak like aristocrats in another?

Sometimes youngsters become amateur linguistic geographers. With professional ardor beyond the energies of a trained investigator, they seek out informants from the three representative groups in their linguistic community: an older person with little formal education, a middle-aged person who finished high school, and a young college graduate. From these informants' running speech they try to isolate the names of familiar everyday items. Their methods may be crude and their findings insignificant. But becoming an amateur linguistic geographer can be no more harmful to the child or to the profession than becoming an amateur archeologist, astronomer, salesman, or poet. There is something to be said for the motivation, patience, accuracy, objectivity, and inductive reasoning that go into these student-initiated projects.

Other times, dialectology enriches work being done in other classes. If the pupils are studying American settlements in history, for example, they like to see how the linguistic atlas findings substantiate the findings in the history text. Or they may be doing a unit in local history and want to see how it is reflected in the region's dialects. As they study westward expansion, they can see the connections between language growth and migrations. This is when they see the connections between language and physical geography, social history, political and religious boundaries. Studies in world history or world literature gain new dimensions when pupils can examine the varieties of English as a world language.

Almost invariably, if the pupils are mature enough (and this is often a matter of intellectual climate in a classroom rather than age or grade level), questions about dialect open up larger questions about linguistic change. Now the class is asking for a unit on the history of the language. Perhaps. The teacher has to play it by ear unless his course of study is more specific. Too much too soon is as bad as too little too late. Sometimes a simple factual answer is all the student wants. Other times he is really asking to find out in great detail how our language came to be as diversified as it is today.

This is the difference between a teacher and a text. The good teacher does play it by ear. He can adapt the sequence of his course to these unexpected but welcome demands for enrichment. A day or two with dialects or history of the language may answer immediate questions or motivate a later detailed unit. Even as an interlude between heavy doses of literature, grammar, or composition, it may serve a useful purpose. The teacher who uses lexicography or dialectology in this incidental way is not cheating unless he is passing off this brief exposure as a survey of the entire subject.

But a textbook has a commitment to a body of knowledge presented in a systematic, scholarly manner. When a publisher replaces an old chapter on parliamentary procedure with a new one on lexicography and another old chapter on telephone etiquette with a new one on dialects and continues to peddle this "English text" as a new course incorporating the newest linguistic findings, let the buyer beware. These transitional texts do exist. But the conscientious teacher will not be misled. He will insist, though wait he must, on solid high school texts in these subjects, not on occasional nods or polite bows. Jean Malmstrom's *Language in Society* is one step in the right direction.[8] Her and Annabel Ashley's *Dialects—U.S.A.,* the first publication of the Commission on the English Language of the National Council of Teachers of English (NCTE), is already being used in many classrooms.[9] *Writers the Other Side of the Horizon,* edited by Priscilla Tyler, is also extremely useful.[10] But it will be some time before the subject matter of English can be reexamined, before we know what should remain and what should go. Until then, the extent to which dialectology is part of English programs will have to be settled by teachers locally. A most fitting niche for this subject!

[8] Jean Malmstrom, *Language in Society* (New York: Hayden Book Companies, 1965).

[9] Jean Malmstrom and Annabel Ashley, *Dialects—U.S.A.* (Champaign, Ill.: National Council of Teachers of English, 1963).

[10] Priscilla Tyler (ed.), *Writers the Other Side of the Horizon* (Champaign, Ill.: National Council of Teachers of English, 1964).

16

Modern language study has banished some of the myths about what grammar is and why it should be taught. It is subjecting the study of the history of our language to the same scrutiny. One irresistible notion is that we turn to the past to seek sanction for present usage. If a word is hallowed by antiquity, it must be good! Yet if we pursued this argument to its logical conclusion, our most prestigious terms would be our monosyllabic taboo words. They have a long ancestry with cognates throughout the Indo-European family of languages. We'd proudly use *ain't* and *ye* and *'em, Who are you looking for?* and *between you and I*. For all these expressions have an honorable history. And if we wanted to be emphatic, we'd start piling up the negatives as we haven't dared to since Chaucer's time. When poor, long-suffering Griselda's patience gave out, she hit her husband Walter with six negatives in one sentence! Another way to be emphatic would be to accumulate our superlatives like Shakespeare's "most unkindest cut of all." We'd even turn to focal areas that have resisted change. In the language of the so-called hillbillies, we'd find our Standard. What would happen if we turned to the past to justify the clothes we wear and the houses we live in today?

Another reason often cited for studying the history of our language is that this is a good way to learn both language and history, to get what we glibly call background in our culture. All too often, however, neither language nor history survives the marriage. Or the off-spring of the happy union is still a bastard: a blend of fact and myth. When culture with a capital C becomes the goal of language study, the highlights are usually Julius Caesar confronting the blue-painted aborigines of Britannia, Hengest and Horsa onshlaging and horsing around with the poor Celtic remnants, King Alfred establishing the Danelaw when he isn't burning cakes, William the Conqueror reversing the Normandy beachhead disaster in 1066. From there on, Scott's *Ivanhoe* takes over with Gurth and Wamba stalwartly resisting the

French occupation not with blood, sweat, and tears, but with pure Saxon talk. Even presented with greater system and accuracy, such stories only provide the background for linguistic change. They describe little and explain less about the history of English.

At a time when so much new knowledge is entering the schools and so much thought is being given to what should stay and what must go, the only reason for studying our language's history is for the facts we can obtain and the uses we can make of these facts both in further theorizing about language and in using language itself. History of the language then becomes the third truth that makes us free—free from the tyranny of false standards of usage and free to use our knowledge to make reasonable judgments. Thereby the subject lends itself well to Jerome Bruner's spiral theory of learning, which maintains that any subject can be taught to any child in some honest form. If education consists of facts and concepts that broaden and deepen as the child matures, then the facts and concepts about our native language belong all over the curriculum. Linguistic change is something we live with every day in and out of school.

The word play in the nursery, the patois in the family, the neologisms of technicians and politicians and hucksters, the idiom of jazz and space travel, the word flood unleashed by a Hiroshima or a Sputnik, even the ingroups' and outgroups' private language—all attest to the fact that no matter what we do to our language, English remains English. Although time does make ancient good uncouth, although style in language does change with our culture, the underlying and essential characteristics of English are there for the pupil to know and understand with deepening awareness as he matures. Amid the endless diversity of linguistic change, an essential unity keeps asserting itself.

A look at two sentences may show us what we mean by change and what we mean by essential unity. The first comes from a recent news item in the *New York Times:*

> A new discothèque, La Gigue, will erupt with the frug, the surf, the monkey and the bostela at the Waldorf-Astoria on April 7.

The second is almost a thousand years old. It is Archbishop Aelfric's translation of news that had remained news for a long time but had not yet reached the heathen in that outpost of civilization called England:

> On anginne gesceop God heofenan and eorðan.

The most obvious change in a millennium, the change in the pronunciation of these words, eludes us on the printed page. The alphabet remains the same except for the barred *d,* which was a new sound to a Roman missionary speaking and writing Latin, but which was an old sound in the native English of his prospective converts. This letter was later discarded for the *th* combination we find in words like *with.* Although we might conclude from this that the essential unity is our Roman alphabet, common sense tells us otherwise. We know that many languages other than English use the Roman alphabet.

Although the alphabet itself may not help us to characterize what we call English, the combination of letters in that alphabet does help. We recognize words like *a, new, will, with, the, and, at, on* in the *New York Times* sentence; words like *on, God, and* in Aelfric's sentence. We use the familiar words in the first sentence to guide us to a subject-predicate relationship that we intuitively identify with an English sentence. Culturally, we may still be far away from the meaning. The unfamiliar words may not be in our newest dictionaries. But one thing we're sure of: If anyone were to ask whether it is an English sentence, we'd say it is. We'd even be able to draw the line between subject and predicate between *Gigue* and *will.*

The Aelfric sentence, so removed from us in time and place, will have some elements that have become obsolete, others that have persisted through the years. The latter will be the essential unity we are seeking in English. Using the criteria we found helpful in the modern sentence, we start with the familiar words as clues to relationships between words, to the subject-predicate relationship. We can assume that *on* introduces a prepositional phrase; that *God* is not part of a pair or a series, for it has neither *and*'s nor commas connecting it with other words. But that it is a noun and a very proper noun we have no doubt. Now if we can only dispose of *gesceop, heofenan,* and *eorthan,* our sentence will make some kind of sense, be it semantic, structural, or both. Those last two words would look something like our *heaven* and *earth* if we weren't bothered by those *-an* endings. Evidently somebody within these thousand years wasn't bothered and dropped them off if the modern words are related to the old English words! And if we recall from our chapter on the two R's that spelling follows sound change very, very slowly, that it may be millennia before "Watchadoin?" formally spells what all of us say, then we can say that what often happens to unstressed syllables—they disappear— may have happened to the *-an* of *heofenan* and *eorthan.* But let's not dismiss those unwashed barbarians in Albion too cursorily. They hadn't been tacking on -*an* just to hear themselves talk. That ending must have served some useful purpose. Meanwhile, back to our sentence at the old monastery. If we have decided that *God* is a noun, that *heaven* and *earth* are probably nouns, and that *on anginne* is a prepositional phrase, then the one word left is *gesceop*. And if we want to live dangerously, we play our intuitive hunches again. We know an English sentence must have a verb. So we call *gesceop* a verb. Now the problem is, can we justify the hunch in any reasonable way? We can say at least it doesn't have that -*an* ending that we attributed to the nouns. At this point, we resort to a little more intuition. Let's stop pretending. You and I know the verb means *created* because culturally we may be more familiar with that *God, heaven,* and *earth* combination than we are with discothèques and gigues. So we say it is an English sentence. "I remember it as a sentence, even if I can't recognize it in its old English form."

In our groping with thousand-year-old words, we can't afford to be fussy. Memory is no less sure a guide than intuition—so long as we realize that we remember something more than the words in sentences. Underlying all those old and new words that come and go through the years, all those endings that we've clipped off, are the unchanging words like *a, and, the, to, on, with, at* that steer us to patterns of spelling and sound that we call English words and larger patterns of words that we call subjects and predicates. The rules by which we create these patterns remain; the lesser rules that come and go are the ones that account for change.

We could, for example, test our hunch about the verb *gesceop* by applying some of the facts. For example, the fact that *ge* is an unstressed prefix that disappeared just as the -*an* did; that *sceop* didn't need the familiar -*t, -d,* or -*ed* to show that this news had occurred in the past any more than we need those endings for the past tense of *bear* or *run* or *rise*; that although words like *scoop* or *skip* won't support our intuitions, *scop* will. The scop, you will recall from your old poems, was a maker, a *shaper,* a creator of old English songs. What worked for *gesceop* may work for *anginne,* too. If we lop off the *an* as we did the *ge* in *gesceop* and the *ne* as we did the *an* in *heofenan* and *eordan,* we're left with a root *gin,* not as in a Martini, but as in *begin* or as in Macbeth's "I 'gin to be aweary of the sun." The prepositional phrase *on anginne* may then be the ancestor of *on* or *in the beginning.*

Once we've stripped the old sentence of endings that might have concealed the modern word from us, we have to go through with our modernization. We have to use word order to express the relationship between subject and predicate that might have been revealed in those old endings. Otherwise, we'd still be left with the antique flavor of

> In the beginning created God heaven(s) and earth.

rather than

> In the beginning God created heaven(s) and earth.

Studying the history of English, then, can be an ever deepening process of seeing how the external history of a people—the wars, the migrations, the inventions, the natural phenomena, and religious and social developments—is reflected not only in the growth of vocabulary but also in the way new words are absorbed into the framework of the language. New pronunciations, new spellings, new forms of words and sentences are not *new* to the child learning his language from his parents. They are *the* language, *his* language with an underlying system of rules into which his parents' innovations have already been absorbed. To characterize language in our time, then, ultimately means to specify what a native speaker must know in order to use the language. To study change in our language, as we go backward in time, is to specify what a native speaker must have known in order to use his language. The fundamental likenesses that keep English English are these deep, subsurface rules that we internalize. To bring them to the surface of our conscious awareness is to broaden and deepen our knowledge of the history of English.

There is no limit, then, as to how far we might push our questions about the Aelfric sentence. We might want to take each word back not only to his time but beyond into the Germanic group, the Indo-European family, and even a conjectural proto-Indo-European form. We've said just a little about consonant and vowel change in those seven words. We haven't begun to describe the change and account for it in a plausible, testable, systematic way. To do that, we'd have to invoke many more facts from comparative linguistics, many more theories that account for change.

If, then, theorizing about language, like all theorizing, is open-ended, the best thing we can do for our youngsters is to arouse their interest and curiosity, satisfy some of it with the facts we know, leave a good deal of the adventure to them, and be absolutely sure that no matter how far they go in this subject they will not have to waste time and effort unlearning what we have taught them.

Wherever youngsters meet new words or new uses of old words, they are ready to start this quest. So you laid the foundation when you introduced Junior to Mother Goose and Doctor Seuss, when you made up nonsense words and sang silly songs and just had fun with language. This is the earliest and liveliest material for any embryo linguist to experiment with. And when the school can extend these experiences, history of the language is off to a good start. But even if the child can't recall the way he played with words and varied them, he has himself, his family, his clique, radio, and television to listen to. He can't help seeing and hearing how language keeps changing from person to person, from place to place, from time to time. And if his natural curiosity hasn't been thwarted, sooner or later he'll want to know: How come we all speak English so differently and we still understand each other? Why don't people all over the world speak just a little differently from each other? Where do all the different languages come from? We need this natural bridge between language in and out of school to keep updating the facts of linguistic change that we find in our texts.

There are many ways to start answering these questions, though the final answers can never be found. One way is to let the child formulate his own theory and then push that hypothesis as far as it can logically go in the light of the facts we have. Another way is to arm the child with some of the fundamental facts. Many of them come out of lessons in spelling, pronunciation, word study, meaning, grammar, dictionary and dialect study, composition work, and speech. The good teacher introduces historical explanation whenever it will help the child master a new point. The formal teaching of this subject, however, has to wait until the eleventh or twelfth grade. Then the pupils' knowledge of grammar, history, world literature, and possibly a foreign language helps him to bring into focus what he has been learning incidentally about language history in snips and pieces. This formal presentation may be by way of large-group instruction, of chapters or pamphlets or texts specially written for the group, or by older but highly readable texts like Jespersen's *Growth and Structure of the English Language*.[1] Texts designed for the precollege years are now being written. But lectures and texts are only a first

---

[1] Otto Jespersen, *Growth and Structure of the English Language* (9th ed.; New York: The Macmillan Company, 1948).

step. Individual and group research projects usually enable the pupil to *use* or at least *test* his knowledge against the facts of language in his own community. Infants and octogenarians, old newspapers and magazines as well as today's mass media, historical dictionaries, and atlases—all offer the opportunity for serious but lively investigation into language change and variety.

Invariably, however, whether the pupil is discovering these facts for himself or is being told them and asked to verify them, whether he is learning them sporadically or systematically, the facts of historic change in pronunciation, vocabulary, and grammar confront him. Growth in vocabulary is the most obvious because it keeps happening in our very own midst. Yet there are very few variations on the age-old pattern. Sometimes we increase our word stock by extending the grammatic function of words we already have in the language. Maybe that's how we got *run* or *feed* as nouns a long time ago; how we got *bug* and *case* as transitive verbs today; how we got *but me no but's, ups and downs,* and *on the go.* Or a mere shift in stress may give us another part of speech, as in *pro'test* and *protest',* *ob'ject* and *object'.* Or a mere change of the root vowel may give us *song* from *sing, sang, sung;* or *food* from *feed.* But we seem to have outgrown this gradation as we've used fewer and fewer strong verbs that change their vowel.

Another way to increase our word stock is by compounding, either adding suffix and/or prefix to a root or combining two word roots. So we get *unkind, kindness, unkindly, mankind,* and *antidisestablish-mentarianism.* How did we get along without *supermarket, intercom, realize, finalize, panorama, delirama, nymphet,* and *sermonette?* Often, instead of lengthening a word we cut it down to size to form a new one. So *diagnosis* gave us *diagnose; burglar, burgle; domination, dominate; enthusiasm, enthuse.* Sometimes we keep only one word of an expression as a new word; we don't say *private soldier* or *principal teacher* any more. The long expressions we invariably cut to monosyllables if we need to use them often enough; after a while we forget what 'words *CARE* or *SNIK* or *WASP* stood for. If we can't reduce them to monosyllables or acronyms, we settle for letters like *DDT* or *TV* or *TVA.* But while we're clipping some words to *ad, cute,* or *phone,* we're expanding and combining in words like *teach-in, jet plane, babysit,* and *blackbird.* We make generic terms of proper names like *Uncle Tom* and *Quisling,* identify man and his inventions in words like *fuchsia* and *sandwich,* or man and his discoveries in words like *Fermium* and *Einsteinium,* or places and things in words like *china, scotch,* and *bourbon.*

We can't resist the impulse to play with the sounds of words. Echoes, rhymes, hybrid blends, onomatopoetic words keep creeping into our language: *dilly-dally, namby-pamby, boogie-woogie; snide, chortle, brunch, motel; buzz bomb, squelch,* and *squatsch.* We can finally resort to sheer inspiration for words like *kodak* and *nylon.* But when we coin new words, we have to be sure of their English pronounceability. If we had to ask for *Dlia* instead of *Dial,* for *Rpell* instead of *Prell, Xlu* instead of *Lux,* those products would hardly sell —at least in English-speaking countries.

But changing the forms of old words and forming new words is only one set of ways of increasing our vocabulary. We keep extending the semantic boundaries of words we already have in the language. Some ameliorate, or go up, in the scale of meaning, like *praise* or *lord;* others pejorate, or go down, like *silly, lust,* and *hussy.* Some become generalized like *barn,* which used to store only barley, and *girl,* who was a youth of either sex. Others become more special in meaning, like *deer,* which was an animal of any kind in Shakespeare's day, and *starve,* which once meant to die in any manner. Some words become more concrete like the biblical *fastness;* others, more abstract, like the *lemons* we often get when we hunt for bargains. Some words shift their emphasis; a *veteran* was once just an old man. Other words shift through poetic figures of speech. The *daisy* was the day's eye. When everything in the teenager's world is *terrific* or *fantastic,* metaphor is gone and superlatives become superfluous. Words can shift their meaning, too, by radiating new meanings. *Pin* means different things to the dressmaker, the golfer, the bowler, the locksmith, the sailor, the musician, the jeweler, and the collegiate.

Finally, when we have exhausted our own word stock, we borrow from others. These loan words are the biography of a people. They are recorded cultural, political, religious, military history. Invasions, travel, commerce, and inventions carry words across any boundaries. The popular words are usually transmitted orally as they fill our daily needs for the good life. The learned words usually reflect a more cultural and literary influence. In our own time, we need only look at the continental importations on our food shelves and our fashion pages for those popular words; at the addenda to a recent unabridged dictionary for the popular and learned ones. Yet there were other times when we borrowed and reborrowed words from Roman conquerors and missionaries, from Scandinavian marauders and mates, from French governors and scholars and artists, from Renaissance explorers who brought back new products from all parts of the old and new world. Ours is a long tradition of accepting foreign words freely into our language.

That our vocabulary has increased and how it happened can be interesting and revealing to pupils of any age. Such knowledge reaches the pupil through every subject from the primary grades on; it does not have to wait for a course in history of the language. But the changes in pronunciation and grammar are slower, less noticeable, less accessible to the youngster than to the more mature student who reads widely in periods other than his own and perhaps even in languages other than his native one. Only as he reads the old Scottish ballads or the Middle English of Chaucer or the early Modern English of Shakespeare does the student really have to face up to some of the facts of sound change. And as he notes changes and correspondences in sounds, he begins to see that these changes are indeed systematic. He can work out the relationships between Chaucer's pronunciation of vowels and our pronunciation of the same vowels in the same words. In other words, he need not stop by noting the impact of the Norman invasion and occupation on our vocabulary. He can hear how our own English words shifted their pronunciation; he can account very precisely for the singing quality of Chaucer's verse; he can also account for the discrepancy between spelling and pronunciation of many words in modern English. When he comes to Shakespeare, he notes that our vowels were still undergoing changes in pronunciation, that we were still working toward what we would call modern English. When *Rome* rhymes with *room* and *please* rhymes both with *knees* and with *grace,* we realize that the great shift in vowel pronunciation produced enormous flux rather than an overnight change. We still have alternate pronunciations of words like *vase, roof,* and *tomato.*

Ultimately, however, changes in the sound system have not been stressed in classes. They have been noted rather as aids to extracting meaning from elusive puns and rhymes and as aids to oral interpretation. This should neither surprise nor alarm us when we realize how few Shakespearian actors of our day have mastered or cared to master the nuances of the bard's pronunciation. How many of us would understand these actors if they did talk the way we assume

Shakespeare's actors did? Though we may listen to recordings of what may have been Chaucer's or Shakespeare's English, we cannot say that we study change in sound thereby. It is the printed page and the modern pronunciation that communicate to most of our students.

To do more than note the big surface differences in pronunciation would require a systematic analysis of distinctive features of speech sounds, a more precise terminology, and an examination of the relationship between the underlying grammatical structure of a sentence and the actual pronunciation of a particular sentence. That these are two different kinds of knowledge can be seen in many adults' mastery of the reading and understanding of a foreign language and their enormous difficulty in mastering or even approximating the pronunciation of the sounds in that language. Broadcasts from the United Nations show this discrepancy between linguistic knowledge and oral performance. Since our study of literature of the past stresses knowledge or understanding of the text rather than the oral performance, it is only reasonable that we look more closely at the syntactic than at the phonological rules. The latter are the ones that can come in college courses if the student really wants to broaden and deepen his understanding of language change. But he will have no unlearning to do if he has mastered the syntax; he has only to discover that "Sound change is the addition of rules to grammars." What really changes is not sounds but the abstract set of rules for producing sentences. In other words, the way we pronounce a sentence depends on the structure, the way it is put together. How it is put together does not depend on its pronunciation.

If changes in vocabulary are adaptable to any part of the course of study and changes in pronunciation can be pursued only by the advanced classes, changes in sentence structure become basic. Structure is the language. It is what underlies our choice of words and the sounds that represent them physically. It is what determines our comprehension of what we read or hear. If we understand the essential structure of an English sentence then, we should have no difficulty in moving about in space and time in literature. Thus, when pupils read Hawthorne or Dickens, the length of the nineteenth-century English sentence may seem strange; but once they have been alerted to the meanings of obsolete or regional words, they can cope with sentence length. Even reading Shakespeare presents more vocabulary problems than grammar or punctuation might. Yet the student who has been alerted to structural changes since Shakespeare understands the text with less backtracking and helpless rereading of a passage. The more flexible word order; the empty unemphatic *do* for the present tense; the distinctions between *you, ye,* and *thou, thee;* the different kinds of plurals and possessives enable the informed student not only to get the literal meaning but also to note the rhetorical devices and subtleties of interpretation from Shakespeare's sentences. Understanding, enjoyment, literary appreciation, and critical appraisal can be encouraged, therefore, when the student realizes the precise differences between the language of his time and the language of the writer's time. Although a thorough knowledge of sentence structure cannot assure a student's success in literature or composition, it can do no harm and possibly much good.

The history of the language, then, can be studied in many ways and more and more teachers are introducing carefully thought-out units not only on the external changes in vocabulary but also on the internal changes in structure. Sometimes these accompany a course in European, American, or world history. To see how our language has developed as British English, American English, and a world language makes sense for the pupil when it can be coordinated with his history work. Sometimes these units accompany the reading of a classic that might otherwise be as formidable as a foreign language. Barriers to reading *Beowulf,* Chaucer, Milton, or Shakespeare can and should be removed. Sometimes these units are part of the senior's rounding off of his knowledge of English before he leaves the shelter of the high school for town, gown, or uniform. And somehow an exposure to the history of the language awakes the pupil from his sense of linguistic absoluteness and certitude and nudges him into a more tolerant and responsible attitude toward language. The varieties of change in vocabulary, spelling, pronunciation, and grammar may even encourage him to take a few calculated risks in his own expression.

Since this subject matter is fairly new in the schools, teachers are experimenting with it at various levels. The cultural history, the romance of the language, the picturesque etymologies appeal to pupils of all ages. Investigating the correspondences or laws of change that have been discovered by comparative linguists and are being reexamined today demands greater knowledge and maturity. Here the student goes from the colorful and dramatic story of language to the intellectual challenge of discovering order, reason, system among these many changes and correspondences. The student who has seen the chain reaction in theories about man's development may appreciate the same sequence in theories about man's language development. Darwin's theory of evolution was only a partial explanation of the varieties of species and the progression from simple to complex forms of life. Yet early twentieth-century studies of the internal structure of the cell and of mitosis and later studies of the internal structure of amino acids and of the function of DNA, RNA, and the synthesis of protein molecules have strengthened Darwin's hypothesis. The student who sees how genetics helped explain evolution and how biochemistry helped explain genetics may be ready to see how theorizing about language diversity and development has followed a similar path. De Saussure's nineteenth-century hypothesis about long-lost consonants in proto-Indo-European was a reconstruction based on internal evidence. It remained in the realm of theory until these long-lost consonants were actually discovered in the twentieth-century decipherment of Hittite, a language which was being used almost four thousand years ago! The external evidence for validating De Saussure's theory had turned up! History of our language, then, is another way to involve our most able students in the theorizing that characterizes our times.

As we arrive at more powerful explanations for change and diversity in language, we shall no doubt have to reformulate much of the content of courses now being developed. We have come a long way since antiquarians attributed particular languages to man, God, and beast in Eden. Later assumptions that language change was chaotic and harmful had to be abandoned for still later studies of comparative linguists who corrected false etymologies and established relationships based on correspondences in Indo-European languages. These corrections, in turn, made way for better classification of sounds and more rigorous analysis of changes that proved to be systematic. What had been dismissed as chance submitted to verifiable analysis. In our own time, new studies in syntax and phonology are beginning to explain much change that was heretofore attributed to accident or even to error.

Thus far teachers on their own, in retraining institutes and on fellowships, have been adapting college texts and preparing their own materials on the history of the language. But good texts based on most recent scholarship and written especially for high school students are forthcoming. As we teachers come to understand more about the history of English and about the nature of linguistic change, perhaps we will be more tolerant of Jespersen's optimism about language and pessimism about teachers. Looking about him, he could only see English evolving toward a more perfect stage. He saw it becoming more simple and regular; he cited the disappearance of arbitrary grammatical gender and the enrichment of pronoun uses; he welcomed the new conjunctions, compounds, and uses of the infinitives. "Let us hope," he concluded, "that in the future the more and more almighty schoolmaster may not nip too many beneficial changes in the bud."

17

If English classes learn nothing else from their study of dictionaries, linguistic geography, and history of the language, they are at least cured of some of their notions about "correct" English. Once they have been exposed to the truths about language change and usage, there's no turning back to a right-wrong dualism. In these classes we find less talk about correct usage and more talk about good usage. For the most glaring fact is that no language widely spoken is uniformly spoken. Correctness, then, becomes a dubious goal; the only realistic one is effectiveness in speaking, reading, and writing.

When standards prove so debatable, variable, and elusive, clarity, accuracy, and conciseness become the more urgent and reasonable goals. Teaching in today's English classes, then, emerges not from a narrowly applicable set of techniques but from a broadly based approach to language as a whole. Still, there is no agreement on how to teach good English. What not to do has only become clearer than what to do. We simply cannot deal with a very real subject like language in our dictionaries, linguistic atlases, and histories—and then ask the pupils to return to unreal prescriptions as to usage. Even the pupil who has not learned the facts gets little out of these prescriptions. Twenty-five years ago Charles Fries discovered that narrow prescription and drill in usage in our schools only increase the number and proportion of errors from year to year. No matter what we do, we cannot oversimplify a problem as complex as usage. The only way, then, is to face it honestly and consistently, armed with all the facts modern linguistic study can provide.

The first step is to acquire the knowledge upon which an intelligent judgment on usage can be based. To be able to discuss a student's speech or writing in clear, precise terms that fit our language is also helpful. A comment like "awkward" or "interesting" does not tell the pupil how he can improve his performance. If he respects the teacher's knowledge, taste, and judgment, precise criticism only strengthens that confidence. It is the most constructive without being prescriptive. On the other hand, the teacher's comments on a pupil's paper do not always tell the story. Often, instead of writing a single word, "vague" or "precise," the teacher devotes an entire conference period to going over a paper with the student. His suggestions, whether oral or written, can only alert the student to the need for variety and adaptability of usage, depending on the paper's purpose. Every comment is really one aspect of the teacher's total linguistic and social philosophy. We know that dogmatic pronouncements rarely teach anyone to write well. But the nagging questions remain: Can anyone be taught to write well? Or is it like Clym Yeobright's answer when his well-meaning mother wanted him to abandon the idea of bringing education to the denizens of the heath: "Mother, what is doing well?" If one cannot be taught to write well, can one learn to write well? Usage is only one part of this whole problem, but it is a very real part. Not precept but example, not preaching but teaching of usage.

Various teachers of English who are also linguists have recognized the different dimensions of usage and have offered helpful guides to classroom teachers. None of them says, "Do nothing. Whatever is is right." And all of them agree that usage always depends for its effectiveness on the speaker, audience, time, place, and occasion. Harold B. Allen of the University of Minnesota sees usage as a three-dimensional continuum moving from speech to writing, from formal to informal, from standard to nonstandard—this continuum movable in space from here to there and in time from then to now. To limit one's linguistic range to one level, then, is like limiting himself to a single set of clothes.

One of my colleagues insists he is a Thoreauvian; one set of clothes suits him fine. But Thoreau's clothes had to fit him; he had especially large pockets sewn onto that one suit. And his conversations with the woodchopper Therien destroy the analogy between Thoreau's language and his one suit of clothes. Truly individual usage is the most obvious result of choice among varieties of usage.

James Sledd of the University of Texas suggests how many teachers regard usage when he notes the seven most common attitudes. The first denies all standards; it assumes that whatever a person says is right for him. The second does not question either, but it relies on an observance of rules. They are simply to be obeyed, not to be reasoned about. The third is the standard of "unrationalized taste." Let your feelings be your guide and cultivate those feelings in others. The fourth, which appeals to the "factual minded," turns to the prestige dialect for its standard. "Whatever is in the language of the chosen people must be right." The fifth reveres the tradition of the past. It wants only to preserve useful distinctions and to retard linguistic change. The sixth is committed to social mobility; it encourages the usage that will enable the student to rise in the world. The last is the one that surmounts these confusions and narrow loyalties. It can only commit itself completely, from one paper to the next, to the particular fitness of means and end, the appropriateness of the language to the writer's specific purpose. It implies a long series of writing experiences which train the student to measure the effectiveness rather than the correctness of his language. How appropriate is his usage to the situation, the writer, the audience, and the subject matter? This is how we explain to the pupil what we mean by good English.

This seventh method demands of teacher and pupil knowledge of the subject matter of English: its structure, literature, and rhetoric, as well as know-how in using reports on the facts of modern usage. The seven standards, so rooted in a teacher's linguistic and social philosophy, are debatable. And perhaps at different times in the child's development one or another standard makes most sense. But the teacher of adolescents has little choice. Anything but the seventh way of looking at a student's language is doomed to failure not only because of the nature of language but also because of the nature of adolescence.

This is the time when, as if to right a pious wrong, and to heal an old wound, the adolescent renounces his childhood faith in elders at home and in school. Narrow prescription of any form of behavior only hastens and intensifies his revolt. The questions, the rudeness, the defiance are infuriating. But they are healthy signs of autonomy. Only half child, half man that he is, he repudiates the language of his elders only to accept with utter faith and fealty the jargon of his peers. Their slang becomes holy writ, be it as stereotyped as their hair-do's, and as ephemeral as their braces and acne. And the mother who, for the sake of togetherness, tries to adopt their lingo, becomes as ridiculous as a dowager with a pony tail or a matron with an above-the-varicose-kneed hemline. While the adolescent questions, rebels, and passionately aligns himself with new causes and groups, the teacher's attitude toward language can either help him to find himself or alienate him even more from the adult world.

When a student discovers that his English teacher's goal is not to uphold the purity of the language or to oil the tracks to success or to spread a private gospel about style but to listen to what he has to say, the first reaction may be surprise or deep suspicion. Maybe putting content before correctness and flexibility before consistency is the school teacher's equivalent of pony tail or hemline! But when classroom discussions and private conferences only confirm what we are calling the seventh method, suspicion may give way to writing on subjects that concern him deeply, no matter how far removed they may seem from the syllabus. Although the adolescent still gives his days to adolescent allies, he may begin to give his nights not to Addison and Steele but to his journal. The teacher who has won this victory knows better than to take red pencil to that journal; correctness is a minor virtue here. Of course journals are only a rare and happy way to develop flexibility and judgment about standards. But the English teacher can't afford not to gamble on this kind of success.

Meanwhile, flexibility and judgment have to be sought in more direct ways for the entire class. Standards begin or end, then, with the kind of teacher the school can provide. Louise Higgins, who has trained both teachers and students, has solved the problem first with

> We are not interested in the reactionary teacher who does little but polish the subjunctive for the dress parade; we are not interested in the radical who purports that language only lives when it is doing syntactical somersaults. We want teachers who can handle all the levels . . . one who has thorough training, proficiency on the various usage levels, and an understanding of the milieu in which she works.[1]

In her own classes, she sets the example for the teachers she has hired:

> . . . using a myriad of examples from all forms of communication— good, bad, and appalling, I constantly call the attention of my students to the difference between written and spoken English. . . . The first big distinction I make is that between public and private utterance. . . . From the vantage point of public language, I make other subdivisions. There are obviously legal, business, journalistic, scientific levels of usage, to name a few. Within these levels, I place formal and informal expression. . . . Informal English is used in the bulk of our public utterances. . . . Third, in dealing with usage, I

[1] V. Louise Higgins, "Approaching Usage in the Classroom," *English Journal,* **49** (March 1960), 182. Used by permission of the author.

have found that the primary need of the language neophyte is some kind of order. My plan of order is the approach by levels. . . . Fourth, I make frequent use of reference books, but I try to make my selection eclectic. . . . Besides specific references, a teacher has to make use of what I can only term "common sense" observation of language. . . . No matter how eclectic her references, the teacher-arbiter can become unduly restrictive if she does not keep in mind that her important job is not corrective but constructive. . . . I make it very clear that I neither built the house nor did I designate the doors. In this case, I am merely an agent showing off the real estate. I have the key to the front door, and once the student has the concept of usage levels I have given him the key. The back door is always ajar.[2]

Maybe this is what the Commission on the English Curriculum of the National Council of Teachers of English were hoping for when, in 1952, they took a stand on usage:

1. Language changes constantly.
2. Change in language is normal.
3. The spoken language is primary.
4. Correctness rests upon usage.
5. All usage is relative.[3]

How, then, is the English teacher to "correct" these two ninth-grade compositions?[4]

The Horror Chamber

Sitting nervously in the high white chair, his hands sweat feverishly, while he gripped the arms of the chair as if he were holding on to life itself. His leg muscles rippled from the strain. His stomach was in a state of nausea and the cold sweat on his brow did not help matters. Suddenly, a man dressed in a white suit peered over him, tension kept growing. A second did not elapse, the pain was intense. Closing his eyes tightly shut, all he could visualize was a black whirlpool that seemed to be devouring his body. Then all of a sudden the pain ceased, the beads of perspiration were gone and so was the fear. He slowly opened his eyes. Simultaneously, the dentist said, "We'll get the other cavity next time, Mr. Jones."

[2] *Ibid.*, pp. 183–185.
[3] Commission on the English Curriculum, *The English Language Arts*. NCTE Curriculum Series Volume I (New York: Appleton-Century-Crofts, 1952), pp. 275–277.
[4] The two compositions are from "An Articulated Program in Literature for Grades Seven through Twelve," Newton Public Schools, Newton, Massachusetts, 1964. Used by permission of the Public Schools of Newton, Massachusetts.

That's Reality for You

You know, kids learn alot of interesting things from television.
And gee, if it wasn't for the good old T.V., they might have to live
in utter ignorance all their lives. For one thing, they find out,
through repition, that there are big bad gangsters in Chicago and
New York. Wow, how would you like to go through life not knowing that? And kids learn too that the bad guy or gangster always
loses in the end and that there are a bunch of nice clean-cut cops
on every corner to shot someone dead. Without good old television,
look how kids today wouldn't know how reality really is. That these
great Medicial Shows, for instance, that have made such a hit these
days. Boy, before they went on the air I didn't even want to be a
doctor. But now I really have changed my mind. Just think of all
those adventures you would go through. And what about those
pretty patients and nurses you have to work with. Wow, I wish I
could grow up real fast so I could be a doctor. But there is only one
problem. Everyone who watches television knows that you have to
be handsome to be a doctor. Well, maybe I can be a villian out
west. You know, there's badmen out West even now. I learned that
from a show I watched last night.

One pupil has evidently been taught to write correctly; the other
has not learned to write correctly. Yet one will have to do some unlearning before he substitutes outer control for inner control of language. To achieve a real sense of freedom, which has nothing to do
with license, the pupil has to discover, through his own successes and
failures, what Edwin Sauer feels all English teachers should remember: "Language is forever a matter of risk, adaptation, experiment,
judgment, and common sense . . . its vigor and resourcefulness are in
proportion to our willingness to take chances with it."

In our time, such discovery does not come easily to pupil or to
teacher, in spite of the great advances in linguistic knowledge and the
new textbooks reflecting that knowledge. It is still the old story: "The
lyf so short, the craft so long to lerne,/Th'assay so hard, so sharp the
conquerynge." Nor do the models on the mass media simplify our
choice. Glibness, slickness, sloppiness, deadness, oneness—what
Randolph Quirk of University College, London, calls "tongue rot"
and what Thomas Pyles of the University of Florida fears as "a
nationwide caste dialect"—reach wider and wider audiences. But so do
the words of a Churchill, a Kennedy, and a Stevenson. The teacher's
job is not to protect the student from these alternatives in usage
but to equip him to choose wisely among them. Only a respect for
individual expression, an urgency toward sharing ideas, a readiness

to consult authoritative rather than authoritarian references can make standards in and out of the classroom pertinent. And if an old poet like Horace reminds us that usage determines the standard, a young poet like Denise Levertov helps us to hear it:[5]

A Common Ground

i

To stand on common ground
here and there gritty with pebbles
yet elsewhere 'fine and mellow—
uncommon fine for ploughing'

there to labor
planting the vegetable words
diversely in their order
that they come to virtue!

To reach those shining pebbles,
that soil where uncommon men
have labored in their virtue
and left a store

of seeds for planting!
To crunch on words
grown in grit or fine
crumbling earth, sweet

to ear and sweet
to be given, to be eaten
in common, by laborer
and hungry wanderer . . .

ii

In time of blossoming,
of red
buds, of red
margins upon
white petals among the
new green, of coppery
leaf-buds, still weakly
folded, fuzzed
with silver hairs—

when on the grass verges
or elephant-hide rocks, the lunch hour
expands, the girls

[5] From *The Jacob's Ladder* by Denise Levertov. © 1958, '59, '60, '61 by Denise Levertov Goodman. Reprinted by permission of the publishers, New Directions Publishing Corporation and Jonathan Cape Limited.

laugh at the sun, men
in business suits awkwardly
recline, the petals
float and fall into
crumpled wax-paper, cartons
of hot coffee—

to speak as the sun's
deep tone of May gold speaks
or the spring chill in the rock's shadow,
a piercing minor scale running across the flesh
aslant—or petals
that dream their way
(speaking by being white
by being
curved, green-centered, falling
already while their tree
is half-red with buds) into

human lives! Poems stirred
into paper coffee-cups, eaten
with petals on rye in the
sun—the cold shadows in back
and the traffic grinding the
borders of spring—entering
human lives forever,
unobserved, a spring element . . .

> . . . everything in the world must
> excel itself to be itself.
> —PASTERNAK

iii

Not 'common speech'
a dead level
but the uncommon speech of paradise,
tongue in which oracles
speak to beggars and pilgrims:

not illusion but what Whitman called
'the path
between reality and the soul,'
a language
excelling itself to be itself,

speech akin to the light
with which at day's end and day's
renewal, mountains
sing to each other across the cold valleys.

TOWARD A COURSE OF STUDY

18

Do the new developments cited in this book ignore the facts admitted by the National Council of Teachers of English? According to their recent poll only one half of 7,417 high school English teachers had majored in English or literature, one third of the other majors were only remotely connected with English, and English teachers below the high school level proved even less prepared to teach their subject. In another study, nearly two thirds of the secondary teachers consider themselves poorly equipped to teach composition and speech, and 90 per cent feel even less qualified to teach reading. And who even mentions language? Since two thirds is larger than one half, may we infer that even a college major in English does not prepare many of our teachers for their English classes? The U.S. Commissioner of Education warned of the shortage of adequately prepared English teachers and urged federal aid not just for the sciences but also for the humanities, especially English. An amendment to the 1958 National Defense Education Act (NDEA) provides this aid.

If English teaching is found wanting today, it is not by comparison with that of the past but by contrast with two realities that never faced us in the past: an explosion in pupil enrollment (more are going through high school and on to college than ever before in our history) and a revolution in course content (as we have noted, linguistic knowledge has broadened and deepened within the last decade as never before in our history). At such a time who dares to generalize about what goes on or should go on in the English classroom? But merely to pursue past excellence in language study is to deny the essence of language: change.

Still, changes in enrollment and in content involve means rather than goals. Although we have more youngsters to take farther than ever before, the ultimate goal of most language study remains precise, effective, and occasionally joyous communication: to be able to converse and write fluently, to listen and read easily, and to get some pleasure therefrom. Only wishing won't make them so. Each of these skills represents a complex of acquired abilities and functions, all of which we feel should be related. But until we know more about how we learn in general and how we acquire language in particular, we can only approximate the relationships. Some helpful clues have already come from studies of aphasia. "Disintegration of the verbal pattern," Roman Jakobson tells us, "may provide the linguist with new insights into the general laws of language. . . . aphasic regression . . . shows the child's development in reverse." We become aware of the rules where something happens to disturb the rules. But the clues are reciprocal. To understand language breakdown, we have to understand what language is and how it works. Other clues come from data processing for computers or electronic brains, which ideally require a complete description of a language. A machine, unlike a baby, will not talk or think unless it is fed more precise linguistic information than can now approximate the baby's built-in equipment for integrating, patterning, and selecting. Input and output, encoding and decoding must be carefully calibrated. The child is the linguist's ideal; the computer is the linguist's guinea pig. And Pavlov's dog has gone to his eternal reward; learning is more than conditioning. Incomplete as our knowledge is, we already know how much goes into language production—exclusive of feeling. Every day linguists, pediatricians, psychologists, neurologists, electronics engineers, audiologists, and teachers are telling us more. And while the language system itself implies a rigor, precision, and explicitness we intuitively command, we seem to be unweaving a rainbow. As a behavioral science, English presents unique frustrations.

What are the implications for a course of study? The English teacher can learn from, but cannot wait for, the linguists. He has to do his best with what is now known, and his best calls for humility. There is no magic formula or perfect sequence for applying our fragmentary knowledge of language to the pupil's growth in using language. The English teacher knows better than to play magician or God though sometimes, especially when tired, or on the defensive, he sounds like God's deputy. Yet he knows, too, that in reformulating knowledge he is not sacrificing past certainties. To a large extent, past successes can be attributed to the English spoken in the homes of most college-bound students years ago and to their considerable studies in ancient and modern foreign languages. Often these cultural and educational advantages are mistaken for a better grammar or sounder classroom technique or higher standards of yesteryear.

Moreover, we Americans would be the last ones to profit from a magic formula even if we had all the answers to our questions about language. So far our entire democratic tradition has avoided the shibboleths and decrees of an academy. When Laurence Wylie of Harvard University visited a French school a few years ago, he reported:

> The rules are considered important because it is believed that a person cannot express himself properly unless he knows them thoroughly. It is difficult for an Anglo Saxon to comprehend how essential this language study is to the French. The French judge a person to a far greater degree than we do on the basis of his ability to speak and write correctly.[1]

A sophisticated American immediately asks, "What do you mean by *correct?*" Or he converts *correct* to *Standard* English. But, as we have seen in the section on usage, dictionary makers themselves hardly agree on *Standard* without context.

A national standardized English course, then, would not make real sense. To deny schools their local autonomy might help a few poor schools, but it would harm more good schools. Such a course would assume uniform speech and identical needs. It would only establish hurdles that test persistence rather than potential or achievement— like the barriers confronting the Nigerian schoolboy. He has to pass

[1] Arthur J. Carr and William Steinhoff (eds.), *Points of Departure* (New York: Harper & Row, Publishers, 1960).

a written test on *The Rape of the Lock* and the first two books of *Paradise Lost* to prove he is ready for a British university. A standardized course would also assume that we really know how a human being learns, that we know the deep subsurface structure of the English language, that we have a complete description on which to base our usage rules, our reading and writing skills. But our language study is in a state of growth and transition. Style and usage are in flux. Moreover, there is less agreement on how and what to teach in language than in literature or in composition, which have been thriving on diversity, if not incertitude, for a long time. There is much deliberation, experiment, debate, and dissent today. We have outgrown complacency and we will not retreat to a false certainty. This is why teachers feel unprepared. They mistrust the pat solutions of yesteryear; they are aware of a new ferment.

Meanwhile what makes an English language program truly contemporary? Still the names you recall from your own school days—but with a difference. Reading, writing, punctuation, spelling, grammar, usage, logic, semantics, rhetoric—the first are two of the three R's, basic tools for every man. But what of the rest, which constitute language? What knowledge, what understanding, what skills do they include? How do they lead to our ultimate goal of precise, effective communication? All are usually built into the English course of study, whether it is handed down by the school, the community, or the state. But a course is only a guide, never an edict. It provides some progression, avoids needless repetition, enables the new pupil and teacher (with one out of every four American families on the move each year) to fit their English knowledge and skills into a larger framework. It is never more than a blueprint for a particular structure.

Let's assume that Mr. Quidditch heads the high school English department or supervises English in a district that is willing to pay for good education for its children. His job is not simply to keep book inventories and teacher dossiers. To hold on to the point of view from both sides of the desk, he has a limited class load. But he leaves time to visit other classes, to read, to think, and to aim for a sound language program from kindergarten through grade twelve—and in more and more cities—through grade fourteen.

Whether by choice or necessity, Mr. Q. is involved in today's ferment. He still believes that reading, writing, and language study are basic essentials of an English program. But he knows their relatedness is based more on tradition than on evidence. And what is *basic* to the language program: punctuation, spelling, grammar, usage, logic, semantics, rhetoric? Call his favorite *it*. How does he know when to introduce *it,* how much of *it* to teach at each level, how to provide continuity, how to respect individual differences, which texts to use, how much emphasis to place on oral work, how to combine *its* past and present, how to alert teachers to new studies in *it,* how to correlate *it* with subjects other than English, and finally how to correlate *it* with the other *it*s that might seem equally important to another English supervisor?

If he regards reading and writing as the mere recognition and recall required by our colonial district schools, his choice will be easy. And it will comfort those who find their answers to today's complex problems by ignoring them and citing the excellent solutions of the past. Reading (or literature), writing (or composition), and language do not compete; they coexist and, we hope, interrelate. If Mr. Quidditch decides mechanics, punctuation, or spelling is basic, he is training a generation not of readers but of proofreaders. But who will train the readers and writers for him? If he decides on grammar, usage, logic, semantics, or rhetoric, he will be asked, "Which one of each do you mean among our competing grammars, usages, logics, semantics, rhetorics?" And when the competition gets rough, he can say, "A curse on *all* your houses" and decide to do without them all —sans grammar, usage, logic, semantics, rhetoric, sans taste, sans everything—until the sages in the universities and in the marketplace recall that the educated man does not look for greater simplicity than his subject will allow. What to do with English—and the children— meanwhile? Chaucer and Emerson send them huckleberrying. In our time, Rachel Carson says, "Better not."

But Mr. Quidditch need not dwell in darkness nor need he wait for the great light. If he can keep his good teachers, he can count on their knowledge, experience, common sense, and commitment to the continued search in their own education. Constant self-appraisal and reexamination of *what* is being taught and *why* and *how* have always characterized the best English programs. He can also turn to specialists at the nearby universities, to scholarly texts, to professional publications and meetings, to special studies by his state, regional, and national associations of English teachers, to the USOE Program in English (sponsored by the United States Office of Education), to the Commission on English (created by the College Entrance Examination Board), and to teacher institutes under the NDEA. Sabbatical leaves for teachers' intensive study, feedback from graduates of the school, new ideas from alert teachers—all these will help Mr. Q. to hammer out a good course of study. How good will depend on the commitment of the teachers to testing materials over an extended period of time, on the flexibility the course allows teachers and pupils in working toward clearly defined objectives, on realistic conditions of course load and pupil load. A recent issue of the *NEA Journal* singles out for praise a California high school teacher who, after working with 160 pupils per day, corrects their compositions, plans his lessons, and criticizes scripts for the *Mr. Novak* TV series. The best course of study in the world fails under such conditions.

Portland, Oregon, was a pioneer in tackling enormous problems with the help of the experts. The supervisor of English, Miss Marian Zollinger, tells the story in part:

> The public schools in Portland, Oregon, have recently had a rare opportunity to plan and produce a program for high school English which includes a four-year sequence of language study. Many of the high school English teachers there during the last three years have extended their professional education by taking courses in linguistics, have come to feel a new responsibility regarding high school instruction in language, and have developed a series of studies to be included in the four years of the high school curriculum. This year these study units are being used at each grade in twenty-four pilot classes. Although the project has yet to be formally evaluated [this was written in 1962], the experiment is under way and units are being taught as an integral part of the English class work. The present description of language study in Portland high schools must as yet, however, be considered merely a progress report.
>
> The circumstance which gave impetus to the work in linguistics was a system-wide evaluation of the total high school curriculum for students whose academic interest and achievement were average or high. In 1958, the School Board, with financial aid from the Fund for the Advancement of Education, sponsored a study of the high schools by college professors, who were then to furnish recommendations for improving high school training of potential college students. Their survey and report and the ensuing work done by the high school teachers, with the assistance of college professors, have affected the curriculum for about half of the high school students. A similar study is continuing currently, with the aim to improve the curriculum for the other half, that is, the students who are less able or less interested in academic work.
>
> The survey by the college professors was directed for almost two years by Dr. Albert Kitzhaber, now of Dartmouth College. During that time a selected group of professors visited classes, examined textbooks, perused courses of study, discussed educational problems with teachers, and finally made a series of recommendations. The reports were directed toward the work of English, social studies, science, mathematics, art and music. Teacher committees in each

subject were then invited to study the recommendations and use them to advantage in preparing a revised program for students who were potentially of college ability. A large part of the fund was used to provide released hours during the school year for those who took special responsibility in curriculum planning and for stipends awarded to applicants to attend summer institutes in 1960 and 1961. The institutes included classes or seminars at graduate level; in English eight courses dealt with literature, language, and speech. In the summer of 1961 teachers' guides were also prepared during the six-weeks' workshop by those appointed to the writing session. The writers in the English group, including six college professors and nine classroom English teachers, produced *A Teacher's Guide for English A, Grades 9–12* [later renamed *Guide for High School English, Vol. I*], a volume with complete course outlines and scholarly notes on every study topic in the four-year course.

The following summary of curriculum development describes only the work on language in the English classes. During the initial survey, Dr. Paul Roberts, of San Jose State College, studied the existing curriculum and wrote recommendations for change in the teaching of language. Later, after the teacher committees were formed, Dr. W. Nelson Francis, Franklin and Marshall College, served as the consultant in linguistics and as a member of the writing group. In the two summer institutes, Dr. Graham Wilson and Dr. Donald Alden, both of San Jose State College, gave forty-five class hours of instruction on linguistics to about sixty high school English teachers. During the school year, two members of the high school staff each conducted weekly inservice training classes amounting to twenty class hours to introduce about a hundred others to a study that held much that was new and interesting to most teachers of English. This year the inservice classes are continuing with full enrollments. This training, of course, is only a beginning in an extensive field of scholarship. It has, however, proved useful in introducing the teachers to more accurate facts about language from recent research and helping them to establish important points of view about the approach to language study. The textbooks and the teacher's guide also provide the teachers with a good deal of assistance in the language units they teach.[2]

Since this report was written, the Portland schools have modified and advanced their program and have been sharing revisions of their course of study with teachers everywhere.

Here is a course typical of those that have emerged since World War II where teachers in a department of English decide to revise.[3]

[2] Marian Zollinger, "Language Study in High School English Classes," *The English Leaflet,* LXI, 1 (1962), 43. Used by permission of *The English Leaflet* and Marian Zollinger.

[3] From the course of study in English developed by the University of Illinois High School, Urbana, Illinois, 1960–1964, under the direction of Professor

Again, it represents not an ideal but a real course with the usual combination of strengths and weaknesses:

Since 1960 the English staff at University High School has been developing a sequential curriculum for use in junior and senior high school classes. University High School, which is the laboratory school of the College of Education at the University of Illinois, has an accelerated program which handles junior and senior high school English in five years. Because our students are selected for ability, the subfreshman-junior sequence corresponds to conventional grades roughly as follows:

> subfreshman ....7th and 8th grades
> freshman ....9th and 10th grades
> sophomore ....11th grade
> junior ....12th grade

The major work of the project is the preparation of daily lesson plans which, when complete, will constitute the teaching materials and procedures for grades 7 through 12.

The curriculum develops from two basic assumptions: that English is not a collection of vaguely related subject units, but a single discipline which has its unity in the communication process; that the sequence of lessons from grades 7 through 12 spirals out from basic concepts which are learned in grades 7 to 9.

The first assumption suggests the overall organization of the curriculum, which may be diagrammed as follows:

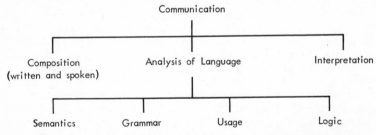

As the chart suggests, the curriculum is language-centered. Students are at all times engaged in one or a combination of three kinds of activities. They are putting ideas or experience into a language structure (composing); they are getting ideas or experiences out of a language structure (interpreting); or they are analyzing language in terms of its grammatical, semantic, and rhetorical structure. But ... the core of the curriculum is the study of the relation of form and meaning in language. Such a study views semantics, grammar, usage, logic, and rhetoric as interrelated aspects of communication.

The second basic assumption suggests the sequence of the cur-

James M. McCrimmon. Used by permission of James M. McCrimmon as submitted to the author in 1964.

riculum. The function of the work in the junior high school years is to establish the tools of analysis—the basic communication concepts—and to begin to develop proficiency in using these tools in composition and interpretation. The function of the work in the senior high school years is to extend analysis to increasingly mature levels. A brief summary of the work in each area will illustrate the sequence.

Semantics. The work begins in the 7th grade with an elementary analysis of the relation between words and things, the role of context, the process of classification, the nature of class names, and the concept of abstraction. In the 8th and 9th grades this study is extended to provide a fuller understanding of the relation of language and its tendency to simplify and stabilize experience. In these grades also, the characteristics of informative and affective statements are identified and used in the interpretation of prose and poetry. In the 10th grade the study of the relation of language and experience is extended to include the influence of language on perception, thus completing the view of language as a means of selecting, organizing, and recording experience. This completes the formal study of semantics. Thereafter semantic analysis is a continuing part of the interpretation of literature.

Grammar. The study of grammar is chiefly the work of the junior high school years, it being our judgment that continuing the study of grammar through the senior high school years wastes time through unprofitable duplication of earlier lessons. The work begins with a review of the inflected parts of speech (morphology) and then proceeds through syntax ... to sentence building. In the 9th grade grammatical analysis moves into a study of the rhetorical effect of particular sentence structures, such as the parallel and periodic sentences. Thereafter, attention to grammar is limited to specific problems in composition and interpretation.

Usage. Usage, as contrasted with grammar, is concerned with bringing a student's language habits into accord with the practices of educated writers and speakers. This work is largely remedial and is handled chiefly by constant attention to proofreading and by periodic exercises in spelling and punctuation. Some individual students may need to continue work on usage in the senior high school years, but a major effort is made to establish satisfactory language habits by the end of grade 9.

Logic. This part of the curriculum is just beginning to be developed. It will probably begin in the 10th grade and will be closely related to the work of persuasion in the 12th grade.

Composition. Written composition is a major part of the curriculum in each grade from 7 through 12. All writing is directly related to current work in language and literature. The earliest emphasis is on *specific* communication, especially the use of examples to illustrate general statements. This is followed by close attention to the structure of paragraphs and by practice in using the most common paragraph structures. In the 9th grade the concept of purpose is introduced, and in that grade and the tenth considerable attention is given to the control imposed by the writer's purpose in the selection, organization, and development of the material, and on the style and tone of the writing. From the 10th grade on, most of the writing is thematic—that is, the function of the essay is to develop the implications of a theme or thesis. In each grade, students write more than is customary in high school classes, and as a general procedure selected essays are projected, duplicated, or read aloud for classroom evaluation.

Work in speech composition is largely confined to the 11th and 12th grades, and much of it is concentrated in a sustained experience with persuasion during the second half of the 12th grade. In this work students select a controversial question of public policy, study the background of the problem and the proposals which have been offered for its solution, and then evaluate the proposals through debate. The purpose of the debate is to discover the most acceptable solution rather than to engage in competitive conflict.

Interpretation. During the junior high school years the work in interpretation is approached from two points of view—developmental reading, which includes vocabulary building and reading for comprehension and speed, and the interpretation of literature. Thereafter the work is confined to the study of literature.

The general approach to literature in all grades is through analysis of the structure of the work, using the word "structure" in its most comprehensive sense to mean the sum of all elements in the work which affect interpretation. We propose to attempt a more precise definition later; at present we recognize the following as structural elements: vocabulary, grammatical structure, the metrical pattern of a poem, the selection and omission of material and the emphasis given to particular material, the point of view, the author's attitude towards his subject and audience, the theme, the relation of parts to the whole, the integrity of the work, the purpose as induced from all these observations, the world or universe within the work, the system of values that prevails in that world, and the relation of these values to dominant human concerns. The progression from 7th to 12th grades is from simple to complex structures—from simple action stories in the 7th grade ("The Most Dangerous Game") to "Hamlet" and "Oedipus" in the 12th grade. As a staff, we are now trying to establish a scale of complexity, partly to determine what should be taught at what grades, but chiefly to discover the nature of the teaching problem in any work we select.

This report, written in 1962, represents one kind of teamwork. Since then, grants have enabled schools to work on curriculum together with university professors and researchers. Donald Bateman of Ohio State University, for example, has been heading a project which is trying to find out how a knowledge of transformational grammar affects a student's writing in grades nine and ten. Is the sentence structure in his later compositions more sophisticated? Can he subordinate and sustain ideas? "We are trying to keep a running account of our understanding of the nature of generative grammar, its place in the English program, and the problems attending its teaching. . . . If one thinks of a generative grammar as a theory of sentence formation, then it seems to follow that the study of composition, which is sentence formation certainly, could not be carried on independently of the grammar." These are Mr. Bateman's tentative assertions in August, 1963. His project, completed in 1964, is one of many seeking evidence of the practical applications of a knowledge of sentence structure.[4]

The Cooperative Research Branch of the United States Office of Education is sponsoring in its Program in English (Project English) twelve different curriculum study centers. The University of Nebraska and the University of Wisconsin are working on grades kindergarten through twelve. The University of Georgia and Columbia University are concentrating on the elementary grades; Florida State University and Hunter College, the junior high; the University of Oregon, the University of Minnesota, Indiana University, grades seven through twelve; Carnegie Institute of Technology, on the high school years.

A typical curriculum center brings together classroom teachers and university professors to devise and test new teaching materials, which are then tried out in various school districts close to the project center. Each school system assigns several teachers to work with the professors at the university. Inservice summer courses show the rest of the teachers how to use the materials that have been prepared. The aim is not to produce a perfect course of study but to suggest standards and substance for a modern English curriculum. The Nebraska project has prepared over five thousand pages of curricular materials. One curriculum center, for example, with Carnegie support, produced films on transformational grammar.

These projects explore curriculum by many means. Some concentrate on composition, others on language or literature. Some compare the effectiveness of separating and combining the three. Some

[4] Donald R. Bateman and Frank J. Zidonis, *The Effect of a Study of Transformational Grammar on the Writing of Ninth and Tenth Graders.* NCTE Research Report No. 6 (Champaign, Ill.: National Council of Teachers of English, 1966).

concentrate on special needs: the gifted, the special, or underprivileged student. Some, on special interests: drama, creative writing, English as a second language. Some, on concepts from psychology, anthropology, sociology, and linguistics. Some are testing thematic units. Some, Bruner's spiral theory of cognitive growth. Here basic concepts, clearly presented with ever deepening meaning, are the framework for the course of study.

The most careful work in new language study has been coming out of the University of Oregon's Project English curriculum center, where explicit materials (separate descriptions and instructions for teachers and pupils and specific units) have been prepared by teams of expert teachers, scholars, and researchers. They are not rushing toward a deadline; they have been proceeding cautiously, grade by grade, trying out materials, reformulating, and explicating. Their work is certainly a starting point for any English teachers who are concerned with new linguistic knowledge and its implications for curriculum writing.

Mr. Quidditch, by getting on the mailing list of the *Newsletter* put out by the U.S. Office of Education Program in English, can keep up with all these developments. But he need not stop with reading. He can see for himself how these projected ideas work in the classroom, and he can confer with others about his special interests in curriculum. Through a federal Office of Education grant to Western Reserve University, the Demonstration Center in English at Euclid Central Junior High School held a series of three-day and week-long conferences. Workshops, discussion groups, classroom observations, and guest speakers concentrated at different times on specific parts of a total English curriculum for grades seven through nine: structure in language and literature, theme-centered curricula, reading skills, and composition. Research in English, Modern Approaches to Literature, and Composition engage those who come for "concentrated study of major problems in English instruction." Another center at Syracuse University demonstrates how reading can be taught in grades seven through twelve. Films and teachers' manuals will be of use in college methods courses.

In addition to curriculum development and demonstration programs, the Office of Education sponsors work in basic research, small contracts, and research and development centers. Already there are available monographs and reports from these many projects. Among those which have invited a new look at our textbooks is Ruth G. Strickland's *The Language of Elementary School Children,* which examines children's listening control and effectiveness in speaking, reading, and writing during the first six years of school.[5]

The Commission on English, appointed by the College Entrance Examination Board (CEEB) in 1959, has prepared teaching materials, sample examinations, reading lists, and kinescopes and has planned and run summer institutes for career teachers of high school English. The experience of these institutes has been invaluable to those designing later institutes under the National Defense Education Act. The 1959–1963 Progress Report had this to say about language study:

> In the study of language, an area neglected by most teachers and in most training courses, the summer institute program and the syllabus developed three principal aims: (1) to make the teacher aware of language as a field of study; (2) to show him the basic assumptions and methods of modern linguistic study; (3) to encourage him to undertake further study in language, and to offer guidelines for that study. Phonology, systems of syntax, linguistic variety and problems of standard usage, and the history of the English language were included in the study units.[6]

The far-reaching effects will be interesting to watch. English teachers do want training and retraining. Applications for one summer NDEA institute in language ran to 1100, in literature to 700, although there could be only 30 accepted in each group. And this was a typical or even less-than-average demand.

Similarly, the College Entrance Examination Board is not shirking its responsibility. Already work is under way to prepare a separate language achievement test that will at first be optional. Eventually a section on language may be added to the regular English Achievement Test. Schools that incorporate new language study into their regular English programs will want to see the results. They will want to see how their students perform on a nationwide test of linguistic knowledge.

Ultimately, however, what makes sense for other schools will not make the same sense for Mr. Q.'s school. His course must be ready for the transfer pupil from and to these different schools; but it must first serve the needs of his own community. There was a time when a man had to live where he worked. Speedways and subways have

[5] Ruth G. Strickland, *The Language of Elementary School Children: Its Relationship to the Language of Reading Textbooks and the Quality of Reading of Selected Children.* Bulletin of the School of Education, Indiana University, **38,** 4 (July 1962) (Bloomington: Indiana University, 1962).

[6] Commission on English, *A Progress Report for 1959–63* (Boston, Mass.: CEEB Commission on English, 1963). Out of print.

enlarged his choice. Now he prefers to live where his children will get the best education, even if he has to commute to work. The community's best real estate salesman is often its schools, whose excellences cannot simply be copied. One school system, for example, has built into its program a rich unit on dialects in Oregon: on variations in word history, pronunciations, and meanings. But such a unit could serve only as a springboard for teachers in Texas or Massachusetts.

Yet, no matter where the school, the child must progress from the simplest comprehension exercise in the elementary grades:

Fish live in water. They swim and swim all day. They cannot live on land. If you take them out of water, they will soon

A. walk
B. die
C. run away
D. get lost

to the most demanding exercise in the twelfth grade:

Directions: *Study the following poem carefully before starting to answer the questions.*[7]

On My First Son

Farewell, thou child of my right hand, and joy:
My sin was too much hope of thee, loved boy.
Seven years thou wert lent to me, and I thee pay,
Exacted by thy fate, on the just day.
O could I lose all father now! for why
Will man lament the state he should envy—
To have so soon 'scaped the world's and flesh's rage,
And if no other misery, yet age?
Rest in soft peace, and asked, say, "Here doth lie
Ben Jonson his best piece of poetry;
For whose sake henceforth all his vows be such
As what he loves may never like too much."

One of the questions is *Write a paraphrase of lines 3–4, making sure that both the literal and the figurative meanings of such words as "thee . . . exacted . . . just" are clear.*

In the first grade, he fits words into a simple, clear context

It is hot in _____.	winter
It is cold in _____.	supper
I like to eat _____ and _____.	summer
	dinner

[7] The following sample question is reprinted with permission from the 1964 edition of *Advanced Placement Program: Course Descriptions* published by the College Entrance Examination Board, New York.

with the usual penalties for deviation from standard idiom and standardized thinking!

Eleven years later the English Achievement Test of the CEEB expects him to be able to cope not only with structure and meaning, but also with rhythm, mood, and tone which provide multiple levels of meaning in a poem. For a good poem is an intricate contraption. It is "a structure, an ordered experience, built up through various kinds of meaning controlled in turn by various uses of language," says Reuben Brower. "To confront a work of literature," he continues, "means responding to particular uses of language, to words and their arrangement . . . from the barely referential to the rhythmic." Language, then, is one part of literary study. But it is only one part, not the whole. The test is concerned with this inseparable end product. Yet the course of study has to devise ways of separating and combining the study of language and literature.

The same is true of composition. In the first grade, your youngster marshals his ideas in a simple sentence. The classroom bulletin board may display news items like

> *Today it is snowing* or
> *My baby sister ate a tube of toothpaste.*

Time goes on and the happy years are fled. All too soon the Achievement Awards Program of the National Council of Teachers of English may give this assignment to your high school junior:

> In his Nobel Prize Address, William Faulkner states that any poet or writer has a duty to write about the truths of the human heart. He goes on to say, "It is his privilege to help man endure by lifting his heart, by reminding him of the courage and honor and hope and pride and compassion and pity and sacrifice which have been the glory of the past."
> As a nominee for one of the NCTE Achievement Award citations, you are asked to write for no more than one hour on "The Truths of the Human Heart Revealed in Literature." Use examples from your own reading to support your observations.[8]

Obviously, no one subject or method paves the way to such achievement. Although it tests general performances in language, it is called an English composition test.

Whatever such tests measure, the credit or the blame must be shared. Mr. Quidditch's course of study—even if Holy Ghost written

---

[8] Impromptu theme topic of NCTE Achievement Award contest, 1961. Used by permission of the National Council of Teachers of English.

—can only be as effective as the English teachers who follow, modify, or ignore it; as the texts, readings, and homework that enliven or kill it; as the other departments that also have standards for pupils' listening, speaking, reading, and writing; as the libraries in home, school, and community; as the capacity for learning engendered in the first four years of life. Answers to the test questions just noted tell more about the pupil's capacity and desire to learn and about the size, quality, use, and growth of the library in his home, school, and community than about Mr. Quidditch's excellent course of study. His is only a quiddity. Yet even in schools where minimal English standards are ignored in science, math, and history class, Mr. Quidditch and his English teachers are most often held solely responsible for the results in these reading and writing tests.

The second half of the revolution, the advance in linguistic knowledge, is indeed Mr. Quidditch's direct concern. As we have seen, the last decade has marked revolution and counterrevolution in language study. The teacher realizes that although use of English is a shared responsibility, nowhere but in his class will the pupil master *knowledge* of the system underlying the sounds we utter and the meanings they convey.

To ask the pupil to engage in talk about such matters as his own style, usage, and appreciation of literature without this systematic knowledge is to build upon a foundation of shifting sand. For the first time we are becoming deeply aware of how our language does work, how words combine to provide meaning. This awareness is a study sufficient unto itself; our language system may prove as interesting a science as our circulatory system or our monetary system. In each we learn how the system works before we decide how it works best. Such knowledge of man's most characteristic activity may in turn affect other kinds of knowledge and activity. We have long felt that to relate our native language to literature and composition, we must first know what characterizes the language we relate them to. To reformulate scientific knowledge from time to time has seemed perfectly reasonable. As language study becomes scientifically based, i.e., capable of predicting and verifying, we are reformulating it and seeking its fundamental relationships to reading and writing. If understanding the structure of the English system will enable the student to connect language, literature, and composition, so much the better.

The English teacher still realizes that reading and writing are his responsibility, though they operate in the pupil's total community. In a sense every teacher is an amateur English teacher. But only the English teacher can be an expert in the English language. Objectively and systematically taught, language is not confined to the English classroom. It can reinforce much of the logical approach in the new math, science, social studies, and foreign language classes. The teacher recognizes the importance of such a language foundation because he has himself been disenchanted with the old grammar and exposed to some of the new. We do not yet have national language tests in English, but the clearest signs lie in the abandonment of the old standardized grammar tests and in the ferment at schools and universities. Language workshops and institutes, new courses, new texts, new requirements for English majors and for teacher certification attest to this second revolution. For Mr. Quidditch and his staff, life will never be dull. The informed teacher knows, then, there is no return. In abandoning the old classroom grammar, he has discarded a dubious certainty for the challenging search, two hundred years of pedagogic refinement for a decade of pioneer study in language.

We could not trace your child's language growth grade by grade. We could not list the knowledge, understandings, and skills to be gained day by day, week by week, year by year—including vacations with you! For learning—language learning especially—does not exist in a vacuum. Your work, your home life, your hobbies, your travels, the examples you set as speaker, listener, reader, and writer inevitably have reinforced or counteracted what went on in the classroom. Look at the talk, the books, the intellectual companionship and stimulation in your home as well as your community. To sharpen perception, deepen thought, and heighten delight, we have to perceive, think, and delight. So long as growth depends on the school, home, and community, a prefabricated course of study will be unrealistic and wasteful. A good language program grows from verifiable knowledge of subject matter adapted to a community's need and resources. And it dares to ask some probing questions. Is the school an educative as well as a social force? What are the goals of most of its students? How much is a good English program worth to the taxpayers? A large, diversified community will need not one but several programs, equally good but with different sources of strength, each in turn allowing for different goals and rates of progress. They are only diverse means to the same ends. And in a democracy they are everybody's concern.

19

The hallmark of English studies in the fifties was revolution and counterrevolution; in the sixties it may be trivia. Derived from the Latin words *tri* (three) and *via* (way), *trivia* means "trifles" or "unimportant matters." For a crossroad or a place where three roads meet is common enough; it confronts every traveler. The road he takes, however, is never common; it is always a choice which becomes part of his particular destiny. Therefore the ancient Romans also named a goddess Trivia and connected her with the three Fates or wayward sisters who confront us at a crossroad. English language study has reached this crucial stage. Either all the alarums and excursions of the fifties will prove to be trivia in the modern sense, or they will shape the destiny of English as a subject for years to come.

Yet there is no turning back. New linguistic knowledge is here, whether we avail ourselves of it in English classrooms or ignore it. New demands for equal education for all are also here, whether we interpret education narrowly as literacy requirements or broadly as development of potential. And new forms of government support have become available to English teachers, whether it be used for upgrading teacher preparation, for redefining content and basic research, for improving learning conditions through smaller classes and better school facilities, or for graduating the profession from genteel poverty to vulgar affluence. The sixties mean undreamed of opportunities for change in English teaching.

The dilemma is understandable. From the first chapter in this book, when we saw that language is an oral, conventional, systematic, symbolic form of communication, we saw that linguistic study was both science and art; that it could no more be confined to the English classroom than to the psychology, anthropology, sociology, physiology, philosophy classroom; that it plays a significant role in metrics and in rhetoric, in mathematics and in electronics; that pediatrician, phonetician, logician, and politician make use of it. The question remains: Who shall keep it and who shall teach it?

Preceding chapters have shown that whoever decides to keep and teach language, whether for its own sake or for practical applications, can now avail himself of a more precise description. Although this book has dealt only with those areas of English that cannot deny new language study, some mention belongs here of the many schools that are already extending their goals beyond linguistic knowledge for its own sake. Some teachers, recognizing that they are not theoreticians but practitioners, not specialists but amateurs, are looking into the practical applications and implications for literature and composition. How can this new knowledge be useful in the classroom? Will it improve reading and writing?

Robert Hogan of the National Council of Teachers of English observes: "Imaginative teachers are finding in the literature textbook, rather than the grammar book, the richest source of materials for linguistic analysis, regardless of the particular grammar they teach." But linguistic analysis serves another purpose in a literature text. A more precise syntax should provide clearer understanding by removing ambiguities. The student who analyzes the structure of Hamlet's

> How stand I then
> That have a father killed, a mother stained?

is not simply trying to find out what the subject, verb, object, and trouble are here. He needs this precise information to know whether or not Hamlet is another Oedipus!

In poetry especially, plain syntactic sense is often a matter of identifying parts of speech, noting inversions of modern word order, hearing the pronunciation in rhymes and puns, and dealing with lexical meanings that are not the obvious ones. In the same play, the student has to know whether Hamlet's "I'll make a ghost of him that lets me" is a threat or a request for permission to murder. Phonemic theory has also invited teachers to reconsider what they have called metrics in verse. The suprasegmentals—stress, pitch, and pause—have been useful. Caesura in Pope's poems, for example, has become much more clearly defined.

The question still remains: How much of this linguistic information and analysis is of serious consequence? Is linguistic analysis a necessary part of literary appreciation? Or is its greatest strength a precise terminology that can help to clarify the critic's methods and fortify his conclusions?

Teachers are also exploring the link between generative grammar and composition. Many grants and graduate theses are concerned with this question. Some teachers feel that composition, which is sentence formation, cannot be studied independently of the grammar. Others cite the need for a new and improved or revived rhetoric if grammar is to contribute to better writing. Meanwhile many English students are transforming sentences to see how they can achieve unity, coherence, emphasis, and variety. They are experimenting with sentence lengths and combining ideas in a more precise and deliberate fashion because they have terms and tools in the grammar. And while classrooms are involved in the practical end of the link between grammar and composition, theoreticians keep extending their own goals. Zellig Harris of the University of Pennsylvania has been analyzing connected discourse. Language samples longer than a sentence may provide more insight into the relation between a knowledge of grammar and competence in writing.

Kenneth Pike of the University of Michigan is convinced composition can be taught through linguistics. Extensive reading and writing, drills on different types of sentence structure, and his tagmemic theory of grammar are the means. Here he analyzes structures as sequences of functional classes in slots. This, too, may contribute to our teaching of composition.

In addition to these practical applications to reading and writing, some are more concerned with implications. The logical basis for the new grammar as well as the new math and science cannot be ignored. The formal study of logic is being introduced not only into regular English programs but also into the early grades. If grammars are being written for elementary students, logics are being tried on these same age groups. Richard G. Morrow of the Cornell Critical Thinking Project is testing the idea that certain kinds of logical-thinking abilities can be taught successfully in grades four through twelve. His group has been teaching some kind of deductive logic (a course usually taught in college) to students at each of these levels for about four weeks.

Another implication strongly connected with other new subjects is semantics. The study of meaning is not new to the schools. Aristotle was very much concerned with it in fourth century pre-Christian Greece. His grammar, logic, and rhetoric dominated European medieval education. These three subjects, known as the trivium, were the liberal arts of the curriculum. Historical linguistics, however, put changes in meanings on a scientific basis. But it remained a philosophical problem as to how words not only transmit thought but also influence it. In our time Bertrand Russell, Alfred Whitehead, and Alfred Korzybski extended the concern. Korzybski's rejection of Aristotelian approaches to meaning became known as General Semantics and was popularized by S. I. Hayakawa and Stuart Chase. Throughout the 1940's Hayakawa's *Language in Thought and Action* was the semantics text in many schools and colleges.[1] Thus far all studies of meaning limited themselves to words. But as soon as we began theorizing about grammar not in terms of morphemes, words, and word classes but in terms of phrase structure and transformations, the horizons of semantics were extended. New semanticists like Jerry Fodor and Jerrold Katz ask instead, "How can a listener derive a single interpretation of a sentence, not an interpretation of all the single words?" Thus they want to account for the relationship not between words and meaning but between structure and meaning. From this theorizing may come new content in semantics for the English classroom. At least we are concerned with more fundamental questions about meaning than with the semantic traps that engaged us in the forties.

Another experiment in the application of current linguistic knowledge is the Formalist Secondary School English Project designed by Professor Chenault Kelly of Eastern Illinois University. This is an attempt to coordinate symbolic logic with discourse about grammar. In forcing the student to "attend to the structures of sentences in a way not accomplished by traditional grammatical discourse . . . it helps them in developing the skills of reading, verbal expression, and problem solving."

From these random samplings of practical applications and further implications, we can see that we have been riding several hobbyhorses toward this crossroad. On the one hand, we are giving serious thought to the nature of our subject, English, and to a redefinition of its content in the light of new knowledge. Every major professional group has become involved in some way: CEEB, NCTE, NEA, MLA, ACLS, NASSP. The College Entrance Examination Board, through its Commission on English, has sought to define the subject as a consensus among teachers of English, to note the essential characteristics in terms of language, literature, and composition, and to offer ideas for improvement of instruction. Its instruments have been summer institutes for almost 900 teachers, kinescopes "to demonstrate sound

[1] S. I. Hayakawa, *Language in Thought and Action* (2nd ed.; New York: Harcourt, Brace & World, Inc., 1964).

practices in the teaching of language, literature, and composition," a book of end-of-the-year examination questions and answers and comments to illustrate "the general range of competence in essay answers written at each grade level" (nine through twelve) . . . and to "provide rich demonstrations of the response good teachers give to the compositions they read," and a report, *Freedom and Discipline.* "The Commission believes that schools and teachers should be free to choose what kind of grammar and what literary works are most appropriate for their own students, but that these choices will be effective only if the teachers have undergone the discipline of professional training, which many now lack." Such an inquiry has taken five years. Lesser but equally serious inquiries are also being conducted by standing committees of the National Council of Teachers of English, and by cooperative studies with the National Education Association, the Modern Language Association, the American Council of Learned Societies, and the National Association of Secondary-School Principals. The greatest help is coming from federal funds through the Office of Education and the National Defense Education Act. Conferences, institutes, workshops, fellowships, reports, position papers—all concern themselves with content, teacher preparation, research, or improving teaching conditions.

The road, then, is heavy with traffic. On the one hand, we are redefining our subject and finding better ways to integrate language, composition, and literature. On the other hand, we are trying to articulate grades K through twelve. Although we have abandoned long established ideas about grammar and usage, we have several competing grammars without the school texts that would do them justice, and we have questions of usage still left unanswered without any serious inquiry into the nature of standards and of error in language. So we find that the quotations in the Introduction of this book still raise the basic questions. Is English a tool subject, as the *Daily News* suggests, or is it so refined that grammar is a separate humanistic subject, as Mr. Lees suggests? And what of the questions raised by the Modern Language Association and the Linguistics Society of America? To some degree, they reaffirm what the *Daily News* and Mr. Lees have said. But they raise further questions. Will language be taught by English teachers or by any teachers? And what of cultural lag, alluded to by the Linguistics Society and by Mr. Oppenheimer? In a period of enormous intellectual flux, social upheaval, and technological change, what shall we accept as a minimum essential of communication? What can we call style in language? What are the essential conventions in present-day English? How shall they be preserved? And as the world moves more and more toward newer means of communication and processing knowledge, what shall we call reading, writing, and speaking, and where should the emphasis be in the classroom?

These questions have been with us for some time, and they clamor for answers as we commit ourselves to equal education for all. No one sage or group of sages can begin to answer them. But never have we had a better opportunity to seek answers that are obtainable. We now have the wherewithal—if knowledge, concern, and funds can be called wherewithal—to establish communication and cooperation between schools and colleges, to train and retrain English teachers at all levels, to avail ourselves of the new learning in language, to give serious thought to curricular change, and to show deliberate commitment to improving English instruction in all the schools of our land. New content, new standards for teacher certification, new books and facilities, and true compensation for the educationally deprived can become available. We dare to assert all these possibilities at the very time that we have been humbled. For we know that we are only at the threshold; that what we don't know about language infinitely exceeds what we do know.

This kind of awareness and humility is perhaps our greatest strength as we come to the crossroad. The next few years will tell which road we have taken. When we have seen the results of all the projects and institutes, what kinds of knowledge and skills we may assume in every grade school graduate, in every high school graduate, in every college graduate, we will know which road was taken. Either language study will have become the legitimate concern and responsibility of every English teacher, or it will have left the English classroom for a long time. To assume a prolonged state of flux and indecision such as we are now in is to assume infinite patience, largesse, and effort. James R. Squire, who has been an observer or a participant in many of the decisive meetings that have been held by professors, teachers, administrators, public officials, foundation heads, government agencies, and scholarly and professional groups, says, "I am convinced that we stand on the threshold of a magnificent new English program. I am equally convinced that unless we begin to pull together instead of pulling apart, we shall never achieve the breakthrough."

The pulling apart is to a large extent the inevitable result of the technological changes we have been living through. For if we look to the past, we will see that each age that produces technical change also produces a breakdown in communication between generations and conflict within groups. We can, then, accept our destiny, repeat the experience of our ancestors, and accept the Babels in which we now live. Either we can divide the spoils in English and go our separate ways as teachers of language or literature and composition, or we can say, "To the victor belong the spoils." We can submit to the most strident voices and the most powerful groups, whether they decree that language belongs in whole or in part within the province of English. But so long as the choice depends on teacher, scholar, researcher, administrator, and supervisor deciding jointly what is best for the boys and girls in our schools and colleges, we must presuppose that each of these decision makers has carefully examined what he is accepting or rejecting in language study. If not, he is denying to himself and others man's inalienable right to choose his own words wisely and freely. The intelligent parent can only insist on these rights to knowledge when he is aware of them himself. In English classrooms at least, we "could an if we would" banish the babbling and start the intellectual dialogue. When school, university, and community have committed themselves to dialogue rather than babbling, we shall have disambiguated the word *trivia*.

GLOSSARY

The following words, used in this book, have specialized meanings in the study of language:

AFFIX   A sound or sequence of sounds attached to the beginning or end of a word (for example, prefix or suffix) or, in some languages, inserted within a word.

ALLOPHONE   Any one of the various sound-types that together constitute the sound-class called a phoneme. The *p* in *spin* and the *p* in *pin* are different allophones of the /p/ phoneme.

BLEND   A cluster of two or more adjacent consonants in the same syllable.

DETERMINER   A limiting modifier of a noun or a noun "marker" as *the* man, *his* new car.

DIGRAPH   Two successive letters representing one phoneme, as *ea* in *bread* or *ch* in *chin*.

DIPHTHONG   A glide from one vowel to another in the same syllable, as *oi* in *boil* or *i* in *mine*.

FUNCTION WORD   A word signaling grammatical relationship: Fries uses the term to cover all words not usually found in the subject, verb, predicate adjective, or adverbial complement position.

GENERATIVE GRAMMAR   A language model which shows by a sequence of rigorously applied rules how language operates to formulate all of the grammatical sentences and none of the ungrammatical ones.

GRAMMAR   The study of language: classes of words and their forms, functions, and relations in sentences.

GRAPHEME   A minimum unit of the writing system, not able to be sub-divided, as the letter *d* in *dim* or *g* in *dog*.

LINGUISTICS   The scientific study of human language, or of human speech and its recorded forms.

MORPHEME   A significant unit of form, not able to be subdivided, as *man* (noun), *do* (verb), *-ing* (suffix).

MORPHOLOGY   The study of word formation, including inflection, derivation, and adding of prefixes and suffixes.

MORPHOPHONEMICS   The study of the differences between allomorphs (varying forms of a sound at different points, as the *es* of *churches,* the *s* of *books,* and the *z* sound of *dreams*) of the same morpheme or sound form.

PHONEME   The minimum distinctive sound unit in speech, as the *f* in *fin* and the *d* in *din*. It is a class of sounds, not a sound.

189

PHONEMICS   The study of language structure in terms of its phonemes or units of sound.

PHONETICS   The study and classification of sounds used in human communication.

PHONICS   A method of teaching reading by teaching the pronunciation of individual letters and syllables.

PRESCRIPTIVE GRAMMAR   A study of language which compares a living language with a "model" language (like Latin) and prescribes how the living language should be used.

RHETORIC   The study of the art of speaking and writing effectively, the principles of communication.

SEMANTICS   The study of the meanings of words and phrases and especially of historical changes in meaning.

STRUCTURAL GRAMMAR   The study of language which analyzes the structures or patterns of spoken sentences and thereby describes the distinctive features of a language.

SYNTAX   A study of the way words are arranged to form phrases, classes, and sentences; the ordering or arrangement of morphemes.

TRANSFORMATIONAL GRAMMAR   One kind of generative grammar, using the procedure of beginning with a kernel (or basic simple) sentence and showing a number of transformations or changes, such as active voice to passive or modifying word to phrase to clause.

SUGGESTED READING

GENERAL LINGUISTICS

Sapir, Edward. *Language: An Introduction to the Study of Speech*. New York: Harcourt, Brace & World, Inc., 1921; also Harvest HB 7.

Schlauch, Margaret. *The Gift of Language (The Gift of Tongues)*. New York: Dover Publications, Inc., 1956.

These books are worthwhile both as introductions to linguistics and as introductions to two remarkably articulate, entertaining writers. The Schlauch book reads more easily, but the Sapir has remarkably staying power.

GRAMMARS

Fries, Charles C. *The Structure of English: An Introduction to the Construction of English Sentences*. New York: Harcourt, Brace & World, Inc., 1952.

Jespersen, Otto. *Essentials of English Grammar*. London: George Allen & Unwin Ltd., 1960.

Roberts, Paul. *English Syntax*. New York: Harcourt, Brace & World, Inc., 1964.

When you have read Jespersen and Fries, you will have met the men who led whole schools of grammarians: the first is scholarly but neither structural nor traditional; the second is the source for structuralist texts. Roberts adapts Chomsky's theory of transformational grammar to a programed school text. My friend Jim who hasn't met an intelligent parent yet warned me not to list Chomsky's *Syntactic Structures* or Fodor and Katz's *Structure of Language*. So I'm not listing them. But intelligent parents with a background in math, science, or logic will find these two books the most exciting of all. Even Chomsky's more cautious *Aspects of the Theory of Syntax*, though it goes way beyond his *Syntactic Structures*, loses some of the early young man's excitement.

HISTORIES

Baugh, Albert C. *A History of the English Language*. New York: Appleton-Century-Crofts, 1957.

Pyles, Thomas. *The Origins and Development of the English Language*. New York: Harcourt, Brace & World, Inc., 1964.

Baugh traces our external history through language. The migrations, the invasions, the wars, the intellectual debates and new inventions and discoveries are all there. Pyles deals more with the internal history. The structure of the language and the nature of linguistic change are very systematically and wittily presented.

DICTIONARIES

Gove, Philip B. (ed.). *Webster's Third New International Dictionary of the English Language, Unabridged.* Springfield, Mass.: G. & C. Merriam Co., 1961.
Sledd, James, and Wilma Ebbitt. *Dictionaries and THAT Dictionary.* Chicago: Scott, Foresman & Co., 1962.
Wilson, Kenneth G. *Harbrace Guide to Dictionaries.* New York: Harcourt, Brace & World, Inc., 1963.

The *Webster Third* should be next to Aunt Hepzibah's wedding present, for contrast if for no other reason. The Sledd and Ebbitt case book will show you the difference between lexicographers' and readers' notions of what a dictionary is for. If you aren't a sophisticated user of a dictionary, Wilson will make you one.

USAGE

Evans, Bergen, and Cornelia Evans. *A Dictionary of Contemporary American Usage.* New York: Random House, 1957.
Fowler, Henry Watson. *Dictionary of Modern English Usage.* 4th printing. Rev. and ed. by Sir Ernest Gowers. New York: Oxford University Press, 1965.

The Evans is informal yet scholarly, but the information is getting dated. The Fowler is British, but it is most recent. And many Americans do get their cues from Fowler.

DIALECTS

Brook, G. L. *English Dialects.* New York: Oxford University Press, 1964.
Mencken, H. L. *The American Language.* 4th ed. abridged by Raven I. McDavid, Jr. New York: Alfred A. Knopf, Inc., 1963.

If you want a whole book, read the Brook or the Mencken. If you want a chapter, see McDavid's in W. Nelson Francis, *The Structure of American English* (New York: Ronald Press, 1958).